Benjamin Franklin:

ENVOY EXTRAORDINARY

Benjamin Franklin:

ENVOY EXTRAORDINARY

by Roger Burlingame

Coward-McCann, Inc. New York

To A.W.B.

My Partner in
All Things

COPYRIGHT © *1967 BY ROGER BURLINGAME*

All rights reserved. This book, or parts thereof, may not
be reproduced in any form without permission in writing
from the Publisher. Published on the same day in the
Dominion of Canada by Longmans Canada Limited, Toronto.

Library of Congress
Catalog Card Number: 67-10561

PRINTED IN THE UNITED STATES OF AMERICA

ACKNOWLEDGMENTS

I HAVE had kind and patient assistance from the librarians of the New York Public Library and the libraries of the Century Association and the Harvard Club of New York City. In particular I had help from Mr. Robert W. Hill of the Manuscript Division of the New York Public Library, who made available to me the Franklin papers in the library's possession.

I owe much to the courtesy shown me by Professor Leonard W. Labaree, director of the Yale University project, "The Papers of Benjamin Franklin." During a recent visit I made to New Haven, Mr. Labaree gave me his full attention and made me familiar with what I understand is the most extensive collection of Frankliniana in the world, which is housed in the Yale University Library.

My friend and long-time literary adviser Kenneth Littauer gave my manuscript a careful reading and made many valuable suggestions, all of which I adopted.

As always, my wife has helped me over many a hurdle and shown her usual tolerance of even my most cantankerous moments.

My thanks go to Mrs. Rodman Valentine, who has given me valuable typographical help and to Mrs. Dorothy Rutherford for the index.

CREDITS

Permission has been granted for quotations from books, provided such quotations are used either for illustrating the text or citing authority. The following publishers have agreed to such use in this volume:

American Historical Association: quotation from "A Missing Chapter of Franco-American History" by David Jayne Hill in *American Historical Review*, Vol. XXI, p. 714, in Chapter IX.

CONTENTS

Illustrations will be found following page 96.

PREFACE

FOR Americans, few events in American history have been so hard to understand as the war that made us a nation. Apart from the patriotic bias which led most nineteenth-century American historians to fabricate victories out of defeats, there are other obscurities which twentieth-century scholars are only just beginning to clear. For most interested nonscholars, the civil war of the 1860's, the Spanish war and both world wars are easier.

The American Revolution, or War of Independence, was different from other wars with whose pattern we are familiar. It was, indeed, a civil war on both sides of the Atlantic, but one in which geography played no part in the conflicts of interests or loyalty. In both England and America, institutions, even houses were split. An arresting example is the partition which thrust Benjamin Franklin and his son, William, apart. Throughout the war there was sharp division in Parliament and, until an emotional and irrational king unified them, in the ministries as well. And even after the Declaration of Independence in 1776, there were men in the Continental Congress who were nostalgic for dependence.

Geography also added to the obscurity by vastly enlarging the panorama. The War of Independence had for its scenes not only Lexington, Boston, Long Island and Saratoga, Philadelphia and Yorktown, but remote and mysterious islands in the Caribbean, in the tropical Atlantic, or off the coast of South America, busy French ports, the courts of France and Spain, the decks of privateers and merchantmen in every western sea, and even distant India. And we know now that the moral consequences of that war penetrated every cranny of civilization.

Added to the difficulty of grasping the import of this enormous area of operation and influence, was a communication so slow that the duration of the conflict for only eight years seems miraculous.

Finally there is the potent but complex factor of the English and French background. Both nations stood on the brink of an upheaval which would alter the economic, social and political traditions of centuries. In such an imminence, there were contrasts between the old and the new that seem hardly credible even in a world as disordered as ours in the mid-twentieth century. Yet, in those times, whatever stability or tangential action might ensue was the work of gifted individuals of the sort that seem to have disappeared from our world, stifled by organization or machine control. There were such persons in England and in the colonies. In Britain, Burke was one and, for a time, Chatham and Rockingham and Shelburne, and even bad boys like Wilkes and Charles James Fox. In America, the members of the Continental Congress, midwives of the painfully emerging new nation looked about them for geniuses that might resolve what appeared to be irreconcilable conflicts.

Happily they could find such men. There was Jefferson, who had drawn from Locke the materials of the Declaration; there was John Adams, who, in spite of his own and his wife's puritan traditions, understood the science, if not the art, of politics; and, the one best adapted to an international mission, Benjamin Franklin. Without these and, no doubt, the firebrand Tom Paine and the American bad boy Sam Adams, the war, no matter what outer circumstances might favor it, could not have been won.

Why it was won may be learned from a study of the letters, papers and autobiographical writings of Benjamin Franklin, the greatest, some think, of them all. He was the *deus ex machina*, the power behind thrones and republics and, above all, the imponderable social genius that moved the heavy impedimenta of war with so light a touch that few were aware of its irresistible force.

Many of the scholars who have cleared away the cobwebs from the history of American independence have done so by exposing and interpreting the philosophy of this scarcely credible person. Above all they have found peace of mind. With it he could take the bitterest abuse with unruffled temper, the most extravagant adoration with humility. He could stand before kings and their ministers in his simple garb and with the common touch at the ends of his fingers. His wit could bite through the toughest moral skin or reduce to absurdity the most pompous pronouncement. He could play chess with women of the nobility or the salons while spies within his own household listened to his every step; often he commented on the game with humorous confidence. "But you cannot take the king," a fair opponent said to him one evening as he playfully swept the piece from the board. "We do," he replied, "in America."

He played, too, round the edges of love at an age when most men have become immune to feminine hypnosis. He guided the thoughts and wills of the host of women to whom he was "Dear Papa"; he never turned away from a child who asked him for a story. But at the very moments when he seemed wholly to relax in these pleasures, he was directing the movements of ships in most of the seven seas as they sailed toward the ultimate destinations in the American colonies, laden with guns and powder for the Sons of Liberty.

Franklin was not bewildered by the wide canvas the War of Independence was painting. He held, in his mind's vision, every pirate's cove in some little-known island where a ship might hide from the enemy and every European port where gunpowder in tea chests might be loaded on a fast schooner.

In Paris, for the specific purpose of drawing the French into a military, naval and economic alliance against Britain, he exercised a patience that was rare, in that time, among patriots. Through the first years of the war when the news from New York, Philadelphia and Valley Forge was at its worst, when

Washington's men were starving, freezing and deserting by the hundred, Ben Franklin, in Paris, waited. He neither urged nor persuaded the French king or his ministers. He knew the time would come when all France would clamor to be let in to fight against their ancient enemy. Indeed, certain Frenchmen such as Caron de Beaumarchais impetuously urged *him*. But he stood his ground in the confidence that was of his nature. Meanwhile, he lived life all the way, drinking the best French wine, eating the famous French food, taking even the consequent gout in his stride with, above all else, peace of mind.

Believers in planned destiny will see in Franklin a nearly perfect pattern. Athletics, especially swimming, gave him a strong body; this combined with abstinence and frugality in his youth laid the foundation for a sturdy old age. Theories about food, fresh air and exercise which were far ahead of his time gave him a constitution which enabled him to throw off diseases and disabilities which would have killed most men. His early training as a journalist and printer taught him to pick and choose out of the riches that the English language spread before him and made him a precise and eclectic writer. His boyhood visit to London clarified the physical plan of that great metropolis, commenced friendships that were of signal aid in later, more troubled years; there, too, he learned the poise in the presence of important persons that must be one of the virtues of a diplomat.

And what of his inquiries into science? His practical inventions that he gave to society without patent or paid license? The American public was too busy for science and if they used his devices, it was, often as not, without credit. But abroad, where a veritable frenzy of discovery had followed Isaac Newton's experiment, Franklin's fame had long preceded his arrival so that he was welcomed and heeded by every English and European philosopher. Finally, it was the closeness to nature during these years of scientific questioning that gave him his patience and his peace of mind.

Many biographers have written "definitively" about Benjamin Franklin. Others have contented themselves with phases.

Some have been fascinated by the paradoxes he presented: passion and tranquillity, abstinence and epicurean tastes, silence and prolific articulation, rigid moral codes and the tolerance of sinners—including his lapsed self-wisdom and friendliness—the list is scarcely finishable.

This book—yes, there is room for another and another through all the long corridors of literary record and analysis—will be about his most productive period (for us Americans) in London and Paris. In this elderly time, he showed most the human being that we always try (sometimes with unsuccess) to find beneath the embellishments of our heroes. Benjamin Franklin cannot long stand in stony aloofness on a pedestal; our warm love, the intense desire for his friendship must pull him off.

Benjamin Franklin:
ENVOY EXTRAORDINARY

I

FRANKLIN'S ENGLAND

THE England that received Franklin in his maturity enjoyed a prosperity that had been forecast to the boy of nineteen. The interest in science that Newton had aroused as the centuries turned had borne fruit. Skepticism had made a deep dent in the dominant old theologies. Already, in the seventeenth century, superstition, magic, astrology, alchemy had followed witches out of society. Whatever hangovers of these things still existed were under constant attack. And, as no one knew better than Franklin, revealed religion was being replaced by "deism" among the intellectuals, and deism was filtering down into the lower ranks. There was talk of the God of Reason and those who sought him kept looking across the channel, war or no war, for Voltaire and the encyclopedists and the French scientific experimenters.

At the same time the prosperity that was, eventually, to corrupt English society, was rising day by day. British trade covered most of the world. In England, it was not always easy to tell commerce and government apart. For example, the ruling power in India was a commercial body, the English "East India Company," organized at the end of the seventeenth century for trade. In America, both Virginia and New England had been founded by stock companies operating for profit. By the mid-eighteenth century, Parliament and the ministries were deeply involved with the commercial interests and these dictated colonial policy in large measure.

For British colonies to be dedicated to English prosperity

might have been accepted in the plantations of the West Indies, but rugged Yankees and proud Pennsylvanians and Virginians remained unconvinced. When word came across the Atlantic about what the English were doing with their prosperity and what English prosperity was doing to British government, American colonists felt that the fruit of their labor should be kept at home.

In England as general wealth increased and immense individual fortunes were built, the rule of the aristocracy and the landed gentry became nearly absolute. The England of the Magna Carta, which had once appeared to be moving toward a goal of liberty, equality and general justice, had become an oligarchy. A few thousand rich men engaged largely in extravagant dissipation or the exploitation of luxury had gained control of Parliament and the ministries to the hurt of the great masses of the people, who suffered extreme poverty and gross injustice. The curious contradiction inherent in this condition was that the persons in this ruling group were highly educated, talented and representative of the first English families, whose morality had been undermined by wealth and leisure.

To the historian George Otto Trevelyan, what he called the "phenomenon" of this mid-eighteenth century period was "that men of age and standing, of strong mental powers and refined cultivation lived openly, shamelessly and habitually, in the face of all England, as no one who had any care for his reputation would now live during a single fortnight of the year at Monaco." Yet these very men occupied positions of dominating importance. The Duke of Grafton, for example, who paraded a notorious mistress before the crowds at the Ascot races, was at one time First Lord of the Treasury and at another, Chancellor of Cambridge University, and the scandalous Earl of Sandwich would, but for the opposition of certain clergymen, have been chosen for the same Cambridge office.

While this group maintained its immunity to censure and continued its costly orgies, the poor were crowded into disease-breeding slums where hundreds of children died daily and others were executed for petty misdemeanors. The theft of a

penknife meant the gallows for a boy of ten and a girl of fourteen was hanged for stealing a handkerchief. A hanging was
occasion for a holiday and crowds thronged Tyburn in London
to laugh and sneer as their fellows were strung up.

Yet parallel with the degrading antitheses that English society was presenting, dynamic forces were at work. The wave of
invention destined soon to sweep the country into industrial
revolution had begun as Benjamin Franklin arrived. New-
comen's atmospheric engine, crude as it was, had pumped out
the water that had rendered useless the vast coal fields of the
North, and Abraham Darby's coke had taken the place of the
wasteful charcoal that so long had smelted iron. James Watt
was obsessed with the idea of substituting steam expansion for
atmospheric pressure and was assisted by John Wilkinson, who
was learning to bore accurate cylinders. For the making of cloth,
John Kay had invented the flying shuttle and Hargreaves, Arkwright and Crompton were on the verge of completely revo-
lutionizing the textile industry, taking it out of the country
cottages and putting it into the "dark Satanic mills."

And there was a movement to assist commerce by immense
construction of canals and roads which would bring about the
new discipline of civil engineering. Interested in all these things
was a group of what were known as "new men." They too were
inspired by commerce and they too would build fortunes but
they were hard-working folk who never found or wanted
leisure: Wedgwood, the potter; Wilkinson, the ironmaster;
Arkwright, Boulton and Brindley. Fighting their way upward,
the new men were endowed by no inheritance, and their sympathy was with fellow workers at the bottom; they were a
menace indeed to the complacent rich dilettanti.

In Parliament, and even in the ministries until they were
eliminated by Hanover misrule, was a scattering of liberal and
even great men, some of whom have become heroes of American
history. There was William Pitt, who became Lord Chatham;
there was Edmund Burke, perhaps greatest and certainly most
eloquent of all; and there was Charles James Fox, who managed to get into trouble with most of the conservative ruling

class; and there was the more dubious John Wilkes, self-styled champion of liberty who, at least, was hostile to the oligarchical rule. And Franklin was to see three good ministers, Chatham, Shelburne and Rockingham, come successively into the disfavor of George the Third while the acts of the king's favorites soured his love of England.

2

But Benjamin Franklin's love of England was at its peak when, on the 26th of July, 1757, he arrived with his son, William, in London. He knew little of the darker side of the English scene. For him the busy metropolis was bracing and brought back his usual energy after the month-long sail from New York to Falmouth during which he had tired of "the uniform view of a vacant ocean." To him, then, England was the motherland to which, as a proud Englishman, he owed all allegiance and love.

Since his first visit in 1725, when he was a working and sometimes wayward boy of nineteen, he had built a few close friendships with Englishmen he had not seen but with whom he had carried on abundant correspondence. There was Peter Collinson, fellow of the Royal Society, to whom he had sent all his observations on electricity and who had caused them to be published in the Society's *Transactions,* thus giving them to the scientific world. The year before his arrival, the Royal Society had done Franklin the honor of electing him a member, so his foothold in England was secure. There was William Strahan, publisher of the works of Samuel Johnson, David Hume, Edward Gibbon, and William Blackstone, with whom, through letters, he had become so intimate that he tried to arrange a marriage between his daughter Sally, and Strahan's son.

But personal friends were not necessary to the warmth of Franklin's reception in England. His fame had preceded him. The news of his experiments and scientific observations had spread, not only through England, where intellectual men had inspired an atmosphere congenial to such matters, but on the

Continent as well, where the work of Lavoisier and Laplace was soon to be followed with such eagerness.

Months before, Franklin had put Collinson and Strahan on the alert for his coming. Sure enough, he had told Strahan, he would turn up at the Strahan press. "Then look sharp," he wrote, "and if a fat old fellow should come to your printing house and request a little smouting, depend upon it 'tis your affectionate friend and humble servant." "Smouting" was jargon for journeyman jobs.

Peter Collinson was not surprised, therefore, when, late in the evening of July 26, a coach drew up at his house at Mill Hill and the Franklins got out. He made them stay the night with him. Tomorrow, they would look for a place to live and tomorrow, too, Strahan would come. While they talked, Collinson, long familiar with Benjamin Franklin's cast of thought, fell under the spell of his person. Now he could watch the play of humorous fancy in the eyes and round the lips of the man he thought he knew so well. As he talked, looking, occasionally, slyly over his spectacles, Franklin's lively words surprised Collinson, who remembered his writing as very formal. He told of the trip, of his relief from the monotony by composing a new preface for his *Poor Richard;* of the passenger who lost a bet to the skipper when the packet had actually attained thirteen knots—faster than any vessel had ever sailed; of constant observations of sky and wind and sea, in tune with his persistent effort at nearness to nature.

The next morning, getting word of Franklin's arrival, William Strahan came and confirmed his estimate of the friend who had written him so often. As he wrote to Deborah Franklin, "I never saw a man who was, in every respect, so agreeable to me. Some are amiable in one view, some in another, he in all." Of William: "Your son I really think one of the prettiest young gentlemen I ever knew from America."

A place to live could wait. They got him temporary quarters at the Bear Inn and now he must get about his mission. For Franklin was in London as representative of the proprietary province of Pennsylvania to ease what Pennsylvanians thought was proprietary tyranny. The proprietors in this case were the descendants of William Penn and of a very different character from the founder.

Proprietorships were a feudal legacy. Once they were grants from the Crown to a "proprietor" who possessed sovereign rights; they were, in effect, estates under a one-man dictatorship. The proprietor could appoint officers, create courts, make laws, raise a militia and command it and establish towns. The sale of land and its settlement were in the single control of the proprietor, or overlord. In America, distinct from "royal colonies" accountable directly to the king, there were several proprietorships: New York, New Jersey, Maryland and Pennsylvania. Like most instruments of British imperial government, they were devices for the promotion of trade; they were successors to the old trading companies such as those which established Virginia and New England early in the seventeenth century and which collapsed when the settlers began to regard themselves as independent "freemen" and returned little or no profit to the home offices.

But William Penn, who was given the grant of Pennsylvania in payment of a royal debt by King Charles II, refused to think of himself as a feudal overlord. He drew up a "Frame of Government" for the province which gave the people an immediate voice in the government and which established a legislature, one house of which was to be elected by the people and which should make their laws. Such emphasis was laid on religious freedom and freedom of immigration that the province became a refuge for thousands of persecuted Quakers from Europe and later for oppressed Germans and restless Scotch-Irish.

But when William Penn returned to England, his provincial deputies found ways of escaping the restraints he had put upon them and angry disputes arose between them and the new immigrants, who believed they had come to a free land—free, at least, from the old rigid controls that had driven them from home. This conflict so disturbed William Penn that he threatened to return the province to royal rule and would probably have done so had illness and death not intervened.

As it was, the proprietorship passed to William Penn's sons, Richard and Thomas, and under their near-feudal control, conditions for Pennsylvanians grew intolerable. The Assembly —the elected legislature of the province—therefore commissioned their most persuasive member, Benjamin Franklin, to make the long, dangerous voyage to England to present the case of the freemen to the new proprietors and, if they proved obdurate, to agitate for the return of the proprietorship to the Crown: to make it, in short, a royal colony, which the founder, in his late years, had advocated. It was a ticklish assignment, much more difficult because of the changed conditions in England and because of the uncertain tempers of the teutonic Hanover kings who had come to rule the nation.

Benjamin Franklin, on that day in July, 1757, when he set out on his mission, was unaware of the extent of these changes in his beloved mother country; he had no realization of the intention of the ministries to put as much of the burden of the expense of the war with France on the colonies and of the cynical attitude of the men in high places that the colonists were a lesser breed than Englishmen. Benjamin Franklin was proud of his English heritage; to him, the fact that he was a British subject made him an Englishman, the peer of any other who might never have stepped outside the City of London.

3

When Peter Collinson told him that Lord Granville, president of the king's Privy Council, had asked to be informed, instantly, of Franklin's arrival, he went to see his lordship, who "received me with great civility." The civility, however, did not mean that Granville approved of Pennsylvania's complaint.

"You Americans," he said, "have wrong ideas of the nature of your constitution; you contend that the king's instructions to his governors are not laws, and think yourselves at liberty to regard them or disregard them at your own discretion. But those instructions are not like the pocket instructions given to a minister going abroad, for regulating his conduct in some trifling point of ceremony. They are first drawn up by judges learned in the laws; they are then considered, debated, and perhaps amended in Council, after which they are signed by the king. They are then, so far as they relate to you, the *law of the land,* for the king is the LEGISLATOR OF THE COL-ONIES."

Franklin wrote down this speech, capitals, italics and all, the instant he left Lord Granville's presence so that it should be preserved exactly as he remembered it. And he made a record, too, of his sharp reply.

"I told his lordship this was new doctrine to me. I had always understood from our charters that our laws were to be made by our Assemblies, to be presented, indeed, to the king for his royal assent, and that being once given the king could not repeal or alter them. And as the Assemblies could not make permanent laws without his assent, so neither could he make a law for them without theirs. He assured me that I was totally mistaken."

Franklin's "alarm" at this assertion showed that he had now encountered a condition for which he had not been prepared. Along with the oligarchical rule and the general corruption accompanying the erratic behavior of the Georges, William Penn's liberal Frame of Government—which had been called a "Holy Experiment"—had been wholly distorted. The constitution which the people of Pennsylvania had cherished, as all great constitutions have been cherished, had been subverted to the aims of absolute power. Where, now, was the Magna Carta? Where, now, was the "new" England, reformed by the "Glorious Revolution" of 1688? These questions must have harassed Benjamin Franklin as he thought back over the interview with the president of George II's Privy Council!

But Granville's rebuff was nothing to the ugly reception he received from the proprietors, Thomas and Richard Penn, sons of the founder, at Thomas's house in Spring Garden a few days later.

"The proprietaries justifyed their conduct as well as they could, and I the Assembly's. We now appeared very wide, and so far from each other in our opinions as to discourage all hope of agreement."

And then that rarest thing happened: Benjamin Franklin lost his temper. He told Thomas Penn that his father's original charter gave the Assembly "all the powers and privileges of an assembly according to the rights of free-born subjects of England and as is usual in any of the British plantations in America."

To this, Thomas Penn replied:

"Yes, but my father granted privileges he was not by the royal charter empowered to grant, nothing can be claimed by such grant."

"Then," said Franklin, "if your father had no right to grant the privileges he pretended to grant, and published all over Europe as granted, those who came to settle in the province on the faith of that grant, and in expectation of enjoying the privileges contained in it, were deceived, cheated, and betrayed."

Penn answered, Franklin remembered, "with a kind of triumphing, laughing insolence, such as a low jockey might do when a purchaser complained that he had cheated him on a horse," that the settlers should have looked into it to find out whether the charter was legitimate; that if they were deceived, it was their own fault.

"I was astonished," Franklin recalled, "to see him thus meanly give up his father's character, and conceived at that moment a more cordial and thorough contempt for him than I ever felt for any man living, a contempt that I cannot express in words, but I believe my countenance expressed it strongly, and that his brother, who was looking on me, must have observed it. However, finding myself grow warm, I made no other answer to this than that the poor people were no lawyers themselves and, confiding in his father, did not think it necessary to consult any."

The interview ended by a demand that Franklin draw up a paper listing the Assembly's complaints and that the proprietors would consider it in due time. It was now mid-August and their lawyers were away on vacation and could not review the matter till they returned. Franklin gave them the required paper and waited "a year wanting eight days" for a reply. Actually, they never replied to him directly but went over his head and communicated with the Pennsylvania Assembly instead, complaining of Franklin's lack of formality and rudeness in his manner of presenting the complaints.

The most pressing of the Assembly's complaints were financial; the people had been put to enormous expense providing for their own defense against the Indians yet, as they had been forbidden to tax the proprietary estates which made up most of the province, they had been unable to raise the money. It was hardly a matter which could be postponed for a year.

This was indeed a test of Benjamin Franklin's patience, perhaps his supreme virtue. But the interval gave him time for many things. He had a few friends and many admirers in London. Membership in the Royal Society was, for an American colonial, no small honor. He who could find interest and amusement anywhere could find more in London than in any other city he knew. He was able, with the generosity of the Assembly, plus what he modestly called the "competence" that in a half century of industrious and frugal life he had made and saved, to live extremely well and do much as he liked.

He was soon established in a boarding house in which he and William occupied four rooms. They had, also, two servants. For a while he would be able to forget his frugality, to live like an English gentleman, to travel as he pleased and to move freely on the highest social plane.

Unhappily, however, his pleasure had a painful interruption.

II

INTERVAL OF PAIN AND
PLEASURE

AS the Franklins settled into their quarters at Number 7
Craven Street, Benjamin hardly knew that he had suddenly made a lifelong friend or that the fine large house was to
be his shelter and the center of his activity for the greater part
of the next fifteen years. But perhaps his landlady, Mrs. Margaret Stevenson, knew, after the few preliminary words that she
and Franklin had together, that he would never be just another
lodger. Like all women, she was drawn to him, not remotely
in a sexual sense, but as a protector, as a guide who would give
wise answers to puzzling questions and so, to that extent, take
the place of her dead husband. And Polly, her daughter, at once
accepted him as the father she needed. With the girl, it was,
from the first, a matter of frank adoration.

The home these people made for him and their friendliness
diverted him from the disappointments and frustration that had
attended the first approaches to the performance of his mission.
Here in Craven Street, he could do as he liked: go back to the
scientific studies and experiments that assuaged his acutely
inquiring mind; entertain the men who sought him out as soon
as they knew that he had come—men that his fame had reached,
who had questions and doubts about "philosophy," as natural
science was then called. He could go and come as he pleased
and need explain to no one why—a freedom of which he took
quick advantage. He drove about the London that he loved

and would always love, however hostile the folk he must deal with; he made appointments for meetings in a tavern or coffee-house with trusted friends for long talks over a bottle of good claret, on the parlous relations of a government and an empire.

He sought out the printing house where he had worked as a boy, and, sure enough, some of the old pressmen were still there. He treated them to a gallon of beer, a gesture in contrast to the temperance lectures he had treated them to thirty years before. Thirty years later, he had become more genial.

Another reminder of that earlier sojourn in England was a call from James Ralph, who had been his companion in 1725. They had fallen out in those days because Franklin, beset, as he said, with what he called "ungovernable passions," had borrowed Ralph's mistress, an episode he rationalized by Ralph's supposed neglect of the woman. Back in Philadelphia, however, with his beloved Deborah, he deeply repented of this "erratum." When he "took" Deborah "to wife" the happy home life she made for him helped him to govern his wayward desires and although there were occasional other "errata," he was devoted to her through many years. Indeed, he had begged her to come with him this time to London but she had refused, saying the voyage was too much of a hardship and that it was her duty to stay at home and keep house for their daughter, Sally.

Meanwhile, Ralph had comforted himself by writing bad poetry and now, in 1757, he had become a literary figure of some importance in London. And toward Franklin, he cherished no ill feelings because of the boyhood quarrel.

Though the Stevenson women did everything to make his life comfortable and happy, he missed Deborah and Sally constantly. Later in the year, he sent them rich presents: china, silver, cut glass, linens, silk and satin clothes, carpets and things for the household. Also he wrote to "Debby" when he could but, for some two months, he was unable to do anything. It was then that Margaret Stevenson and her daughter showed him kindnesses that he never forgot.

2

Driving, on business, through the wet, cold streets of London in a drafty hack, he caught, as many have who are unused to the English climate, a violent cold. No sooner was he better and able to get about than he came down with a relapse,

> which continued longer than the first, attended by great pain in my head, the top of which was very hot, and when the pain went off very sore and tender. These fits of pain continued sometimes longer than at others; seldom less than 12 hours, and once 36 hours. I was now and then a little delirious: they cupped me on the back of the head which seemed to ease me for the present; I took a great deal of bark, both in substance and infusion, and too soon thinking myself well, I ventured out twice, to do a little business and forward the service I am engaged in, and both times got fresh cold and fell down again; my good doctor grew very angry with me, for acting contrary to his cautions and directions, and obliged me to promise more observance for the future. He attended me very carefully and affectionately; and the good lady of the house nursed me kindly; Billy was also of great service to me, in going from place to place, where I could not go myself, and Peter [a servant] was very diligent and attentive. I took so much bark in various ways, that I began to abhor it; I durst not take a vomit, for fear of my head; but at last I was seized with a vomiting and purging, the latter of which continued the greater part of the day, and I believe was a kind of crisis to the distemper, carrying it clear off; for ever since I feel quite lightsome, and am every day gathering strength; so I hope my seasoning is over, and that I shall enjoy better health during the rest of my stay in England.

It was long before Deborah got this acount of his trouble, for letters had to be entrusted to a traveler and by that time he was again having pleasures after his pain. One was helping "Billy" to enter the Middle Temple, from which he expected to emerge ready for the bar. Another was to attend the banquet of the Royal Society, at which he was enthusiastically welcomed by the members, especially his friend John Pringle, who was about to become president of the Society. He had corresponded much with Pringle about electricity. His latest message, appropriately following his illness, was about his attempts to cure persons who had been paralyzed by stroke with shock treatments: placing the patient "in a chair on an electric stool," after which he drew "a number of large strong sparks from all parts of the affected limb or side." Unfortunately, as later physicians, reading Franklin's letter, may have suspected, the relief, if any, was only temporary.

And, as he later told Deborah:

> Your kind advice about getting a Chariot, I had taken some time before; for I found that every time I walked out, I got fresh cold; and the Hackney Coaches at this End of the town, where most people keep their own, are the worst in the whole City, miserable, dirty, shabby Things, unfit to go in when dressed clean, and such as one would be ashamed to get out of at any gentleman's door.

So he hired a coach of his own, for which he paid the enormous sum of twelve guineas a month but it was worth it if it kept him well, or so he and Deborah thought. It shows, however, a change in the thrifty Franklin of *Poor Richard,* once he got away from the Philadelphia in which he was famed for his frugality and into London, where he was celebrated as a statesman and a "philosopher," the companion of other famous men and of prosperous gentlefolk. His account books, which he still carefully kept, show other extravagances such as coats and breeches, silver shoe buckles, and even wigs, which he did not wear at home. And there were the best of wines and spirits, which suggested that the Poor Richard who once preached *"Industry,* and *Frugality,* and *Prudence"* had become a connoisseur.

With the coach, he was able to drive to the new British Museum in Montague House, which naturally fascinated him. Having no knowledge of what was being done to further his mission in the secret conferences of the proprietors, he cherished the hope of going home in the spring. As time went on, however, and with his health improving, there were more and more compensations.

The agreeable conversation I meet with among men of learning, and the notice taken of me by persons of distinction, are the principal things that soothe me for the present, under this painful absence from my family and friends. Yet these would not keep me here another week, if I had not other inducements; duty to my country, and hopes of being able to do it service.

This assurance may have confirmed Deborah in her resolve not to dare the terrors of the Atlantic, though Strahan kept writing to persuade her to join her husband. In February (1758) Mrs. Stevenson went shopping with him and he sent Deborah a box full of luxuries which must have kept her busy and helped her endure her self-imposed separation.

In the large Case is another small box, containing some English China; viz. Melons and Leaves for a Desert of Fruit and Cream, or the like; a Bowl, remarkable for the Neatness of the Figures, made at Bow, near this City; some Coffee Cups of the same; a Worcester Bowl, ordinary. To show the Difference of Workmanship, there is something from all the China Works in England; and one old true China Bason, mended, of an odd Colour. The same box contains 4 Silver Salt Ladles, newest, but ugliest Fashion; a little Instrument to core Apples; another to make little Turnips out of great ones; six coarse diaper Breakfast Cloths; they are to spread on the Tea Table, for nobody breakfasts here on the naked Table.... There is also a little Basket, a Present from Mrs. Stevenson to Sally, and a pair of Garters for you, which were knit by the young Lady, her daughter, who favoured me with a Pair of the same kind, the only ones I have been able to wear, as they need not be bound tight, the Ridges in them preventing their Slipping. We send them therefore as a Curiosity for the Form, more than for the Value....

In the great Case, besides the little Box, is contain'd some Carpeting for a best Room Floor.... Also two large fine Flanders BedTicks, and two pair large superfine Blankets, 2 fine Damask TableCloths and Napkins.... There is also 56 Yards of Cotton, printed curiously from Copper Plates, a new Invention, to make Bed and Window Curtains; and 7 yards of printed Chair Bottoms, printed in the same Way, very neat.

These were my Fancy; but Mrs. Stevenson tells me I did wrong not to buy both of the same Colour. Also 7 yards of printed Cotton, blue Ground, to make you a Gown. I bought it by Candlelight and liked it then, but not so well afterwards. . . .

I forgot to mention another of my Fancyings, viz. a pair of Silk Blankets, very fine. . . . I also forgot, among the China, to mention a large fine Jugg for Beer to stand in the Cooler. I fell in Love with it at first Sight; for I thought it look'd like a fat jolly Dame, clean and tidy, with a neat blue and white Calico Gown on, good natur'd and lovely and put me in mind of— Somebody.

We may imagine the excitement in Philadelphia when Deborah and Sally unpacked these treasures that carried the evidence of Benjamin's thought and care over each detail. To the provincials, many of them must have seemed exotic indeed. Such things came to Philadelphia but rarely, and then to the rich and great.

3

Presents to Deborah and Sally were not the only gifts Franklin sent overseas. Deep as always in the study of science, he wanted others to conduct experiments parallel with his own so that the whole body of "philosophy" would expand. He had none of the secretiveness or jealousy which sometimes made other scientists desire personal credit for discoveries. His wish was to share whatever knowledge of natural phenomena he had acquired and he expected his philosophical colleagues to share theirs with him. In his desire, therefore, to promote scientific education, he prepared a quantity of equipment for Harvard College and sent it with elaborate instructions as to how to use it. He consigned the package to his friend Thomas Hubbard at Boston. It contained:

> A mahogany case lined with lead, containing thirty-five square glass bottles, in five rows, seven in a row.
> A glass globe of the same size and kind with that I used at Philadelphia, and mounted in the same manner.

A large glass cylinder, mounted on an iron axis with brass caps; this form being most used here, and thought better than the globe, as a long, narrow cushion will electrify a greater surface at the same time.

He sent, too, a quantity of tinfoil with careful directions as to how to use it to line the bottles. And then, remembering that a college was concerned with the classics as well as with the natural sciences, he added, in a postscript to his letter to Hubbard:

> I beg the College will do me the favour to accept a Virgil, which I send in the case, thought to be the most curiously printed of any book hitherto done in the world.

These things were sent in April, 1758, and a month later, still immersed in scientific thought, he went with his son to Cambridge, as anxious to contribute his knowledge to an English university as to an American college. In Cambridge, he performed a series of experiments in evaporation with the professor of chemistry, John Hadley. His first contribution (which suggests the homely, practical way in which Franklin often thought) was the memory of a hot day in Philadelphia when the temperature was 100 degrees in the shade, sitting in an open window with the sweat rolling off him and a "brisk wind blowing through the house." Yet, his body had kept cool and this, he had guessed, was because the wind has caused a quick evaporation of the abundant moisture on his body.

Finding that ether caused a quicker evaporation than alcohol or anything else, he and Hadley got a thermometer to read 25 degrees below freezing by applying the ether to the thermometer's ball and then blowing on it with a bellows.

> From this experiment [he wrote his friend John Lining in America] one may see the possibility of freezing a man to death on a warm summer's day, if he were to stand in a passage through which the wind blew briskly, and to be wet frequently with ether. . . .

Franklin had found, then, the principle applied centuries later to the manufacture of artificial refrigeration.

The Franklins had such a good time at Cambridge that they could not resist an invitation from the University to return for Commencement in July. In a letter to Deborah about his second visit, the pleasure over his reception there overcame his usual modesty.

> We ... were present at all the ceremonies, dined every day in their halls, and my vanity was not a little gratified by the particular regard shown me by the chancellor and vice-chancellor of the University, and the heads of colleges.

In that same midsummer, Benjamin and William went on a genealogical tour to Wellingborough, where they found a cousin who remembered the departure of Thomas, Benjamin's father, for New England about 1685. They then went to nearby Ecton,

> being the village where my father was born, and where his father, grandfather, and greatgrandfather had lived and how many of the family before them we know not. We went first to see the old house and grounds. ... The land is now added to another farm, and a school kept in the house. It is a decayed old stone building, but still known by the name of Franklin house. Thence we went to visit the rector of the parish, who lives close by the church, a very ancient building. He entertained us very kindly, and showed us the old church register, in which were the births, marriages, and burials of our ancestors for two hundred years, as early as his book began.

In Birmingham, they talked to some of Deborah's cousins. There, too, Franklin met John Baskerville, the publisher who had printed the Virgil he had sent to Harvard.

Did Benjamin Franklin, through the sequence of pain and pleasure of his first year in London, remember the pamphlet he had written as a boy of twenty: *A Dissertation on Liberty and Necessity, Pleasure and Pain*? He had regretted the essay as an "erratum." In it, he had speculated on whether pleasure and pain were different degrees of the same emotion.

❧ III ❧

MANY INVENTIONS

IN his first years in London, Benjamin Franklin held beliefs
that were truly faiths supported on emotional foundations.
Looked at from the distance of centuries, they seem blind; we
wonder that so sensible a man could have kept them so long.

First was his belief in empire: not, as many Britons thought,
for its economic benefits, but for its political strength and for
its potential good to its peoples. In India, England could carry
what was later known as the "white man's burden" and improve
the lot of people long exploited by commercial interests. America, truly and wholly British, could carry a great flexible government with implications of liberty and justice across endless
spaces, thus extending that "petty island" into an infinite future
of land and men and treasure. He even thought—as have others
before and since—that the capital of the British Empire might
some day move westward into North America.

Rejoicing, in 1760, in the news that Canada had fallen to
the British, Franklin wrote to his friend Lord Kames:

> I have long been of opinion, that the *foundations of the
> future grandeur and stability of the British empire lie in Amer-
> ica;* and though, like other foundations, they are low and little
> seen, they are, nevertheless, broad and strong enough to support
> the greatest political structure human wisdom ever yet erected.

Even in 1762, after he had returned, for a time, to Philadelphia, he wrote to Mary Stevenson, a little homesick, it would
seem, for England, a reason for his love of it.

Of all the enviable Things England has, I envy it most its people. Why should that petty Island, which compared to America, is but like a stepping-Stone in a Brook, scarce enough of it above Water to keep one's shoes dry; why, I say, should that little Island enjoy in almost every Neighborhood, more sensible, virtuous, and elegant Minds, than we can collect in ranging 100 Leagues of our vast Forests?

His second firm faith was in the king. To George III, as to his predecessor, he owed, as all colonists should, full allegiance and, indeed, at the third George's coronation, which he attended, he expressed his confidence in the young monarch. In reply to a word from his friend Strahan, expressing doubts, he wrote:

You now fear for our virtuous young king, that the factions forming will overpower him and render his reign uncomfortable. On the contrary, I am of Opinion that his virtue and the consciousness of his sincere intentions to make his people happy will give him firmness and steadiness in his Measures and in support of the honest friends he has chosen to serve him; and when that firmness is fully perceived, faction will dissolve and be dissipated like a morning fog before the rising sun, leaving the rest of the day clear, with a sky serene and cloudless. Such, after a few of the first years, will be the future course of his Majesty's reign, which I predict will be happy and truly glorious.

Keeping this faith, it was natural for Franklin to believe that his Pennsylvania would be better off as a crown colony than in the hands of the proprietors he hated. The proprietors, in these first English years, were Franklin's only enemies and his first secret moves were against them only. Though he was aware of the existence of corrupt "factions" which would try to dominate the king he was sure they would disappear like the fog, once the glorious royal sunshine burned away all evil.

It was, however, the very strength of these convictions that made the disillusion, when it came, so bitter. But Franklin merely reflected the dominant feeling in the American colonies, heightened, of course, by the warm friendships he had formed and his enjoyment of the London atmosphere which made his memory of Philadelphia and Boston seem dull and cold.

The progress of Franklin's change of heart may be followed in the sequence of letters which appeared, at frequent intervals, under a pseudonym in the London press. Letters were his weapons as well as evidence of his art. He was not a writer, as we know the profession; he produced no great, published works, never wrote a real book, yet he wrote all the time. Pamphlets —a popular medium in his time—newspaper columns, almanacs with their factual material spiced by witty, satirical and wise comment and, above all, letters—to everyone and about everything—were a constant occupation. Few great men and scarcely any Americans have bequeathed more of their heartbeat to posterity than he.

The London newspapers of the mid-eighteenth century—read more fully and carefully than those which later competed with other means of communication—carried the step-by-step story of Benjamin Franklin's metamorphosis from Briton to American. The first letters were aimed at the proprietors and comprise a conspiratorial performance worthy of the subtlest undercover agent. The next went from the local to the general scene and brought the united grievances of all the coastal colonies before the ministries concerned. Then came those aimed at the Whigs and the merchants, who were expected to sympathize with the American dilemmas. Finally, they reflected the change, which was evident in all his behavior, from British to American patriot.

But this contemplation carries us beyond our story. It has been said that the English years from 1757 to 1762 were the happiest of Franklin's life. Certainly there was much that was gentle, wise and witty in his private relations and in activities that brought him personal pleasure and only later—because everything about this scarcely credible man must—became public.

2

The "ungovernable passions" which Benjamin Franklin confessed to in his autobiography were inherited by his son William. William, himself the consequence of a lapse by his father, fell into a similar "erratum" about the year 1759 and a year later presented his father with a grandson, child of an unknown woman of low estate. But as William had been adopted by the Franklin family, so was William Temple, as soon as he was old enough to be removed from his mother—an operation for which, presumably, she was amply rewarded. Temple, as he was called, became a favorite with his grandfather and posterity is grateful to him for his long, faithful work in assembling and publishing many of Benjamin's papers.

William's affair ended his father's dream of marrying him to Polly Stevenson. Polly had left the Craven Street house and gone to live with Mrs. Tichel, an aunt, in Essex in May, 1759, and Franklin kept in touch with her by a correspondence which became an important part of her life and which has become known as one of the gentler episodes of his.

It was her idea that the letters should have a specific, continuing purpose. She was to ask him questions about science that puzzled her. "But why will you," he wrote in answer to her suggestion, "by the cultivation of your mind make yourself still more amiable and a more desirable companion for a man of understanding when you are determined, as I hear, to live single?" Could there be a clearer reflection of the conventions of the day when a girl was expected to think of education only as an adornment that might attract a potential husband?

Franklin wrote her about the sources of rivers, about the effects of tides upon rivers, about the functions of pores in the skin, the distillation of salt water—an inquiry which has since preoccupied many an engineer—the usefulness of certain insects, the influence of the moon on the sea, barometers, and the human body as a conductor of electricity.

One letter, especially, reveals the intensely curious nature of Franklin's mind and, at the same time, the practical direction of his thought. It recalls an experiment he once made to determine the effect of the sun's rays upon colored cloth.

> My Experiment was this. I took a number of little square pieces of Broad Cloth from a Taylor's Pattern-Card, of various Colours. There were Black, deep Blue, lighter Blue, Green, Purple, Red, Yellow, White and other Colours, or Shades of Colours. I laid them all out upon the Snow in a bright Sunshiny Morning. In a few Hours (I cannot now be exact as to the Time), the Black, being warm'd most by the Sun, was sunk so low as to be below the Stroke of the Sun's rays; the dark Blue almost as low, the lighter Blue not quite so much as the dark, the other Colours less as they were lighter; and the quite White remain'd on the Surface of the Snow, not having entred it at all.
>
> What signifies Philosophy that does not apply to some Use? May we not learn from hence, that Black Clothes are not so fit to wear in a hot Sunny Climate or Season, as white ones.... That Soldiers and Seamen, who must march and labour in the Sun, should in the East or West Indies have a Uniform of white? That Summer Hats for Men or Women, should be white, as repelling the Heat which gives Headachs to many and to some the fatal Stroke that the French call the *Coup de Soleil?*

That Franklin, under the exasperating burden of his mission and his multitude of extracurricular activities would take the time to write in such detail to a girl of twenty-one is characteristic not only of his kindness but of the flexibility of his attention.

3

Franklin's rhetorical question to Mary Stevenson: "What signifies Philosophy that does not apply to some Use?" was answered in a statement he made at another time: "Utility is in my opinion the test of value in matters of invention, and that a discovery which can be applied to no use, or is not good for something is good for nothing." These convictions distinguished him from many an ivory-tower scientist who pursues discovery only for its own sake. Such a one, for example, was the Scottish geologist James Hutton, who once remarked that a certain discovery was "a progress of science far beyond the apprehension of the vulgar." For Franklin, it was the "vulgar" whom science must serve. It was, after all, the vulgar in America who had read and admired his newspapers and his almanacs, for whom he had invented his stove and his lightning rod—though the nobility in England and the aristocracy on the Continent had begun to take notice of these useful inventions, made after long scientific study.

In November, 1758, soon after he had recovered from his illness and when he needed the comfort of warmth most, he was unhappy because, though his fire was burning briskly, so little warmth came into his room. So he made what he called "an easy, simple contrivance . . . for keeping rooms warmer in cold weather than they generally are, and with less fire."

Some two centuries later, the reader of his letters about this invention may be surprised that Benjamin Franklin, living in a quiet London dwelling, was able to conduct there an operation requiring the services of a stonecutter and an ironworker and involving enough noise and dirt to distress the most cooperative landlady. That it was successfully accomplished, however, is testimony to the American's will, perseverance and the persuasive charm which must have accompanied his stubbornness. In any case, the fact that the invention worked seems to have delighted everyone who saw it to the point of forgiving any inconvenience it may have caused.

> The opening of the chimney [Franklin wrote James Bowdoin, Boston merchant and later governor of Massachusetts] is contracted by brick work faced with marble slabs, to about two feet between the jams, and the breast brought down to within about three feet of the hearth. An iron frame is placed just under the breast, and extending quite to the back of the chimney, so that a plate of the same metal may slide horizontally backwards and forwards in the grooves on each side of the frame. This plate is just so large as to fill the whole space, and shut the chimney entirely when thrust quite in, which is convenient when there is no fire. Drawing it out, so as to leave a space between its further edge and the back of about two inches;

this space is sufficient for the smoke to pass; and so large a part of the funnel being stopped by the rest of the plate, the passage of warm air out of the room, up the chimney, is obstructed and retarded, and by that means much cold air is prevented from coming through crevices, to supply its place.

The device will immediately be recognized as the forerunner of the damper, later used in all fireplaces to regulate the amount of heat coming into the room.

In our common open chimneys, [Franklin added] half the fuel is wasted, and its effect lost, the air it has warmed being immediately drawn off. Several of my acquaintance, having seen this simple machine in my room, have imitated it in their own houses, and it seems likely to become pretty common. I describe it thus particularly to you, Because I think it would be useful in Boston, where firing is often dear.

In a time when domestic heat could be supplied only (as in England and America) by open fires or (as in Germany) by stoves, Franklin was greatly concerned with the means of making these necessities to comfortable living as effective as possible. With his "Pennsylvania fireplace," later known as the Franklin Stove, he had combined the heating principles of both and, on a small scale, anticipated the hot-air furnace. Working long and patiently over this, he had learned much about the behavior of smoke and, later, in London and on the Continent had found out why chimneys, through faulty construction and misunderstanding of draft principles, failed to draw. The publication of his findings caused wide reform in the architecture and construction of houses and in the habits of those who dwelt therein.

That his ingenuity should move out of the realm of physics into that of the arts was evidence of the wide ranging of his thought. His next Craven Street venture was in music.

4

There was a cultural fad in the mid-eighteenth century which was known as the "musical glasses." Goblets were made to emit notes when touched on the rim with a wet finger. The notes were differentiated from one another by the amount of water each glass contained. The performer sat at a table on which many glasses, carefully tuned according to their water content, were arrayed and, by touching successively the proper rims, produced a melody. The design, according to Franklin, was that of an Irishman named Puckeridge (or Pockrich) but the performance to be heard was given by a Fellow of the Royal Society whom he knew—one Edward Delaval. Franklin was so impressed that he wrote to his Italian correspondent, Giamba-tista Beccaria, about how it had inspired his new invention.

> Being charmed by the sweetness of its tones, and the music he produced from it, I wished only to see the glasses disposed in a more convenient form, and brought together in a narrower compass, so as to admit of a greater number of tunes, and all within reach of hand to a person sitting before the instrument, which I accomplished, after various intermediate trials, and less commodious forms, both of glasses and construction, in the following manner.

Franklin's detailed description demonstrates his talent, not only for making an invention but for explaining it. Whether Beccaria appreciated the pains the inventor took to make his account precise, he was probably pleased by the concluding sentence of Franklin's letter:

> In honour of your musical language, I have borrowed from it the name of this instrument, calling it the Armonica.

The armonica, described in simple terms without the speci-fications in inches and materials about which Franklin was so meticulous, consisted, in effect, of a row of thirty-seven glasses on their sides all continuously turned by mechanical means while the performer could elicit the tones by touching one or another of the rims. Instead of wineglasses he had blown a set of glass hemispheres with holes where the stems would nor-mally be so that they would all fit close together on the shaft that would turn them. These glass globes were graduated in size from the largest (nine inches in diameter) to the smallest (three inches). The notes ranged through three octaves and Franklin tuned them by a harpsichord.

When the instrument was finished, the performing musician could sit before it and, turning the shaft to which the globes were attached by working a foot pedal, could touch whatever rims gave the desired notes without straining his reach. Using both hands, he could play simple chords.

> The advantages of this instrument [Franklin explained] are, that its tones are incomparably sweet beyond those of any other; that they may be swelled and softened at pleasure by stronger or weaker pressures of the finger, and continued to any length; and that the instrument, being once well tuned, never again wants tuning.

The care Franklin took with the tuning, grinding the rims of the hemispheres until the pitch was precise, then engraving with a diamond the letter of each note on the proper glass was characteristic of his perfectionism. Here again we wonder how all this was achieved in the limited scope of his London quarters.

The invention had an immediate vogue. Franklin supervised its manufacture in London and it was sold there as the "harmonica," in accordance with the English practice of anglicizing everything, and musicians performed on it in Italy, Germany and Austria, and, finally, in Philadelphia.

But Benjamin Franklin's inventive activities were not confined to mechanical or cultural devices. These were public and were publicly acclaimed. We may picture the succession of visitors to Craven Street, eager to see what novelty was gestating there. They did not see the secret products of this American's ingenuity, the "inventions" he made in the performance of his mission as agent of the Pennsylvania Assembly whose authorship, however guessed at by shrewd examiners, he never revealed. They were pure propaganda designed to scare his enemies, the proprietors. That they accomplished that design became evident in the course of events.

5

His technique with the London press was the fruit of long journalistic experience. From the tricks he had played on his publishing brother, James, in his apprentice days in Boston, he had built, through the years of his Philadelphia paper, an anonymous self which had attained a wide influence. Writing letters over fictitious signatures or unsigned editorials, he had made the impersonal newspaper take the responsibility for views which were often radical and usually controversial. That he undertook to play the same game in the sophisticated London dailies is evidence of his confidence in his journalistic sleight of hand.

In September, 1758, having failed to get anywhere with the Penns, Franklin decided on an oblique attack by letters implying that the same discontents existed in the adjacent province of Maryland, whose proprietors were descendants of Lord Baltimore. Readers of the London *Chronicle* saw a letter on September 6, stating that a bill passed by the Maryland Assembly had been rejected by the Maryland Council—the chamber of the legislature controlled by the proprietor—because it proposed to tax the proprietary estates. Because of the rejection, supplies from England destined for the province had been cut off.

Five days later, Franklin was pleased to read in the *Public Advertiser* an angry letter denying the *Chronicle*'s purported news in its entirety. He knew, then, that he had reached a sensitive spot in the proprietor's nerve center; also it gave him an opportunity to write another long letter, which the *Chronicle* published on the 19th. In it, he made twenty-nine queries about the political conditions in Maryland, queries which he believed no one could answer except to the prejudice of the proprietary government. And so, indeed, it proved, deepening the sense of fear which already agitated the current Lord Baltimore that proprietaries be abolished and the province made a royal colony, directly accountable to the king.

The last query was:

Whether the frequent clashings of interests between the Proprietors and people of our colonies, which of late have been so prejudicial to his Majesty's service, and the defence of his dominions, do not at length make it necessary for this nation [England] to enquire into the nature and conduct of these Proprietary Governments and put them on a better footing.

Here, finally, was a summary of all the arguments in the suggestion that this archaic, feudal governmental device be ended for good.

In less than two months, the impact of all this correspondence was conveyed across the Atlantic from the proprietor in England to his so-called lieutenant governor in Maryland.

On December 5, the proprietor's secretary and amanuensis, Cecilius Calvert, wrote with all the abbreviations and shortcuts customary to that age of laborious penmanship, to Governor Horatio Sharpe:

> Some months ago an Article was put in the London Chro: that the Supply was not granted in Maryland by reason the Proprietor Estate not be Tax'd the ans^r pub^d that it was devoid of truth, that his Landed Estate was Tax'd in Equal proportion with His Tenants Upon w^h a reply was publish'd of Queries Impertinent and ridiculous not worthy of ans^r tho' easy of confute I mention this as I suppose it will make an eclat in Mary^{ld}.

By this time Franklin had earned the reputation of a general troublemaker—a reputation that was to grow more by design than by accident—and Secretary Cecilius added, "The supposed Author is Mr Franklin...."

A year later, Cecilius believed that a pamphlet entitled "Historical review of the Constitution & Government of Pennsylvania" and published anonymously in London was also Franklin's work and he wrote to Sharpe that it had "met cool reception." "But maybe," he added, "He'll do the same thing about Md & we'd better be prepared. (I am told he holds Public Correspondence with the Province.)"

Franklin denied authorship of the pamphlet but we know

from Strahan, who printed it, that he read it in proof. By 1759, then, everything that appeared in the London press about the North American colonies was scanned with suspicious eyes by Franklin's enemies and he had come to be regarded by most Tories as a dangerous fellow.

In that same year, Franklin was given the honorary degree of Doctor of Laws by the University of St. Andrews in Scotland and he was made a burgess and guild brother of Edinburgh. His visits to Scotland were the most memorable of his life.

IV

WAR AND PEACE

IN Scotland, where he went to get his honorary degree from the University of St. Andrews, Benjamin traveled extensively, always accompanied by William, and met many of the most renowned men of the time. Some of them, such as David Hume and Adam Smith, later won immortality for themselves, but then, in 1759, they gave promise of greatness of which the Franklins were happily aware. They were guests of Sir Alexander Dick, president of the College of Physicians at Prestonfield, of William Robertson, principal of the University of Edinburgh, and of Lord Kames at Berwick on Tweed. Certain men even accompanied the Franklins along many miles of their journey, and everywhere they went, as Franklin wrote to one of his hosts, the "many Civilities, Favours and Kindnesses heap'd upon us while we were among you, have made the most lasting Impression on our Minds, and have endear'd that Country to us beyond Expression."

By far the most enduring friends he made in the fifteen-hundred-mile tour was Lord Kames. He and Franklin were to keep up a correspondence as long as Kames lived. When the Franklins left his house in Berwick to go back to London, Lord and Lady Kames went with them as far as York simply for the sake of being with them. Later, Franklin was sorry they had not gone further.

> How unfortunate I was, [he wrote to Kames] that I did not press you and Lady Kames more strongly to favour us with your

company farther.... So that whenever I reflect on the great pleasure and advantage I received from the free communication of sentiment, in the conversations we had at Kames, and in the agreeable little rides to the Tweed side, I shall for ever regret our premature parting....

Our conversation till we came to York, was chiefly a recollection of what we had seen and heard, the pleasure we had enjoyed, and the kindnesses we had received in Scotland, and how far that country had exceeded our expectations. On the whole I must say, I think the time we spent there, was six weeks of the densest happiness I have met with in any part of my life; and the agreeable and instructive society we found there in such plenty, has left so pleasing an impression on my memory, that did not strong connexions draw me elsewhere, I believe Scotland would be the country I should choose to spend the remainder of my days in....

Franklin's enthusiasm could go no further than to invent the adjective he underlined.

2

While he was having these good times, the anonymous communications which had appeared in the press and elsewhere the previous year and which were generally attributed to Franklin were taking their effect. Though he had not written the pamphlet "Historical Review of the Constitution and Government of Pennsylvania," it was believed, especially by the Penns and their lawyers and supporters, to be his. And, indeed, he might as well have written it for all its ideas were his and the real author, Richard Jackson, did little beyond transcribing them. And Franklin was active in promoting the book; he bought many copies and distributed them widely. The proprietors reacted by spreading acrid though false propaganda against the province and its agent which appeared, also anonymously, in the London press.

Meanwhile, Governor William Denny of Pennsylvania had received the answer to Franklin's complaint, which the Penns had sent him, thus going over Franklin's head and Denny, although theoretically he was merely the tool of the proprietors, went against their wishes and permitted the Assembly to pass a bill allowing for the taxation of the proprietary estates. This, of course, was the principal issue and, as a result, the governor resigned his office in fear of what the Penns' lawyers might do to him. Whether his act was because of the influence of the Franklin-Jackson pamphlet both in Philadelphia and in London or whether he moved out of his own sense of justice, his behavior was branded as a breach of his oath of loyalty to his English superiors.

In a rage, the proprietors petitioned the king to refuse his assent to the Act, which had passed both houses of the Pennsylvania legislature. There was, therefore, a hearing in the Privy Council. Present were Franklin and his counsel and John Ferdinand Paris, the lawyer for the proprietors. Paris argued that, considering the feeling in the province against the proprietors, their estates would be so extravagantly taxed that they would be ruined. The Franklin forces replied that the tax "assessors were honest and discreet men under an oath to assess fairly and equitably" and that the proprietors' fears were "groundless." If the Act should get a royal veto "we insisted strongly on the mischievous consequences," explaining that the people of the province would face certain ruin.

> On this, [Franklin remembered] Lord Mansfield, one of the counsel rose, and beckoning me took me into the clerk's chamber, while the lawyers were pleading, and asked me if I was really of opinion that no injury would be done the proprietary estate in the execution of the act. I said certainly. "Then," said he, "you can have little objection to enter into an engagement to assure that point." I answer'd, "None at all." He then called in Paris, and after some discourse, his lordship's proposition was accepted on both sides.

There was, then, no veto and it all turned out just as Franklin had said it would and it was found that "the tax had been assessed with perfect equity."

3

By the time Franklin had arrived in London in the summer of 1757, what later became known as the Seven Years' War between Britain and France had spread across the world from India to America. The victories of Clive in India balanced the initial defeats in America. But until William Pitt, Earl of Chatham, took hold, there was no promise of total conquest for the British. To him the final defeat of France everywhere and the acquisition of French territory in North America and the West Indies was the unique objective and he was a brilliant enough director of what was, in effect, a world war, to gain for Britain final victory.

The "French and Indian War," as it was known in America, brought suffering to the colonies more from the Indian raids on the frontiers than from the fights with the French in Canada and in the Ohio valley. The colonists did their part in both phases of the war, sending large bodies of troops to the battle zones but, naturally, they were most concerned with the defense of their own property from the "savage" enemy.

Before he had been sent to England as agent from the province of Pennsylvania, Benjamin Franklin had taken an active part in the war. In spite of his abundant aid in supplying the ill-fated Braddock expedition, it had gone down to ignominious defeat. But Franklin had afterward acted as an officer of militia and, although on the edge of fifty, had gone through a rugged campaign on the Pennsylvania frontier.

The war on the sea had provided adventure during Franklin's voyage to England in 1757. His ship had been escorted part of the way by English and colonial men-of-war going to fight the French in the north. In mid-ocean and nearing the English coast it had eluded pursuits by French naval frigates and privateers.

War at sea in the eighteenth century was a sort of free-for-all affair in which individuals, acting on their own apart from any governmental organization, attacked enemy ships wherever they found them and often built private fortunes out of the plunder. The only legitimacy given to their performance by government

was a device known as "letters of marque" which provided ship-
owners and captains with the right to capture any enemy vessel
and tow it to a home port as a "prize," after which its cargo
became the property of the capturer. It was, in short, legiti-
mized piracy and had been, since sea warfare began, an exceedingly attractive enterprise.

Franklin's direct observation of this sort of operation during
an otherwise monotonous voyage gave him valuable instruction
which he was to use a decade later when the house in Craven
Street became a center for maritime conspiracy. But even
earlier, while the war with France was still going on, American
captains were occasional visitors at the Stevenson house and,
from the stories they told him of prize-taking, of large-scale
smuggling in the West Indies, of long pursuits and a hundred
tricks of deception and evasion, he built a storehouse of information that would one day be of immense service to the nation
he would have so large a part in establishing.

4

Meanwhile, however, as the Seven Years' War drew to its
close, he remained wholly loyal to Britain and, with the fall of
Canada in 1760, his vision of empire broadened. There was
discussion in England at the time about what conquests should
be retained in the empire and what should be left to the defeated enemy as too burdensome to be held. Should Canada,
which appeared to be nothing but a vast empty wilderness, be
let go and Guadeloupe, rich in sugar, be held?

To Franklin, who at home had seen enough of the French
and their Indian allies, Canada should be forever British; mi-
grant Englishmen should flock there and people the wilderness;
perhaps, indeed, as he suggested to Lord Kames, it might one
day contain the capital of the empire. Rushing, as usual, to
his pen and his printer, he prepared an eloquent pamphlet
setting forth the colonial advantages of Canada over those of
Guadeloupe. Surely no reader of this ardent tract, which showed
Franklin at the peak of his imperialistic conviction, could im-

agine that anything could ever induce this American to favor
independence for his homeland!

And yet, curiously, in this very time when, all over England,
church bells were ringing to celebrate the victory over the
hated papist French, there were Englishmen who saw a different
future in their crystal balls. One of them was Charles Pratt,
later Lord Camden, who believed that the colonies would one
day try for independence. When he told Franklin this, Franklin, shocked, replied that "no such idea was ever entertained by
the Americans, nor will any such ever enter their heads, unless
you grossly abuse them." Pratt, at the time, was attorney general
of England. Whether he told others of his prophecy, the suspicion spread that this might well happen. The Tories and the
friends and supporters of the proprietors, who naturally seized
upon any pretext for discrediting Franklin, even hinted that
rebellion against the mother country was one of Franklin's aims.
Later, this opinion was publicly expressed in the Privy Council
by Franklin's archenemy, Alexander Wedderburn.

Although this was a fearful suspicion among the English
conservatives, across the Channel it was a hope. The French,
itching for revenge against England, soon saw an opportunity
for encouraging the separation from England of the thirteen
colonies. The Duc de Choiseul, foreign minister under Louis
XV, cherished this hope to the point of sending spies to America
to sound out all rebellious feelings that might arise there and
report them to the French ministry. Thus, by 1763, when the
Treaty of Paris was signed, the idea of American independence
seems to have been in the air—except in America, where loyalty
to England was still considered a mark of patriotism!

That Franklin was aware of this speculation is evident in
his efforts to combat it. In another of his pamphlets, written
probably with the collaboration of Richard Jackson, he recalled
the difficulty he had had with his Albany Plan, made just before
he left for England, to unite the colonies for defense. The plan
had not been ratified because the colonies preferred to maintain their hostility toward one another. Such unity, he insisted,

would be necessary to any rebellion against the mother country
and any separation from it in the interest of independence.

> If they could not agree to unite [he wrote] for their defence
> against the French and Indians who were perpetually harassing
> their settlements, burning their buildings and murdering their
> people; can it reasonably be supposed there is any danger of
> their uniting against their own nation, which protects and
> encourages them, with which they have so many connexions and
> ties of blood, interest and affection, and which 'tis well known
> they all love more than they love one another?
> In short, there are so many causes that must operate to pre-
> vent it, that I will venture to say, an union amongst them for
> such a purpose is not merely improbable, it is impossible; and
> if the union of the whole is impossible, the attempt of a part
> must be madness; as those colonies that did not join the re-
> bellion, would join the mother country in suppressing it. When
> I say such a union is impossible, I mean without the most
> grievous tyranny and oppression. People who have property in
> a country which they may lose, and privileges which they
> may endanger, are generally dispos'd to be quiet; and even
> to bear much rather than hazard all.

As we read these words more than two centuries after they
were written, does there seem to be a hint of those other words
which were to follow in a scant sixteen years: "all Experience
hath shown, that Mankind are more disposed to suffer, while
Evils are sufferable, than to right themselves by abolishing the
Forms to which they are accustomed"? The suggestion is ines-
capable, yet we know that no shadow of a Declaration had ever
crossed Franklin's mind and that this was true of all the people
of the thirteen British colonies on the Atlantic coast of North
America. Franklin was simply presenting an extreme case to
show the impossibility of rebellion.

5

Having achieved the main object of his mission as agent by
persuading the Penn forces to ease the economic burden on

the people of Pennsylvania, Franklin began to think of going home. He wanted to report in person to the Assembly on what he had done in London and on how he had spent the public moneys. But most of all, he longed for reunion with his wife and daughter. Yet life in his beloved London, civilized by the arts and sciences and warmed by his new friendships, was so pleasant that it was hard for him to bring himself to departure —especially as it was so insistently opposed by all his intimates. William Strahan, particularly, kept writing Deborah, trying to persuade her to come over with Sally, after which all the Franklins could establish, in London, a permanent household. So he was torn by wishes and by duties.

His resolve to leave England was not strengthened by the act, in February, 1762, of Oxford University in conferring on him the greatest honor he had ever received. This was the honorary degree of Doctor of Civil Laws. The presentation was at the end of April in the same year and, simultaneously, William was awarded the honorary degree of Master of Arts.

Three months later, however, Franklin went to Portsmouth to take ship for the always perilous passage. "The attraction of reason," he wrote Strahan from the seaport, "is at present for the other side of the water, but that of inclination will be for this side. You know which usually prevails. I shall probably make but this one vibration and settle here for ever. Nothing will prevent it if I can, as I hope, prevail with Mrs. F, to accompany me. . . ." And in a last letter before the sailing he wrote Lord Kames that he felt as if he were "leaving this world for the next: grief at the parting; fear of the passage; hope of the future."

Fear of the passage was quieted somewhat by the convoy of ten of which his ship was a part and the protection of a man-of-war against possible enemy attacks. Also the weather was almost invariably good. It was a long but apparently a gay voyage, visiting from ship to ship, "dining with each other and on board of the man-of-war; which made the time pass agreeably, much more so than when one goes in a single ship; for this was like travelling in a moving village, with all one's neighbors about one." He reached Philadelphia the first of November. He got home well after the ten-week voyage "and had the happiness to find my little family perfectly well." His friends swarmed into the house to welcome him, and one told him that if the Assembly had known when he would arrive, they would have met him "with five hundred horse."

It was good that Ben Franklin could have this time to be with his family and old American friends. It was good, too, that he could see how things were in his province. For, in the next dozen years, he would have missions abroad, among both friends and bitter enemies, that were to keep him far from home.

V

PHILADELPHIA INTERLUDE

IN Philadelphia, Franklin soon discovered that he had enemies as well as friends. What has come to be known as a
"whispering campaign" had been launched against him by supporters of the proprietary organization. The prime mover in
this seemed to be Dr. William Smith, Provost of the Academy
of Philadelphia (which Franklin had founded in 1749), a Penn
supporter. The Reverend Smith's motive seems to have arisen
from his attachment to the Church of England and his consequent hatred of Quakers, with whom the province was largely
populated, and with whom, though a Deist himself, Franklin
was sympathetic. In any case, he took out his rage on Franklin,
enemy of the proprietors and of the Establishment generally.
On a visit to England for the purpose of raising money for the
Academy, he had spread venomous propaganda (which he admitted, after it had done its work to be false), and in Philadelphia he reported to his friends that Franklin had lived
extravagantly in England on the public moneys and his friends
were assiduous in giving the report general circulation.

Those members of the Assembly who may have believed the
rumors must have been surprised when Franklin, rendering
his official report, returned to the Assembly the £ 1,500 they
had given him minus £ 714 10s 7d as the total of his expenses
for his five English years! The Assembly was so astonished by
this small account that they not only refused to accept the
return but voted him another £ 1,500, making £ 3,000 in all.

In a letter to the Assembly, he pointed out that he had been unable to separate private from public expense since much of his accomplishment in establishing good feelings toward the colonies was pleasurable; nor would he charge the province with the cost of his illness or the necessity of living in a manner compatible with the importance of his position. In short, he leaned over backward with his scruples and it was obvious that the major part of the expense had come out of his own pocket.

How he took the vilification spread in England by Dr. Smith appeared in a letter to Mary Stevenson in March, 1763:

> I do not wonder at the behaviour you mention of Dr. Smith toward me, for I have long since known him thoroughly. I made that Man my Enemy by doing him too much Kindness. 'Tis the honestest Way of acquiring an Enemy. And, since it is convenient to have at least one Enemy, who by his Readiness to revile one on all Occasions, may make one careful of one's Conduct, I shall keep him an Enemy for that purpose....

As further compensation for the behavior of those hostile to him, the Assembly voted a resolution that Franklin, acting as agent for Pennsylvania, be formally thanked "as well for the faithful discharge of his duty to this province in particular as for the many and important services done to America in general." Whether or not Franklin was especially impressed by the phrase "America in general" coming from a single province, it is significant that the legislature of Pennsylvania thought so far beyond its own borders. "America" was a word that Englishmen applied to the colonies, but it was one the colonies rarely applied to themselves. Franklin, of course, had long thought of the colonies as a whole, subject to the same royal government, and his experiences in England had crystallized this thought so that he was ready for the unity that was soon to be forced upon them by a Britist act.

It was easy for Franklin to renew the warm intimacies of his youth. As true friends are not lost through physical separation, the members of the "Junto," the club that Franklin had founded in his earlier Philadelphia days, were as cordial and friendly as if the Atlantic had never come between them. As usual, some of his closest friends in America were women, notably Catherine Ray, who, during his sojourn in England, had married Governor William Greene of Rhode Island. In June, 1763, he and Sally visited the Greenes in Warwick, Rhode Island, where, following a bad fall from his horse, he was nursed back to health by Catherine. It was one of Franklin's fortunes that whenever he suffered a disability there was always a woman to give him succor.

In spite of this, and another fall which came in September, he was able in the course of his first year back in America to travel some sixteen-hundred miles in his capacity as colonial postmaster—officially "Deputy Postmaster General"—a position he still held, though during his absence it had been adminis-tered by an assistant.

2

Whether his presence helped aggravate it or, perhaps, circum-stances had moved toward a crisis, the people of Pennsylvania became extremely restive immediately after Franklin's arrival and a political upheaval followed.

On February 10, 1763, the Peace of Paris ended the Seven Years' War between Britain and France. With it came the elimi-nation of France from the mainland of North America and so, officially, there was an end to the French and Indian War in America. The Indian part of that war, however, went right on. Not having been consulted in the surrender of France, the In-dians saw no reason to give up. For years the French had indoc-trinated the people of many tribes with a hatred of the English, telling them that Britain planned an invasion and settlement of the western hunting lands that the Indians cherished as their own. The colonists along the frontiers did nothing to allay these fears; they did, indeed, much to increase them.

In the spring of 1763, after two years of plotting and organi-zation, a formidable body led by Pontiac, an Ottawa Indian chief, captured all but three of the Canadian forts which the

British had taken over from the French, and what has become known as "Pontiac's War" was accompanied by ravages of the American frontier settlements in which many colonists were killed and their property destroyed.

Pontiac's War had immediate repercussions in England because it cost money, and this expense added to the enormous outlays of the Seven Years' War caused the ministries to look about for new sources of revenue. Why, the ministers asked, should not the colonists themselves pay for the defense of their own frontiers? When Grenville, First Minister, revolved this question in his mind, he hatched an idea which became the first great cause of discontent in the thirteen American colonies and, for the first time, united them.

Meanwhile, in western Pennsylvania, the rage against the frontier marauders became bitter and indiscriminate. There were, in the western counties, groups of Indians, offshoots from the Six Nations—always friendly to the English—which had lived peaceably and had, ever since the beginnings of the province, made demonstrations of friendship toward the colonial settlers. Among these were the Moravian Indians, who had been converted to Christianity and had always lived in amity with their Moravian "brothers."

In the course of a century, there had grown up in Pennsylvania, along with law-abiding Quakers and Germans, a population of Scotch-Irish that was far less restrained. A gang known as The Paxton Boys was especially lawless and tried to do by rioting and violence what they could not do by appeals to the legislature and the courts. After swearing vengeance against the Indians—all Indians—for the attacks of certain tribes, and after carrying on, for their "Cause," several nights of riot in Philadelphia, the Paxton Boys traveled westward and massacred whatever Indians they found. As their atrocities injured only the friendly Indians—those that had lived for generations in peace with their white neighbors—Benjamin Franklin was horrified and laid the blame on the proprietary regime.

The pamphlet Franklin wrote, which he said was intended

"to strengthen the hands of our weak government, by rendering the proceedings of the rioters unpopular and odious," described the brutalities in lurid detail.

> These *Indians* [he wrote in *A Narrative of the Late Massacres in Lancaster County*] were the Remains of a tribe of the *Six Nations*, settled at *Conestogoe*, and thence called *Conestogoe Indians*. On the first arrival of the *English* in *Pennsylvania*, Messengers from this tribe came to welcome them, with Presents of Venison, Corn, and Skins; and the whole Tribe entered into a Treaty of Friendship with the first Proprietor, William Penn, which was to last "as long as the Sun should shine, or the Waters run in the Rivers." This Treaty has ... never been violated, on their Part or ours, till now. ...
>
> This little Society continued the custom they had begun ... of addressing every new Governor, and every Descendent of the first Proprietor, welcoming him to the Province, assuring him of their Fidelity, and praying for a continuance of that Favour and protection they had hitherto experienced. They had accordingly sent up an Address of this Kind to our present Governor, on his arrival; but the same was scarce delivered when the unfortunate Catastrophe happened which we are about to relate. ...

The pamphlet went on to describe how "those cruel men" broke into the workhouse in Lancaster where the Indians had assembled to save themselves.

> When the poor Wretches saw they had *no Protection* nigh, nor could possibly escape, and being without the least Weapon for Defence, they divided into their little Families, and Children clinging to their Parents; they fell on their Knees, protested their Innocence, declared their Love to the *English*, and that, in their whole Lives, they had never done them Injury; and in this Posture they all received the Hatchet: Men, Women and little Children were every one inhumanly murdered—in cold blood.

Then, with his usual quiet logic, Franklin asked:

> If an *Indian* injures me, does it follow that I may revenge that Injury on all *Indians?* .... The only Crime of these poor Wretches seems to have been, that they had a reddish-brown

Skin, and Black Hair; and some people of that Sort, it seems, had murdered some of our Relations. If it be right to kill a man for such a Reason, then, should any Man, with a freckled Face and red Hair, kill a Wife or Child of mine, it would be right for me to revenge it, by killing all the freckled red-haired Men, Women and Children, I could ever afterward meet with.

Benjamin Franklin, when he wrote these apparently plausible words, could scarcely realize that for more than two centuries Americans would continue to employ that same lack of logic toward their fellowmen.

The governor, though he issued perfunctory proclamations condemning the acts, was in fact so terrified by the Paxton Boys that he did nothing to implement his pronouncements. One night, indeed, when the rioting in the city was at its height, John Penn fled in panic and, knowing of nowhere else to go, knocked on Franklin's door and begged for his protection from the mob. Afterward, ashamed of his cowardice, he launched a campaign against Franklin, designed to unseat him in the Assembly. He ended by a complete surrender to mob violence and offered a bounty for the scalps of any Indians!

The governor and many Philadelphians who, angered by Franklin's pamphlet and another called "Cool Thoughts on the Present Situation of our Public Affairs," went to the governor's support, were able, in the spring election to drum enough votes in Philadelphia to get Franklin ejected from the Assembly. They could not, however, prevent the Assembly from renewing Franklin's appointment as agent for the province in England and instructing him to present a petition to the king asking that the government be changed from that of a proprietary to a royal colony directly accountable to the Crown and under its protection. Thus his return to London was assured.

3

He determined to sail some time in the year 1764. He would have been at home two years. He was torn again between his desire to do the Assembly's bidding and the necessity for leaving his family. Again, Deborah refused to accompany him and no argument could persuade her. She gave every evidence of attachment to her husband but it became obvious to him that she was even more attached to her home. Also, she complained that her health would not stand the voyage. Her decision, to be sure, was in tune with the custom of the times, when men were expected to go on dangerous missions without their wives and women were expected to keep the home fires buring during the men's absence. And Deborah Franklin was an ignorant, almost unlettered woman dominated by her fears of the unknown.

During Franklin's stay in Philadelphia, his son William, who, at the unsolicited instance of his friend, the Earl of Bute, a favorite of George III, had been appointed governor of the royal colony of New Jersey, arrived to assume his new position and took up his residence in Burlington with the wife he had brought with him from England. The appointment was in no way his father's doing and it greatly annoyed Governor John Penn, but William was well received in the colony and was installed with much ceremony; his father called on him there and went on a tour through New Jersey.

Early in the spring of 1764, the news came of new tax schemes devised by Grenville for raising money to pay the costs of the French and Indian War and the defense of the colonies against the Indians. The one which most caught Franklin's attention was the stamp tax. This called for the affixing of stamps to legal documents, bills of lading, newspapers and many other things. The stamps would cost various sums up to two or three pounds and the money would go as revenue into the English treasury.

This was unprecedented. Taxation had always been the function of the colonial governments. The only exceptions were customs duties intended for the regulation of trade, not for revenue. It seemed to Franklin that Parliament should have no right to tax for revenue unless those taxed had representatives in Parliament. The colonies had none and until they should have, any revenue tax imposed by the government of the mother country would be unconstitutional.

Grenville, however, had as yet introduced no bill providing for this tax. He wished to consult the agents of the colonies before doing so. This gave Franklin an additional reason for going to England. He must insist that such a tax would hurt England more than it would hurt the colonies. As he wrote to Peter Collinson soon after he received the news, "What you get from us in taxes you must lose in trade." With these words, he stated the gist of the argument that he would one day present to Parliament.

The various disturbances had been so costly that there were no funds left in the Pennsylvania treasury on the eve of Franklin's departure for England. The Assembly therefore arranged for a loan for his expenses and £1,100 were subscribed. Of this, Franklin would accept only £500. On November 7, 1764, he was escorted to Chester by three hundred friends and supporters. There he boarded the *Turtle,* the ship that was to carry him away from the whirlpool of controversy that the province had become to his still beloved England.

To his daughter Sally, he sent back this word on the 8th:

> The affectionate leave taken of me by so many friends at Chester was very endearing. God bless them and all Pennsylvania. . . .
> We expect to be at sea tomorrow, if this wind holds; after which I shall have no opportunity of writing to you, till I arrive (if it please God I do arrive) in England. I pray that his blessing may attend you, which is worth more than a thousand of mine, though they are never wanting. . . .

One would suppose that November was no time to start an Atlantic passage in a sailing ship. Yet, in spite of what he described to Deborah as "terrible weather," the crossing took only thirty days, unusual time for the season. "And," he wrote Deborah from the Isle of Wight, "I am, Thanks to God, very well and hearty." His health did not last. Some three weeks later, he wrote again, "I have been severely handled by a most violent Cold, that has worried me extreamly."

4

Anxious as he was to present the Assembly's petition asking for change from proprietary to royal colony for Pennsylvania, he was told by his deputy, Richard Jackson, who had handled the province's affairs in his absence, that there was a more pressing matter. Grenville was determined to introduce a bill which, if it should be passed by Parliament, would establish the Stamp Act. In an interview with the minister Franklin protested, in the name of the province, that Parliament had no right to tax the colonies but that they would be glad to honor, as they always had, any requisitions from the Crown. Grenville replied that he was determined to present the bill to the Commons and that he hoped the colonies would accept the results.

The instant he had arrived in London on December 10, Franklin had gone to the house in Craven Street without warning to Margaret Stevenson; she was out when he arrived and overcome with surprise and delight when she found him there. Several months later, he got news from home; some of it brought him pleasure; some would have greatly disturbed anyone but Benjamin Franklin.

> A vessel from Ireland to New York [wrote Cadwallader Evans from Philadelphia] brought us the most agreeable news of your arrival in London, which occasioned a great and general joy in Pennsylvania among those whose esteem an honest man would value most. The bells rang on that account till near midnight, and libations were poured out for your health, success, and every other happiness.

But his friend William Strahan told him of a letter he had had from son William describing continuing strife in Philadelphia. It was dated February 18, 1765.

> We have not heard anything from my Father since he sail'd, but I hope he has been safely landed in England at least two months ago. Since he left us Mr. Allen one of the principal Prop^y Tools in Pennsylvania has employ'd that Miscreant

Parson Smith, and two or three other Prostitute Writers to asperse his Character, in which they have been very industrious. However they have lately receiv'd a terrible Shock from Mr. Hughes, one of my Father's Friends, who being incens'd at their base Conduct published an Advertisement sign'd with his Name in which he Promised that if Mr. Allen, or any Gentⁿ of Character would undertake to justify the Charges brought against Mr. Franklin, he would pay £10 to the Hospital for every one they should prove to the Satisfaction of impartial Persons, provided they would pay £5 for every Falsehood he should prove they had alleged against Mr. Franklin. But the Challenge they were afraid to accept, and therefore still kept their Names concealed; but as they thought that something must be done, they endeavored to turn all Mr. Hughes's Challenge into Ridicule and raise the Laugh against him by an anonymous Answer. He, however, published a Reply with his Name subscribed, in which he lash'd them very severely for their Baseness. Not being able to answer this, they employ'd one Dove, a Fellow who has some Talents for the lowest kind of Scurrility, to publish a Print with some Verses annex'd villifying my Father and some of the most worthy Men of the Province. By way of Revenge some Writer has attack'd them in their own Way, and turn'd all Dove's Verses against Mr. Allen. . . . This has enraged him excessively as those Verses and the Print had cost him upwards of £25. . . . The Matter of the Propʸ Party against my Father, on Account of his wanting to bring about a Change of Government is beyond all Bounds. . . . If he does not succeed I know not what will become of the Province, as there is such a rooted Hatred among a great Majority of the People against the Propʸ Family. . . .

Much of this seems to a later observer a somewhat juvenile means of carrying on a conflict. So, no doubt, it seemed to the object of the proprietary attacks, living as he was in the more urbane atmosphere of London. Too, he had immediate, important business to attend to. To him, the resolution of the Pennsylvania Assembly about the stamp bill was parallel to their resolution about becoming a crown colony. The copy of the tax resolution which Franklin gave to Grenville read:

That by the constitution of the colonies, their business was with the King in matters of aid; they had nothing to do with any *financier,* nor he with them; nor were the agents the proper channels through which requisitions should be made: it was therefore improper for them to enter in any stipulation, or make any proposition to Mr. Grenville about laying taxes on their constituents by Parliament which really had no right to tax them at all, especially as the notice he had sent them did not appear to be by the King's order, and perhaps was without his knowledge. . . .

Still, the matter was largely theoretical in Franklin's mind; he could not guess at the common anger that would sweep across the entire body of the Atlantic colonies once the bill should become law. Nor was there in Parliament the slightest fear of consequences when it passed both houses. The debate on it was reported to be "languid," almost apathetic. And Franklin himself, in accordance with the provisions of the act, set about appointing the stamp distributor for Pennsylvania.

He would soon discover, however, that the passage of the Stamp Act was the first explosion of the American Revolution. From this point on, though he fought the belief at every step of the way, the conviction grew in him that the British government and even the English king were the final enemies of his homeland.

❧ VI ❧

STORM CLOUDS OVER
THE ATLANTIC

L IKE all Americans, then and since, who visit England in the
winter, Franklin suffered from a cold before he became
reacclimated. But resilience was his primary physical characteristic. Though the cough hung on he was soon up and about
his business. He was able too to resist the harmful effects of
the remedies administered to him by the physicians of the time
—perhaps because his thought on the subject of illness, as well
as on everything else, was far ahead of the time and, following
what he believed was common sense, he usually cured himself.
For example, he had ideas about fresh air which did violence
to current theories in both London and Philadelphia.

Leaving the windows open at night in one's bedroom was
thought to have lethal consequences but Franklin was a heretic.
Of such incongruities of behavior he wrote to Thomas Percival:

> But we abound in Absurdity and Inconsistency.
> Thus, tho it is generally allowed that *taking the Air* is a good
> Thing, yet what Caution against Air, what stopping of Crevices,
> what wrapping up in warm Clothes, what shutting of Doors
> and Windows! even in the midst of Summer! Many London
> Families go out once a Day to take the Air; three or four Persons
> in a Coach, one perhaps Sick; these go three or four Miles or
> as many Turns in Hide Park, with the Glasses both up close, all
> breathing over & over again the same Air they brought out of
> Town with them in the Coach with the least change possible,
> and render'd worse and worse every moment. And this they call
> *taking the Air*. From many years' Observations on myself and

others, I am persuaded we are on a wrong Scent in supposing Moist or cold Air, the Causes of that Disorder we call a Cold.

That he was able to introduce such startling ideas into the house in Craven Street was one more testimony to Franklin's persuasiveness. When he came back, he was received not as the paying guest he had been but as a member of the family. He reorganized the household much as he wished and, whether or not it was done to please him, the family was soon enlarged to include a Franklin cousin, thirteen-year-old Sally, daughter of Thomas Franklin of Leicestershire. As Benjamin later wrote to his wife, the girl was "nimble-footed and willing to run errands for me." Eventually William's son, William Temple, who had been away at school in Kensington, joined the little household during his vacations.

At Craven Street, Franklin was an early riser. The cold bath customary in England as a "tonic" he had given up because "the shock of the cold water seemed too violent and I have found it much more agreeable to my constitution to bathe in another element, I mean cold air. With this view I ... sit in my chamber without any clothes whatever, half an hour or an hour, according to the season, either reading or writing. This practice is not in the least painful, but, on the contrary, agreeable; and, if I return to bed afterwards before I dress myself as sometimes happens, I make a supplement to my night's rest of one or two hours of the most pleasing sleep that can be imagined."

Dinner was in midafternoon, often away from home. In the evenings he would have a glass or so (sometimes a bottle) at a friend's house and get back to bed late. This was the strict Benjamin Franklin who had made his Poor Richard preach every sort of virtue, including temperance and the advice: "Early to bed and early to rise/Makes a man healthy, wealthy and wise"! But this was London, not Poor Richard's Philadelphia, a distinction not remembered as generations of children were taught the verse.

As winter turned to spring, he had so many things to think

about, so much writing and talking to do, so many men to see
and an immediate future so dangerous that the tranquillity of
his home life was a blessing. Despite his advice to ministers and
members of Parliament, the Stamp Act was passed in March
and approved by the king. Franklin, far from the tumult which
arose in his remote homeland, resolved to take it philosophically
and to do what seemed to him proper for an agent to make the
execution of the act as practicable as possible. As Grenville had
provided, to make it more acceptable to the colonists, that the
commissioners should be Americans, not English, Franklin set
about choosing the best persons to collect the taxes, at least in
his province. He picked John Hughes, member of the Pennsylvania Assembly, without realizing what a disservice he was
doing to his friend.

It was midsummer, 1765, before London heard the echo of
the thunder that rolled over the western coast of the Atlantic.
The Act was to go into effect in November.

2

The Stamp Act decreed that stamps costing from three pence
to four pounds be affixed to all colonial bills of lading, licenses,
wills, bonds, deeds, indentures, leases, contracts, newspapers,
advertisements, college degrees, playing cards and dice, and
it provided penalties for noncompliance. The revenue accruing,
estimated to be above £60,000 per year, was to recoup the
British treasury for the costs of defending the colonies during
the late war.

In times of widespread unease, confused and hysterical persons often form mobs and violent, destructive riots ensue. News
of the passage of the Stamp Act and of its impending execution
brought such disorders to most of the American colonies. Governors were threatened, their property destroyed, appointed
tax collectors were burned in effigy and the peace was everywhere disturbed by noisy demonstrations. Later, when the Act
boomeranged back to England, there were riots before the
houses of Parliament in London.

Perhaps the most irrational vandalism occurred in Massachusetts when the beautiful house of Governor Hutchinson was ruined and his fine, irreplaceable library burned. For a time all Boston was at the mercy of a mob, and order was restored there and in other cities only when resolutions of nullification were taken by a concert of colonial legislatures. Then, for the first time, unity came to the thirteen provinces.

Inspired by the oratory of Patrick Henry, seven resolutions were introduced into the Virginia legislature and although only five were finally adopted by the cautious Assembly, all found their way into most of the colonial newspapers and inflamed the populace everywhere. The resolves proclaimed that colonists, according to the royal charters of James I, were "entitled to all liberties, privileges, and immunities of denizens and natural subjects, to all intents and purposes, as if they had been abiding and born within the realm of England." It was inherent in the British constitution, the resolves further declared, that such English subjects were not to be taxed unless they were represented in the taxing body. Thus, the only right of taxation lay within the Virginia General Assembly.

In October, approximately a month before the date set for the execution of the Act, a "Stamp Act Congress" assembled in New York City at the instigation of James Otis of Massachusetts. Delegates from nine of the colonies attended. They made similar resolutions and prepared an address to the king, a memorial to the lords and a petition to the House of Commons, all urging the repeal of the Act.

The protest got its real teeth, however, when there came about an agreement among the people of all the colonies to boycott goods imported from Great Britain. As many of the English merchants owed their prosperity to colonial trade, this concerted action gave Franklin his most powerful weapon in the battle for repeal.

3

As soon as Franklin heard of the violent reception of the Stamp Act by the people of the thirteen colonies, he realized that the British government had done what he failed to do: it had united them, not in the cause of defense but, as they said, in the cause of liberty. He knew, well enough, that once the freedom of a Briton was threatened, there would be no limit to the extent of his resistance. And, as Virginia had declared, an Englishman was no less an Englishman because he had been born three thousand miles from the houses of Parliament. Londoners, living in the margins of a society corrupted by prosperity, may have forgotten this, but the people of Boston and Philadelphia and Charleston remembered. Their ancient charters, legacies from the great Magna Carta itself, guaranteed their precious historic status. To Benjamin Franklin, still a Briton, it was clear, once he heard the echo from overseas of that word, liberty, that the tocsin had sounded.

But when he heard of the universal colonial agreement to stop trading with the mother country, he knew precisely what to do. He was, after all, a practical businessman. The only thing that could shake English complacency was a blow to commerce. Among his friends were many merchants. He soon knew of their alarm at the sudden disappearance of the immense colonial market. They told him of the depression that was creeping up on the manufacturers, throwing workers out of employment and into riots. Through them, he could reach Parliament.

Indeed, by January, 1766, the London merchants had organized and sent an impassioned petition to the House of Commons, stating that the colonial commerce, "so beneficial to the state, and so necessary for the support of multitudes, now lies under such difficulties and discouragement, that nothing less than its utter ruin is apprehended, without the immediate interposition of parliament. . . ."

Franklin biographer Carl Van Doren, having found a scarcity of letters for the year 1765 after August, suggests that, at about that point, he went "underground." Well he might; his job from then on was lobbying for repeal. It was important for him to talk to as many businessmen as possible who were also members of Parliament or persons who had easy access to such members.

This meant a visit to each, for the only other means of communication at the time was by letter, which was too slow, and it was imperative to know at once the temper of the man interviewed. When he spoke to them face to face, he could be extremely persuasive and so he convinced the doubters and strengthened the indecisive. Here we see Franklin at his best: calm, logical, reasoning, without ever showing the fire that was growing in intensity within him. With people he rarely indulged in the acrid sarcasm of his writings, the lethal attacks beneath the metaphors of his pamphlets. He knew that he must not exhibit any reflection of the mob hysteria that had shattered all restraint in America.

Indeed, he was horrified by the stories that came slowly over to him of the violent reaction that had swept his homeland. He had not heard of the indignities that his friend John Hughes had suffered when his appointment as the Act's executor became known. But he wrote to Hughes, on August 9, cautioning calm and speaking of the "Indiscretion of some People with you, concerning the Government here."

> But the Rashness of the Assembly in Virginia is amazing! I hope however that ours will keep within the Bounds of Prudence and Moderation; for that is the only way to lighten or get clear of our Burthens.
>
> As to the Stamp Act, tho' we purpose doing our Endeavour to get it repeal'd, in which I am sure you would concur with me, yet the Success is uncertain—If it continues, your undertaking to execute it may make you unpopular for a Time, but your acting with Coolness and Steadiness, and with every Circumstance in your Power of Favour to the People, will by degrees reconcile them. In the mean time, a firm Loyalty to the Crown & faithful adherence to the Government of this Nation, which it is the Safety as well as Honour of the Colonies to be connected with, will always be the wisest course for you and I [sic] to take, whatever may be the Madness of the Populace or their blind Leaders, who can only bring themselves and their Country into Trouble and draw on greater Burthens by Acts of rebellious Tendency—

Obviously, Franklin could have had no idea of the extent of the disturbances at home and naturally he could have no inkling of what the unfortunate Hughes would be facing when, more than a month later, he got the letter. Though it was easy enough to remain calm in London, it was something else to caution calm to a colonist living in the very cauldron of boiling disorder.

But there was other news from America more personally disturbing to Franklin than even the Stamp Act itself. His enemies in Pennsylvania, adhering, as they did, to the British Establishment, watched the rioting with considerable apprehension and sought a scapegoat. What better villain than the hated agent who, for years, had opposed every aspect of the proprietary government, including the governors and the august Penns themselves!

Raising the pitch of the whispering campaign, the enemies spread the rumor that Franklin had invented the Stamp Act and that he had profited by its passage, having been rewarded by money payments and by the promise of a high government position. In Philadelphia there were threats of burning the family's new Market Street house, which had been built for him and which had not been completed when he left for England. It was thought that Deborah was in danger; she was advised by friends to leave the house, which she refused to do, and William arranged for her protection by sending armed men to stay with her until the danger was over.

In London, fighting for his peace of mind, Franklin made more and more headway with his efforts and, after many ups and downs in the prospect of success, he was finally encouraged, in January, 1766, by the brilliant and devastating speech of William Pitt which attacked the Stamp Act as "unconstitutional, unjust, oppressive...." Early in February, he was ordered to appear before the House of Commons to answer questions as to the necessity of repeal from the American point of view. This "examination," as it has been called, marked the greatest political and diplomatic triumph of his career so far, and it has been thought the major factor in the change of mood of the parliamentary majority.

Franklin's editor and biographer, Albert Henry Smyth, tells:

> The promptness and pertinacity with which he replied to every question, the perfect knowledge of the subject manifested in his answers, his enlarged and sound views of political and commercial affairs, and the boldness and candor with which he expressed his sentiments, excited the surprise of his auditors, and were received with admiration by the public when the results of the examination appeared in print....
>
> The account of the examination was first published in 1767, without the name of printer or publisher. It was translated into French, and widely circulated in Europe. It has been frequently reprinted in both the English and French languages.

In point of fact, a "first edition" was anonymously printed in 1766. The publisher, one J. Almon, was afraid of prosecution and so concealed his name. Later, however, he grew bolder and issued a second edition.

Several of the questions asked in the examination were planted. They were asked by Franklin's friends and the men with whom he had done his lobbying. The answers to them were prepared beforehand and learned by heart. This questioning was led by James Hewitt, Member for Coventry, a dry goods merchant who had much to gain by repeal. His inquiries established the fact that the colonies were already paying extremely burdensome taxes, mostly as a result of recent war costs. The American-born John Huske followed Hewitt. He was the Member from Walden. The answers to his questions were of the utmost importance in showing the insuperable difficulties in distributing the stamps in the back country away from post roads and, indeed, any other practical means of communication.

> Q. Are you not concerned in the management of the Post Office in America?
> A. Yes. I am Deputy Post-Master General of North America.
> Q. Don't you think the distribution of stamps by post to all the inhabitants very practicable, if there was no opposition?

A. The posts only go along the seacoasts; they do not, except in a few instances, go back into the country; and if they did, sending for stamps by post would occasion an expense of postage amounting, in many cases, to much more than that of the stamps themselves. . . .

Q. Can you disperse the stamps in Canada?

A. There is only a post between Montreal and Quebec. The inhabitants live so scattered and remote from each other, in that vast country, that posts cannot be supported among them, and therefore they cannot get stamps by post. The English Colonies, too, along the frontiers, are very thinly settled.

Q. From the thinness of the back settlements, would not the stamp act be extremely inconvenient to the inhabitants, if executed?

A. To be sure it would; as many of the inhabitants could not get stamps when they had occasion for them without taking long journeys, and spending perhaps Three or Four Pounds, that the Crown might get Six pence.

Q. Are not the Colonies, from their circumstances, very able to pay the stamp duty?

A. In my opinion there is not gold and silver enough in the Colonies to pay the stamp duty for one year.

When it came to the turn of the members opposed to repeal to ask their questions, Franklin had to answer ad lib. These interrogators insisted on the theoretical right of Parliament to place an internal tax on the colonies even though they were not represented in the legislature in England. They failed to understand, so they implied, the difference between a duty laid on imports and a tax to be executed within the colonies for purposes of revenue. Is there, asked the questioner, any kind of difference between a duty on the importation of goods, and an excise on their consumption? Franklin was clear and firm on this point which had seemed so ambiguous to Englishmen:

Yes, a very material one; an excise . . . they think you can have no right to lay within their country. But the sea is yours; you maintain, by your fleets, the safety of navigation in it, and keep it clear of pirates; you may have therefore a natural and equitable right to some toll or duty on merchandizes carried through that part of your dominions, towards defraying the expence you are at in ships to maintain the safety of that carriage.

In a long speech near the end of the examination, Franklin made it clear that, although the colonial governments deplored violence in resistance to the Stamp Act, the people would not agree to a right of taxation without representation.

The proceedings of the assemblies [he said] have been very different from those of the mobs and should be distinguished, as having no connection with each other. The assemblies have only peacably resolved what they take to be their rights; they have taken no measures for opposition by force; they have not built a fort, raised a man or provided a grain of ammunition, in order to [insure] such opposition. The ringleaders of riots, they think ought to be punished.... But as to an internal tax, however small soever, laid by the legislature here on the people there, while they have no representatives in this legislature, I think it will never be submitted to. They will oppose it to the last.

Finally, the question was asked:

If the stamp act should be repealed, would it induce the assemblies of America to acknowledge the rights of parliament to tax them, and would they erase their resolutions?
A. No, never.
Q. Are there no means of obliging them to erase those resolutions?
A. None that I know of; they will never do it unless compelled by force of arms.
Q. Is there a power on earth that can force them to erase them?
A. No power, how great soever, can force men to change their opinions.

The examination closed with these simple words:

Q. What used to be the pride of the Americans?
A. To indulge in the fashions and manufactures of Great Britain.

Q. What is now their pride?
A. To wear their old cloathes over again, till they can make new ones.

4

Whether or not, Franklin was proud of the soundness and reasonableness of his answers, he was pleased indeed at their reception and by the news his friends brought him of the examination's effect. On February 27, he was able to write to his friend Charles Thomson:

> We at length, after a long and hard struggle, have gained so much ground, that there is now little Doubt the Stamp Act will be repealed, and reasonable relief given us besides in our Commercial grievances.... I trust the Behaviour of the Americans on the occasion will be so prudent, decent, and grateful as that their Friends here will have no reason to be ashamed, and that our enemies, who predict that the Indulgence of Parliament will only make us more insolent and ungovernable, may find themselves, and be found, false Prophets.

The bill for repeal was introduced into Parliament on the 21st of February, eight days after the close of the examination, and, after passage, received the king's assent on the 8th of March. Almost the first act of Franklin after the repeal was to relieve Deborah of her loyal adherence to the nonimportation agreement of the province.

> My dear Child, [he wrote her, early in April] As the Stamp Act is at length repeal'd, I am willing you should have a new Gown, which you may suppose I did not send sooner, as I knew you would not like to be finer than your Neighbours, unless in a Gown of your own Spinning.... I have sent you a fine Piece of Pompadour Sattin, 14 Yards, cost 11 shillings a Yard; a silk *Negligee* and Petticoat of brocaded Lutestring for my dear Sally, with two dozen Gloves, 4 bottles of Lavendar Water.... I send you also Lace for two Lappet Caps, 3 ells of Cambrick. ... 3 Damask Table Cloths, a Piece of Crimson Morir for Curtains with Tassels Line and Binding.... I send you also a Box

with three fine Cheeses. Perhaps a bit of them may be left when I come home. Mrs. Stevenson has been very diligent and serviceable in getting these things together for you. . . .

Though Franklin never told, in public at least, of his pride in his great performance before the House of Commons, there can be no doubt of his satisfaction with the result. Yet, during the spring and summer of 1766, he saw the storm clouds move across the Atlantic from America to England. As the news came to him of the immense joy and gratitude in America at the repeal, he was aware of the resentment in England at what was regarded in many quarters as a slap in the face of Parliament and a growing desire to put the colonies in their place and show them where the power lay. The old cry of rebellion was raised and the king, just emerging from his first attack of insanity, was obsessed with the will for absolute control in America even if it required a resort to the force of arms. Thus, indeed, it was the powers that be in England that were spoiling for revolution —though with no prescience of what its consequences might be —and not the people of the American colonies, who were still protesting with oratory and bonfires their loyalty to the mother country.

They little realized, nor did Franklin, that it was not the Stamp Act itself, but its repeal that was the beginning of the end.

❧ VII ❧

TRAVELING PHILOSOPHER

ONE of the advantages of the slow communications in the disturbed later years of the eighteenth century lay in the breathing spells between the spells of bad news. In these relatively tranquil intervals it was possible to regain one's peace of mind. Franklin accomplished this by changing the direction of his thought. After the months of incessant activity when the necessity for getting repeal of the Stamp Act crowded everything else out of his mind, it was a relief to go back to other, older interests. It was good to go shopping again for Deborah and daughter Sally with Margaret Stevenson, to explore science and record experiments, to write satires and "bagatelles," to entertain friends with stories and song, to play chess, to carry on an interrupted correspondence or to joke with children.

Soon after the repeal, he wrote to Thomas Ronayne, a glass manufacturer in Cork, to answer some questions which had arisen in the course of electrical experiments made by Ronayne with apparatus of his own construction.

> Your observations upon the electricity of fogs and the air in Ireland, and upon different circumstances of storms, appears to me very curious, and I thank you for them. There is not, in my opinion any part of the earth whatever which is, or can be, naturally in a state of negative electricity; and, though different circumstances may occasion an inequality in the distribution of the fluid, the equilibrium is immediately restored by means of its extreme subtility, and of the excellent conductors with which the humid earth is amply provided. I am of opinion, however,

that when a cloud, well charged positively, passes near the earth, it repels and forces down into the earth that natural portion of electricity which exists near its surface, and in buildings, trees &c., so as actually to reduce them to a negative state before it strikes them.

In this letter, as in various reports on his experiments, Franklin speaks of electricity as a "fluid," an idea to which later students of electronics have returned, though it was long repudiated. Here is another case of his thinking far beyond his time.

Letters he wrote in these years, notably one to Lord Kames in April, 1767, show Franklin to have been a prophet in international politics as well as in electricity. He was much preoccupied with a design which, more than a century later, became that of the British Commonwealth of Nations. But, as the threat of the American Revolution came nearer, he began to despair of the realization of that ideal.

> I am fully persuaded with you [he wrote to Lord Kames] that a *Consolidating Union,* by a fair and equal representation of all the parts of this empire in Parliament, is the only firm basis on which its political grandeur and prosperity can be founded.

This is a reiteration of the project that Franklin and Kames had discussed before and which, for some years, had seemed the only solution to the disturbed relations that were growing toward a crisis. But was it now too late? Had the gulf grown too wide to be bridged?

> The time has been, when the colonies might have been pleased with it; they are now *indifferent* about it; and if it is much longer delayed . . . will *refuse* it. But the pride of this English people cannot bear the thought of it, and therefore it will be delayed.

Franklin then gave a precise description of what the colonies were, rather than what the English supposed them:

> It is a common, but mistaken notion here, that the Colonies were planted at the expence of Parliament, and that therefore the Parliament has a right to tax them, &c. The truth is, they

were planted at the expence of private adventurers, who went over there to settle, with leave of the King, given by charter. On receiving this leave and those charters, the adventurers voluntarily engaged to remain the King's subjects, though in a foreign country; a country which had not been conquered by either King or Parliament, but was possessed by a free people....

Parliament had no hand in their settlement, was never so much as consulted about their constitution, and took no kind of notice of them, till many years after they were established. *

2

The news from America following repeal of the Stamp Act was far from bad; indeed it was so extravagantly good that Franklin, considering the resentful English background, was skeptical of its durability. Watching, from day to day, the temper of Parliament and of the ministries, he was well aware of the anger repeal had caused in certain quarters and of the resolve the government had made to save face at any cost to the colonies.

It has been said of the American people that, in their emotional demonstrations, they rush, overnight, from one extreme to the other. Franklin found this conspicuously true in the late spring and summer of 1766, when the news of repeal came across the Atlantic. From Nova Scotia to Georgia, there was a wave of joyous feeling as intense as the rage that had followed the proposal of the hated Act. Men and women wept, cannon were fired everywhere in exuberant celebration, so many bonfires were lighted that the whole coastline seemed ablaze. Mass meetings were held, orators rose to express loyalty to the king and to the great mother country which everyone, despite temporary disagreements, loved in the depths of their hearts.

Never [wrote James Parton, in his biography of Franklin] did any people so abandon themselves to rapturous exultation, as the colonists did on this occasion. In Boston, the very debtors were brought out of jail, that there might at such a moment, be no one unhappy in the town. When the glad tidings reached Philadelphia, the frequenters of the principal coffee house sent for the captain of the ship [that brought the news] to make one of their company, presented him with a gold-laced cap and gave presents to every man and boy of his crew. They kept a punch-bowl replenished all day free to every one who would drink the health of the king. At night the city was illuminated, and the people were regaled with unlimited beer.

J. F. Watson's *Annals of Philadelphia* tells that three hundred gentlemen

resolved to clothe themselves, on the next birthday of the king in complete suits of English manufacture, and give their homespun to the poor.

Sally Franklin wrote to her "honored papa" that "I never heard so much noise in my life; the very children seemed distracted."

There was, indeed, so much noise that the whisper of an incensed Parliament was drowned. Yes, sure enough, a majority had voted for repeal, but it was an expedient impulse designed to restore a lost commerce, not a concession to governments and peoples who had appealed to what they called eternal principle and raised the cry that taxation without representation is tyranny. After all, the petitioners and voters had talked only about their pocketbooks, whereas that dangerous fellow, Dr. Benjamin Franklin, had said repeatedly that the British legislature had no *right* to impose taxes for revenue on the people of the American provinces.

Despite the repeal of the Stamp Act by a majority, most of whom were commercially motivated, many others believed that Parliament had surrendered its precious control over the rebellious colonies. A bill was passed, therefore, only ten days after the king had given his grudging assent to repeal, "for the better securing the dependency of his Majesty's dominions in America upon the crown and parliament of Great Britain." When passed, the law was called the "Declaratory Act" and it declared that Parliament "had, hath, and of right ought to have, full power and authority to make laws and statutes of sufficient force and validity to bind the colonies and people of

America, subjects of the crown of *Great Britain,* in all cases whatsoever."

This vengeful mood of Parliament led Franklin to final despair of success in his project of union. Representatives from the colonies would never, he was now sure, be admitted to the British legislature. He wrote, therefore, to Cadwallader Evans on May 9, 1766:

> The Parliament here do at present think too highly of themselves to admit representatives from us, if we should ask it; and, when they will be desirous of granting it, we shall think too highly of ourselves to accept of it.

3

Franklin, always distrustful of such emotional demonstrations as that which came in the echo from America, and seeing the danger ahead when it should die down and the colonists realize the true mood of king and Parliament, turned his attention away, this time to Europe. There was nothing he could do at the moment in England; he was regarded by certain ministers as a troublemaker so it would be well to let them cool down before he resumed discussions of issues which were growing insoluble. Too, he had been weakened by colds and attacks of gout and he needed a rest. So when Sir John Pringle, physician to the queen, suggested that Franklin go with him to Pyrmont in Hanover to drink the supposedly curative waters, Franklin accepted. This was in June, 1766. The visit was to be brief because in eight weeks the queen was due to be confined and her doctor must be on hand.

Franklin, apparently dubious about the "waters," wrote to Deborah:

> I hope more from the air and exercise, having been used, as you know, to have a journey once a year, the want of which last year has I believe hurt me. . . .

Travel, to him, was one of the great pleasures; indeed, it was one he could not do without. "Travelling," he once told Polly Stevenson, "is one Way of lengthening Life. . . ." He would not, then, settle down in Hanover as Sir John did; waters or no waters, he would keep moving. So he left Pringle and went on into Germany. At Göttingen, he met the fabulous Baron Münchhausen and the oriental scholar Johann Michaelis. Michaelis told him the day would come when the colonies would separate from England. No, replied Franklin with the sounds of loyalty from across the Atlantic still ringing in his ears, Americans loved the mother country and would never try to be independent of Britain, to which Michaelis answered, "I believe it, but almighty interest would soon outweigh that love or extinguish it altogether."

While Franklin was abroad, there came the prelude to one of the great tragedies of modern English history and a truly shattering blow to the relations between Great Britain and her American colonies.

King George dismissed the Rockingham ministry, which had supported repeal of the Stamp Act and had urged the compromise of the Declaratory Act. Whether or not he did this from pique is uncertain as all things were uncertain at that point in the monarch's career, when he was hovering over the brink of sanity. To the surprise of some, he called William Pitt, now Lord Chatham, and asked him to form a cabinet. Those who enjoy playing the game known as "the ifs of history" are convinced that had Pitt been as sound of mind and body as he had been a decade before, the whole future of both Britain and America would have been other than what it really was.

Friends of America rejoiced that Pitt, one of America's most devoted friends, had been recalled. They were surprised because of the king's earlier repudiation of him. But most rational Englishmen had got over being surprised at the conduct of their ruler.

Unfortunately Pitt was ill. It is difficult to discern at a distance of two centuries what his trouble was. We know he had been tortured by what was then known as gout, made worse by what Franklin called his "quacking." He had, too, either caused by, or independent of his gout, what we should call a nervous breakdown but what then was called insanity.

To be sure, Pitt included in his cabinet such men as Isaac Barré (who had invented the term "sons of liberty" for American patriots) and Franklin's friend, the Earl of Shelburne. This gave the Americans hope. But Chatham, in 1766, fell into a kind of apathy which let the real power go to men like the weak and dissolute Duke of Grafton, America's bitter enemy Charles Townshend, and Lords Hillsborough, North and Howe. Thus, instead of reconciliation, which the Whigs might have brought about, there was a crescendo of oppression, called in the colonies "tyranny," ending in revolution.

Franklin returned from his happy sojourn in Germany to see this drama developing. He knew that his chances of success in reconciliation against such a coalition were slim indeed. In the spring of 1767, Franklin was evidently a marked man. He was being watched. One of the best letters he ever wrote—to Lord Kames—was intercepted and never reached its destination.

Franklin, however, had more personal matters to think about. His daughter, Sally, had fallen in love with an Englishman living in America, Richard Bache.

> ... I must leave it to your judgment [he wrote Deborah on June 22, 1767] to act in the Affair of your Daughter's Match, as shall seem best. If you think it a suitable one, I suppose the sooner it is compleated the better. In that case, I would only advise that you do not make an expensive feasting Wedding, but conduct everything with Frugality and Economy, which our circumstances really now require to be observed in all our Expences....

The rest of the letter is concerned with fears about his income, now that his printing partnership with David Hall had been dissolved, "and if I should lose the Post Office, which among the many Changes here is far from being unlikely, we should be reduc'd to our Rents and Interest of Money for a subsistence...." He concluded these complaints with a summary:

> In short, with Frugality and prudent Care we may subsist decently on what we have, and leave it entire to our Children:— but without such Care, we shall not be able to keep it together;

it will melt away like Butter in the Sunshine; and we may live long enough to feel the miserable Consequences of our Indiscretion.

Nevertheless:

Having lately bought a Piece of fine Pocket Handkerchiefs, I send you 4 of them, being half the Piece; and shall look out for the Quilts you mention, that is, Mrs. Stevenson will, and for the Muff and Snail for Sally.

And he remembered the new house:

I suppose the blue Room is too blue, the wood being of the same Colour with the Paper, and so looks too dark. I would have you finish it as soon as you can, thus. Paint the Wainscot a dead white; Paper the Walls blue, and tack the gilt border round just above the Surbase and under the Cornish. If the Paper is not equal Coloured when pasted on, let it be brush'd over again with the same Colour:—and let the Papier machée [sic] Musical Figures be tack'd to the middle of the Ceiling:— when this is done, I think it will look well.

In London, too, there were personal matters to take his mind away from the menaces that surrounded him. Polly and Margaret Stevenson had accepted a proposal of marriage from a London physician, William Hewson, and Polly, on the rebound from an unfortunate former engagement, was happy and excited. Benjamin Franklin was always emotionally involved with "matches"; he was unsuccessful, to be sure, in making them, but he seemed to take a vicarious pleasure in the marriages of family and friends. He was practical enough, however, to think carefully about the wife's dowry and the husband's income.

Hard on the heels of the new cabinet's accession to power came new, bitter resistance from the colonies. New York refused to obey the new Quartering Act, which provided for living quarters for British troops in the private houses of the colonists, and there was wide resentment everywhere over the "intolerable" revenue acts which carried the venom of Charles Townshend across the Atlantic.

Franklin's decision to travel again in the summer of 1767 saved him from facing some of the anger that bounced back to England from America. It also did much toward paving the way for his own future diplomacy. He naturally had no suspicion what that future might be, but the friends he made on this new journey and the reputation he established were of permanent value to him. For this time, it was to France that his wish—or destiny—moved him.

Scarcely any of his letters give the intimate nuances of his intensely active mind as does this one he wrote to Polly Stevenson from Paris.

> Soon after I left you ... I took the Resolution of making a Trip with Sir John Pringle into France. We set out the 28th past August, 1767. All the way to Dover we were furnished with Post Chaises, hung so as to lean forward, the Top coming down over one's Eyes, like a Hood, as if to prevent one's seeing the Country; which being one of my great Pleasures, I was engag'd in perpetual Disputes with the Innkeepers, Hostlers, and Postillions, about getting the Straps taken up a Hole or two before, and let down as much behind, they insisting that the Chaise leaning forward was an Ease to the Horses, and that the contrary would kill them. I suppose the chaise leaning forward looks to them like a Willingness to go forward, and that its hanging back shows a Reluctance. They added other Reasons that were no Reasons at all, and made me as on 100 other Occasions, almost wish that Mankind had never been endow'd with a reasoning Faculty, since they know so little how to make use of it ... and that they had been furnish'd with a good sensible Instinct instead of it.
>
> At Dover ... we embark'd for Calais with a Number of Passengers who had never been before at sea. They would previously make a hearty Breakfast.... But they had scarce been out half an hour before the Sea laid Claim to it, and they were oblig'd to deliver it up.... If you ever go to Sea, take my Advice, and live sparingly a Day or two beforehand.... We got to Calais that Evening. Various Impositions we suffer'd from Boatmen, Porters, &c. on both Sides the Water. I know not which are the most rapacious, the English or French, but the latter have, with their Knavery, the most Politeness.

There was a characteristic detail of his observation:

> The Women we saw at Calais, on the Road, at Bouloigne, and in the Inns and Villages, were generally of dark Complexions, but arriving at Abbeville we found a sudden Change, a Multitude of both Women and Men in that Place appearing remarkably fair. . . .
>
> As soon as we left Abbeville, the Swarthiness return'd. I speak generally, for here are some fair Women at Paris, who I think are not whiten'd by Art. As to Rouge, they don't pretend to imitate Nature in laying it on. There is no gradual Diminution of the Colour, from the full Bloom in the Middle of the Cheek to the faint tint near the Sides, nor does it show itself differently in different Faces. I have not had the Honour of being at any Lady's Toylette to see how it is laid on, but I fancy I can tell you how it is or may be done. Cut a Hole of 3 inches Diameter in a Piece of Paper; place it on the Side of your Face in such a Manner as that the Top of the Hole may be just under your Eye; then with a Brush dipt in the Colour, paint Face and Paper together; so when the Paper is taken off there will remain a round Patch of Red exactly the Form of the Hole. This is the Mode, from the Actresses on the Stage upwards thro' all Ranks of Ladies to the Princesses of the Blood, but it stops there, the Queen not using it, having in the Serenity, Complaisance and Benignity that shine so eminently in, or rather through her Countenance, sufficient Beauty, tho' now an old Woman, to do extremely well without it.

He went on to tell how he had been at court and dined with the king (Louis XV) and queen, and gave a description of Versailles with its fountains, statues and gardens with guesses as to what they had cost. There was "every kind of Elegance except that of Cleanliness, and what we call *Tidyness.*" He writes of the politeness of the people and their urbanity, greatly exceeding the English, and asks, "Why should they be allowed to outdo us in any thing?"

Franklin then explains what the trip has done to him:

> It is but a fortnight since we left London, but the Variety of Scenes we have gone through makes it seem equal to Six

Months living in one Place. Perhaps I have suffered a greater Change, too, in my own Person, than I could have done in Six Years at home. I had not been here Six Days, before my Taylor and Perruquier had transform'd me into a Frenchman. Only think what a Figure I make in a little Bag-Wig and naked Ears! They told me I was become 20 Years younger, and look'd very galante; So being in Paris where the Mode is to be sacredly follow'd I was once very near making Love to my Friend's Wife.

It was well for Benjamin Franklin, now turned sixty, that he had this respite from all that was sinister in England and America, for after he should return he would face what was probably the most painful ordeal of his life.

NEW FRIENDS, NEW ENEMIES

WE have seen how the moment Franklin arrived in England in 1757, he began to change; how he had taken on the mantle of an English gentleman rather than that of a self-made and homespun American artisan and businessman; of his replacing the dynamic energy of his active, even fighting, career in Philadelphia with a leisure which he thoroughly enjoyed and which made him increasingly attractive to others and, above all, with a tolerance and patience, which had its effect on history.

Franklin's great biographer James Parton records these changes in a description of his subject not more than two years after his arrival in London.

> How heartily he enjoyed the society of literary and learned men, his letters still pleasantly reveal to us. The Franklin of 1759, we must note, was, in some particulars, a very different person from the Franklin of 1724, or even the Franklin of 1744. His figure had become that of a thriving Englishman of fifty-three years, portly, though far from corpulent. He was fonder of his ease than formerly, not disinclined to sit after dinner, and perfectly capable of finishing his second bottle of claret, though better pleased with his usual very moderate allowance. In general society, not talkative, often taciturn; among his intimates, the very gayest, wittiest, happiest, simplest, wisest of men, always ready with sense, fact, badinage, song or repartee, as the moment demanded. "I find," he wrote about this time, "that I love company, chat, a laugh, a glass, and even a song, as well as ever; and at the same time relish better than

I used to do the grave observations and wise sentences of old
men's conversation."

To follow yet another change, in which his sorely tried tolerance and patience turned to bitterness and indignation, may
make a sad narrative but it is a necessary one if we are to understand Franklin's part in the creation of a free and separate nation: the United States of America. The unhappy substance of
this story lies, however, not in the bitterness which turned
Franklin from an internationalist into a patriot but in the
scarcely credible stupidity of the British government. It is, of
course, debatable whether an American people would have
pursued happiness more successfully as part of a British Commonwealth than as a wholly independent nation, but a review
of the tragic sequence of failures by which Britain lost the
most English part of her empire shows what a morass of unwis-
dom, jealousy, corruption of power and general instability had
engulfed the kingdom's court and legislature.

Franklin's return from the pleasing rest France had provided
was not a happy one. The colonies had stopped celebrating what
they supposed was a relenting by Parliament. The church bells
were silent, the bonfires were out and cold, the last toast to the
king had been followed by headaches of anger. The "intolerable" or "coercive" acts of Townshend had met not only resentment but the thirst for vengeance. The readiest instrument of
revenge was, as it had been before, resolves not to buy any more
British goods.

Boston, being the center of unrest, sent, as early as February,
1768, a circular letter to the assemblies of the other colonies,
and in August of the same year Massachusetts unilaterally declared that for one year it would not import any "tea, glass,
paper or other goods commonly imported from Great Britain";
this was followed by agreements in New York, Pennsylvania
and Virginia, as well as the New England colonies. These were
official acts of the colonial legislatures and the resolutions made
allowance for the possibility of repeal of the objectionable
statutes. But sporadic mob violence sprang up in New England

with constant disturbance of the peace and some highly destructive incidents. In 1770, for example, a group of angry citizens baited a detachment of British soldiers with snowballs and other missiles, resulting in the so-called "Boston massacre," in which half a dozen civilians were shot. The following year, a British revenue cutter, the *Gaspee,* while engaged in the effort to collect the hated duties, was boarded by an anonymous Rhode Island gang, its crew captured and the vessel burned to the waterline.

In England this news was greeted with a curious surprise, as if the Townshend Acts had been a perfectly normal legislative method of collecting the money allegedly owed by the colonists, but the surprise was followed by a determination to force submission. As before, Englishmen forgot that the American colonists were also Englishmen. In his book *The American Revolution,* George Otto Trevelyan gives a summary of the sequence of political events.

The cardinal mistake had now been made, and the next was not long in coming. British politicians had much else to talk of; and the hard-working, quiet-living British people, after the Stamp Act was repealed, had returned to their business, and put America out of their thoughts, as they supposed, for ever. They were not prepared for the instant and bewildering sensation which the news of what had been done at Westminster produced across the ocean. For the colonists, one and all, irrespective of class, creed, and calling, it was indeed a rude awakening. In the assurance that past scores were now wiped out, they had settled themselves down to a sober enjoyment of a victory ... for if America had carried her point, England had conquered herself. And now, without warning, without fresh reason being given, the question was reopened.... The situation was far more ominous than if the Stamp-duty had been left where it was. Parliament, by repealing the Act, had publicly recognized and admitted that the claim to tax America was one to which America would never submit; and now, a twelve-month afterwards, that claim was revived on a larger scale, and with a deliberation which showed that this time England meant business.

King George, by then, had become obsessed with the passion to put the colonists in their place even if it meant resort to the military and he easily worked his will on a cabinet of yes-men. Franklin's friend Lord Shelburne resigned because he was unable to restore sense to the inflamed ministers. He well remembered that Franklin had said before the House of Commons "a military force sent into America . . . will not find a rebellion; they may indeed make one." But other ministers insisted that half a dozen frigates and one brigade of redcoats could restore reason not only to Massachusetts—the focus of the king's anger —but the whole of North America.

Accordingly, eight warships were sent to Boston Harbor, artillery was landed and some two battalions marched upon Boston Common. "So," says Trevelyan, "the second stage was reached in the downward course. How serious a step it was, how absolutely irretrievable except on the condition of being retracted forthwith, is now a commonplace of history. But its gravity was acknowledged at the time by few Englishmen. . . ." There was, of course, no retraction, although the duties prescribed by the Townshend Acts were eventually removed, except the tax on tea. By now, however, the discontent of the colonists had reached the point of no return, and, in 1773, the patriots of New York saw to it that the ships of the East India Company did not land their tea; and a band of disguised angry men boarded tea ships anchored off Boston and dumped the precious tea into the harbor. The British then closed the port of Boston and it was too late to mend the broken empire.

It is interesting to note (and inherent in any inquiry into the mind and temper of Benjamin Franklin) that at almost any point in this sequence, the trend might have been reversed. Petition after petition was sent to the king by the colonial assemblies asking for a redress of grievances; none was allowed to reach him. What voices friendly to America were raised in the Cabinet were drowned out and the friends of America resigned.

Propitiatory measures were advocated by the calmer American citizens and some were carried out. One petition made in the Massachusetts Assembly was rewritten several times in order to remove all harshness from its wording. Captain Preston, who had caused the "Boston massacre" by ordering his soldiers to fire on the harassing civilians, was defended by John Adams in his trial for murder and acquitted. Even after the first armed clashes of the Revolution, the Continental Congress sent King George what became known as the "Olive Branch Petition," proclaiming the colonists' attachment to the king's "person, family and government" and begging him to halt the war, to urge repeal of the Coercive Acts and make a "happy and permanent reconciliation." This, like the other appeals, the king refused to receive.

Franklin, in London after Paris, read with distress the attacks on America in the newspapers and condemned much of the disorder in Boston. He particularly deplored the "Boston Tea Party" and even suggested paying for the tea out of his own pocket. He kept in constant touch with such ministers as were amenable to reconciliation and used all his powers of persuasion to induce them to withdraw the offending troops from Boston. With Lord Chatham, who, after his partial recovery, had entered the House of Lords, he drew up an elaborate "Plan" for "settling the Troubles of America," which, however, was rejected 61 to 32 when it was offered to the House of Lords. This was as late as February, 1775.

There was hope in America up to the last moment, kept alive by conservative men like John Dickinson in the Continental Congress; but the voices of such hopeful folk were drowned in the noise of the mob and in the inflammatory oratory of Samuel Adams and James Otis. In November, 1774, Franklin's friend Charles Thomson wrote about the intransigent ministers "who by their cursed schemes of policy are dragging friend and brothers into the horrors of civil War & involving their country in ruin." Then he added, "Even yet the wound may be healed, peace and love restored; but we are on the very edge of the precipice."

2

Meanwhile, the Massachusetts Assembly had appointed Franklin its agent in London. This appointment, Lord Hillsborough, the new Secretary of American Affairs, refused to accept because it had not been endorsed by the British-appointed governor of the province. Lord Hillsborough delivered a tirade at Franklin when he called to present his credentials and Franklin withdrew, saying,

"I beg your Lordship's pardon for taking up so much of your time. It is, I believe, of no great importance whether the appointment is acknowledged or not, for I have not the least conception that an agent can *at present* be of any use to any of the colonies. I shall therefore give your Lordship no further trouble."

These final words offended Hillsborough, who told a friend of Franklin's that they were rude and abusive, "equivalent to telling him to his Face, that the Colonies could expect neither Favour nor Justice during his administration." Franklin's comment on this, "I find he did not mistake me," was written in a letter to Samuel Cooper in which he also said of his Lordship: "His Character is Conceit, Wrongheadedness, Obstinacy and Passion"—strong words which indicate that the bitterness had already set in.

He did not, however, let it interfere with his enjoyment of life or with the pleasures of his intimate friendships. With Polly Stevenson, he devised "A Scheme for a New Alphabet and Reformed Mode of Spelling" and they wrote letters to each other in which she addressed him as "Diir Syr," and he her as "Diir Madam." Franklin later compiled a dictionary based on the scheme and sent it to Noah Webster. Franklin's biographer Alfred Aldridge suggests that the idea for the "reform"

> may very well have come into his mind while he was struggling through the crude phonetic spelling of his wife and sister. In a sense, his innovation was an example of his love for persons of ordinary capacities, to facilitate written expression for them

and spare them embarrassment. Also it represented his linguistic conviction that conventional spelling is irrational.

In the spring, Franklin visited some of England's most celebrated manufacturing towns—the places which would soon become cradles of the Industrial Revolution. Whether the news that, as a result of nonimportation agreements, manufacturing on a considerable scale had begun in Massachusetts and other American provinces, had helped motivate these visits, or whether he had been urged by some of his merchant friends, his interest was eager. He may have told of the news from Lynn, Massachusetts, that, since the refusal to buy British goods, eighty thousand pairs of shoes a year were made in that New England town and that the shoes were cheaper and better than any that had been imported.

After a tour through Leeds, Manchester, Litchfield and Cumberland, he spent three weeks at Twyford with Bishop Jonathan Shipley. This visit was enlivened by two things: the presence in the house of five Shipley girls, the youngest eleven, the oldest, twenty-three; and the beginning of his autobiography, which he wrote in a room that was placed at his exclusive disposal. Naturally, Franklin was delighted by the mutual attraction that came about whenever he got together with children, and the girls, especially Catherine, eleven, and Georgiana, fifteen, never forgot his humorous wisdom and lively stories. He presented Georgiana with a squirrel named Mungo which Deborah had shipped to him; Mungo later escaped and a dog killed it; whereupon Franklin sent Georgiana an epitaph in "the monumental style and measure, which, being neither prose nor verse is perhaps the properest for grief."

It is probable that the rural tranquillity of Twyford, after the clatter and confusion and busyness of cities, turned Franklin's thought in upon himself and he, normally the most detached and extrovert of men, was able to remember the incidents of his past and record them for posterity. He addressed his autobiography to his son William but it is likely that his

Deborah Franklin, oil painting by Matthew Pratt

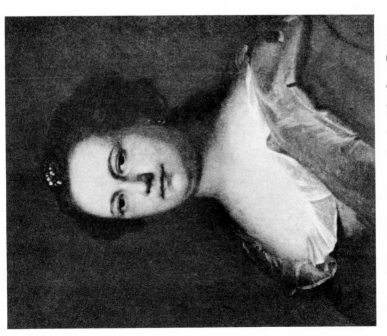

Sarah Bache, Franklin's daughter

Presumed sketch of Benjamin Franklin and a friend by
Charles Willson Peale, 1767

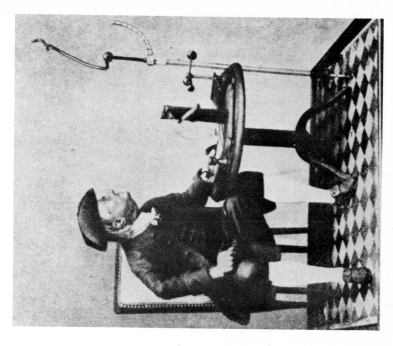

French statuette by Nini of Franklin
experimenting with his electrical apparatus

Benjamin Franklin,
after drawing by C. N. Cochin, 1777

FRANKLIN'S RESIDENCE AT PASSY

Courtesy of Leonard W. Labaree

Independence National
Historical Park Collection
John Adams, portrait by
Charles Willson Peale

John Jay Iselin and the
Frick Art Reference Library
John Jay, portrait by
Gilbert Stuart, 1783

Independence National
Historical Park Collection
The Comte de Vergennes, portrait
by Charles Willson Peale

Independence National
Historical Park Collection
Chevalier de la Luzerne, portrait
by Charles Willson Peale

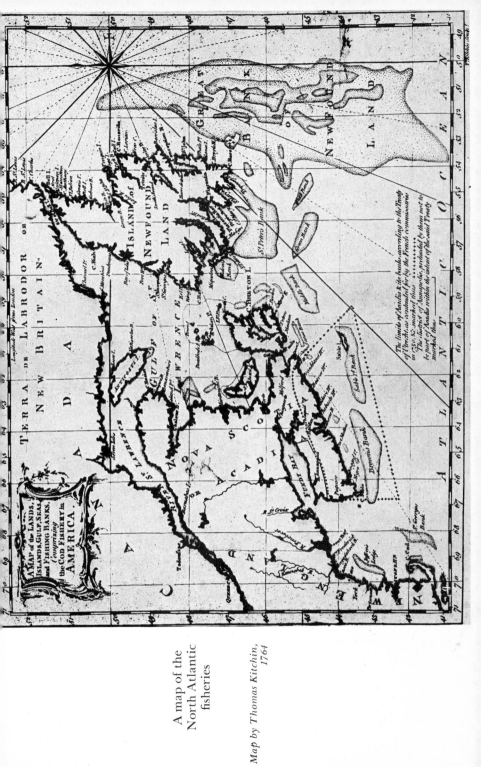

A map of the North Atlantic fisheries

Map by Thomas Kitchin, 1764

The Earl of Shelburne

Charles James Fox, engraving by John Jones
after Sir Joshua Reynold's portrait

grandson, William Temple, took more pleasure in reading and later publishing it.

When he left Twyford he went to Ireland with his friend and collaborator Richard Jackson. He was especially anxious to meet some of the Irish patriots who cherished, he had been told, warm feelings toward America. He was hospitably entertained in Dublin—too hospitably on one occasion when he ate too much and was violently sick afterward—and he and Jackson attended the Irish parliament. Though outsiders were usually not admitted to the legislature, Franklin was welcomed as a veteran member of the parliament of Pennsylvania.

3

Back in London, Franklin was drawn inexorably into the whirlpool of ominous events. He received a petition from the Massachusetts Assembly which he was requested to lay before the king. The Assembly was aggrieved when it discovered that Governor Thomas Hutchinson was paid his salary by the Crown instead of by the Assembly in accordance with the general custom. Lord Dartmouth delayed presenting the petition because he was sure it would give offense to the king and Franklin left it in his hands. The Assembly's complaint against Governor Hutchinson was highly significant, however, as we survey the sequence of incidents that led up to the final break, because it boded ill for Franklin's future in England. Hutchinson was a name he would long remember.

In the London years that were left, Franklin's missions became more and more secret. He moved constantly among men who believed he should be hanged for a traitor; most of his letters were intercepted and he became more careful about their contents. Fortunately he had the support of friends in high places, men like Pitt and Shelburne and Dartmouth.

Increasingly, his liaison with America became less formal and more clandestine. Much of it was implemented by American, sea captains who, for years, had been accustomed to call at Craven Street to tell Franklin the gossip and to do American errands for him, carrying his letters to Deborah and his friends and theirs to him. To some of the skippers he entrusted presents to his family and they reported in Philadelphia on his state of health and of mind. Some of these brave and hardy mariners had been habitués of the Pennsylvania Coffee House in Birchin's Lane in Philadelphia, and, in his younger days, when they were little more than boys, he had drunk many a gay glass with them and listened to their hair-raising adventures. Such were Budden of the *Polly Ann*, Le Gross of *Admiral Benbow* and Falconer of the *Lovely Lass*.

In the days of the boycott of British goods, and especially in the time when even Franklin came to believe that war threatened, smuggling became something of a patriotic duty. If the sea captains were ever troubled by their consciences, which was exceedingly uncommon, they could plead the necessity which Britain had forced upon her colonists. In any case, smuggling was an old American custom—one which, indeed, was expertly revived as late as the Prohibition era of the 1920's and with the same patriotic "alibis"—and, for generations, molasses had been brought into the distilleries of Massachusetts from the non-British West Indies against the express provisions of the various parliamentary Sugar Acts.

It had become, therefore, a part of every American seaman's education to become familiar with all the details of French Guadeloupe and Martinique; of Dutch Statis and Curaçao; and, for good reasons, of the British West Indies as well—where, indeed, many colonial merchants were not too delicate about loyalties to the mother country when they interfered with their fortunes.

British Navigation Laws forbade importation by the colonies from any country except Britain. If the colonists desired French, German or Italian commodities, they must go to England first and be reimported from there. It was possible, therefore, to evade these statutes by sending the goods from a European country first to a non-British West Indian island from which they could be transported to the colonial ports of the Atlantic coast. Although the British navy did its best to intercept this trade, it flourished nevertheless and the sea captains became adept at evasion.

If, in spite of the efforts of Franklin and the less hysterical colonists, a war should be inevitable, the practical Franklin began figuring the costs to the colonists and the chances of an American victory.

England, in this period of extravagance and corruption, was, as Franklin had finally discovered, in an unsound state: deeply in debt, still tired from the war with France, her army small, her navy, under the dissolute and irresponsible Lord Sandwich, suffering from neglect. She would have to send her troops three thousand miles to fight in a country which could not and would not feed them, whereas there was abundant manpower in the colonies and the troops would fight on their own soil. The best statesmen of Britain were badly split on the American issue and it was doubtful if they would give full support to a war in which they did not believe. Finally there was hatred of Britain among most of the nations in Western Europe, and they could be counted on to sympathize with the American colonies.

On the other hand, there had been no durable unity of the colonies and many were still hostile to their neighbors. A war would require a strong central management with the kind of organization Americans knew little about. But most important of all, Americans had almost nothing to fight with: artillery, small arms, powder or ammunition of any sort. A few skirmishes would exhaust the supply. Wool clothing, wool blankets and many other items for the soldiers were necessities. Where could these things come from? American merchants and American sea captains, accustomed for years to handling contraband, knew. Franklin, as agent for more than one colony, realized that part of the job of organizing this immense secret service of supply would devolve upon him. His long acquaintance with the hardy Yankee skippers and with the American merchants, who had already given thought to the coming needs, would be of immense help in this mission. To pursue it in England under the eyes of the potential enemy was a delicate task.

As the year 1773, with its ugly news of the "Boston Tea

Party," came to an end he felt the bitterness and the hatred mounting all about him. He had asked more than once to be sent home as he felt that his usefulness in England was ended and that he was about to become an enemy alien, but the Massachusetts and Pennsylvania assemblies thought otherwise and he was instructed to remain.

In January, 1774, he was summoned to appear before the Privy Council. His appearance, the following month, marked a turning point in his life. Although he had been aware of the personal hatred that had been felt for him in certain quarters, he had no idea of its degree. The insults he submitted to in that ugly session were something of which he had thought English gentlemen incapable. From that moment, the England that he had loved became his bitter enemy. The war clouds that he had seen faint on the horizon were now menacing overhead.

MEETING WITH HATE

FRANKLIN knew that the official reason for the summons to appear before the Privy Council was that the Massachusetts Assembly had petitioned the king to remove the royal governor of the province, Thomas Hutchinson, and the lieutenant governor, Andrew Oliver. He assumed that the king had rejected the appeal and that the Council would reprimand the Massachusetts Assembly for making the petition and Franklin, its agent, for presenting it. What he did not know was that he was to be accused, personally, of a crime and, therefore, he appeared without legal counsel. He was then allowed three weeks to obtain a lawyer to represent him.

Meanwhile every sort of vilification appeared in the London newspapers. Rumors were circulated that, as a result of his crime, he was to be seized and imprisoned and there were hints to the effect that he would lose his position as deputy postmaster general for the colonies.

All this was consequent upon an admission by him that he, Benjamin Franklin, was solely responsible for an episode which had mystified men in Parliament and the ministries ever since it had occurred.

Letters written by Governor Hutchinson and Lieutenant Governor Oliver had been sent to Thomas Whately, a member of Parliament who had since died. Whately's brother, William, and his brother's executor found these letters had been removed and sent to the Massachusetts Assembly. Whately accused John Temple, a former royal governor of New Hampshire, of taking them and sending them to America, where they had stirred up an angry tempest. Temple denied this and challenged Whately to a duel. The duel had taken place and Whately had been injured when Franklin heard about it. Lest there be further injuries, he wrote to the London *Public Advertiser,* stating that he, Franklin, alone was the person who had obtained the letters and sent them to Boston. His enemies, reading this, realized at once that it gave them an opportunity to accuse the hated agent of stealing the letters, and it was of this crime that he was about to be accused at a session of the Privy Council.

What had, in fact, happened, Franklin admitted fully, concealing nothing except the name of the friend who had given him the letters, and this he never divulged. It is true that his enemies made no great effort to find out, for this discovery would have robbed them of the opportunity to place the guilt of the theft upon Franklin's shoulders.

Franklin's explanation, which had been abundantly supported by wholly convincing evidence, was this:

In the autumn of 1772 a friend called and Franklin told him of the grievances of Massachusetts against the Parliament which had imposed unconstitutional taxation upon the people and had followed this injustice by sending armed forces to Boston to see that the statutes were enforced. The friend, who was a member of Parliament, expressed surprise at this and said, "But the governor of the province himself complained of the disobedience of the people in not paying the duties and in abusing the Crown's customs officers and, indeed, requested military aid," or words to that effect. Franklin was amazed and indeed incredulous of this information and his friend offered to prove it. He then brought a packet of letters and invited Franklin to read them.

It was immediately evident to Franklin that his friend was right, that the extreme measures taken by the British government against Massachusetts were done at the specific request of the royal governor and lieutenant governor and had not originated with either the Parliament or the ministries. As his friend had advised, it became incumbent on him to take a more lenient attitude toward the powers that were in England, and if he believed the revenue acts and the sending of the military to Boston were unjust, he should put the blame where it belonged.

The six letters written by Governor Hutchinson to his English friend, whose name had been erased, recounted the outrageous behavior of the Boston patriots in abusing the customs officers of the Crown, seizing their ships, inciting mobs against them and otherwise intimidating them. The letters went on to criticize the Boston town meetings for officially condoning such acts and voting "the collectors, commissioners and officers a nuisance." Yet these victims of the patriots' rage were officers of the Crown! Should not the Crown, therefore, send military aid to these abused officers? Again and again, the letters declared against the liberty and autonomy of the colonists and stressed the necessity of severe punishment from England.

Despite the erasure of the name and address of the addressee, Franklin soon knew that the letters had been sent to one Thomas Whately, a member of the British Parliament.

It especially irritated Franklin that Hutchinson was one of the few royal governors who was a native American. Indeed, his ancestors had been native Americans since William and Anne Hutchinson had migrated to the Massachusetts Bay Colony in 1634. Thomas Hutchinson himself graduated from Harvard College; he had been a member of the Massachusetts House of Representatives and he had held several judicial positions in the service of the colony before becoming lieutenant governor and, finally, governor. There was every reason why such a man should have been a "son of liberty" himself, or at least have sympathized with his fellow colonists in the exploitation of their grievances.

Franklin realized at once that the contents of these letters must be made known to the Massachusetts Assembly and that the colonial legislature should appeal for the discharge of Hutchinson as governor and also of Oliver as lieutenant governor since his four letters were equally incendiary. It was, indeed, Franklin's duty as agent for the colony to get this information across the Atlantic.

At length he persuaded his anonymous friend to let him

send the original letters to Thomas Cushing, Speaker of the Massachusetts Assembly. The friend agreed, but, though several persons in England had seen the letters, he made Franklin promise to insist that they not be printed or published in any way and that they be shown only to a very few.

Franklin should, perhaps, have known that such restrictions could not possibly be fulfilled once the letters were thrown into the hotbed of rebellion that Massachusetts then was. He had not, however, seen the conditions in Boston at first hand. In any case, the importance of getting the letters into the hands of the legislators seemed to him so great that he was willing to agree to any cautions his friend proposed.

When the letters arrived in Boston, they were read aloud to the Assembly and created such a furor that the demand to see them by all the most active of the "sons of liberty" was overwhelming. They were widely circulated, copied, finally printed and published in the Boston newspapers. They were then reprinted in London and the fat was in the fire.

2

Those who could not believe that a man of Franklin's reputation and character would stoop to common theft censured him on another count. The letters were, after all, part of a private correspondence carried on between individuals, and an ancient code of ethics prescribed that such communications should never be made public without the express permission of the writer. Here, an American, acting in his private capacity, had expressed his private opinions to an English friend; should not, therefore, these opinions be held inviolate?

But, asked the Massachusetts Assembly, the Sons of Liberty and Franklin himself, were these letters private in the proper sense of the word? The New Englanders did not know to whom the letters were addressed, the address having been removed; they knew only that they had been sent to an individual. But obviously they were intended to influence men in official positions. Such communications, they believed, could not be con-

sidered private; they were written by a public man, undoubtedly to a public man, and were about public, not private or
personal, subjects. Franklin, who knew exactly who the addressee
was (though he did not tell the Assembly), was aware that
the Massachusetts governors had addressed them to Thomas
Whately because he was in Parliament and had been secretary
to American-hater Grenville; they were certainly meant for
official eyes and, evidently, official eyes had seen them, for their
specific advice had been followed in official quarters. They had,
therefore, been written by public men for public men, and
since they concerned matters for which Franklin, as agent, had
full responsibility, he felt no obligation whatever to regard
them as private and confidential.

It has been said in a somewhat superfluous extenuation of
Franklin's conduct by his more affectionate biographers that
it was not the custom of the time to hold private correspondence confidential; that the London post office opened letters
at will, retained some and sent others on with no attempt to
conceal that they had been read; that Franklin himself had had
many of his letters intercepted and had resorted to sending
letters by private messengers. Such general moral laxity would
not, of course, have justified Franklin's performance; it is far
more rational to accept his own thoroughly reasonable explanation.

3

The petition which Franklin, as a result of the repercussions
of the letters, was instructed to lay before the king still kept
the door open for reconciliation. As usual it was humbly worded
with many protestations of loyalty to "our most gracious sovereign." The burden of it was, as Franklin's friend had declared,
that the oppressive acts had been the result, not of English
tyranny, but of the incendiary representations of the colonists'
own governors.

> Permit us humbly to suggest to your Majesty, that your sub-
> jects here have been inclined to believe, that the grievances

which they have suffered, and still continue to suffer, have been occasioned by your Majesty's ministers and principal servants being, unfortunately for us, misinformed in certain facts of very interesting importance to us. . . .

Your Majesty's petitioners have very lately had before them *certain papers,* from which they humbly conceive it is most reasonable to suppose, that there has long been a conspiracy of evil men in this province, who have contemplated measures, and formed a plan, to advance themselves to power . . . by means destructive of the charter of the province, at the expense of the quiet of the nation, and to the annihilating of the rights and liberties of the American colonies. . . .

Wherefore we most humbly pray, that your Majesty would be pleased to remove from their posts in this government the said Thomas Hutchinson, Esquire, and Andrew Oliver, Esquire, who have by their abovementioned conduct, and otherwise, rendered themselves justly obnoxious to your loving subjects, and entirely lost their confidence; and place such good and faithful men in their stead, as your Majesty in your wisdom shall think fit.

Franklin sent this petition to Lord Dartmouth, who had succeeded Hillsborough as Secretary of State for America, and Dartmouth wrote him that:

I shall not fail to lay it before the King the next time I shall have the honour of being admitted into his presence. I cannot help expressing to you the pleasure it gives me to hear, that a sincere disposition prevails in the People of that Province to be on good terms with the Mother Country. . . .

That one minister should feel thus while others were feeling the bitter enmity that was evidently behind the attack on him indicated to Franklin the total dissolution of unity in the British government.

Franklin was able to retain as Counsel John Dunning, a former solicitor general, and John Lee, who was later to occupy the same post, and appeared before the Privy Council on January 29. The place chosen was a small room in Whitehall known as the "cockpit," scarcely bigger than a large living room, quite inadequate to the crowd of scandalmongers who would gather to hear the hated "thief" and "traitor" humbled.

4

In this famous old arena [writes Helen Augur in her *The Secret War of Independence*] Franklin was trussed and tied, and only the British cock could use his spurs. The Solicitor General, Alexander Wedderburn, had a wide command of the vocabulary of vituperation, then at its peak, and he raked Franklin without mercy. The room was crowded with privy councilors and all the lords and gentlemen who could get in the doors, an assembly smelling of wine fumes, musk, wig powder, and corruption. For his public disgrace the aging Doctor, usually plain in his dress, wore his best suit of Manchester velvet. If America was to be pilloried in the person of Franklin, her dignity demanded velvet.

The formal part of the hearing consisted of a reading of the petition of the Massachusetts Assembly and of Dunning's comment on it that the address to the king was simply an appeal to his Majesty's wisdom and goodness, that it asked no favor and demanded no justice. Wedderburn then attacked the provincial assembly and abused the Massachusetts people and, finally, "turning upon Franklin he assailed him with ribald invective, so gross that large passages were omitted by the friends of Wedderburn when the address was published." Albert Henry Smyth, in his Franklin biography, continues:

It was a scene, as Lecky has said, well suited to the brush of an historical painter. For more than an hour Franklin stood, tranquilly, silently, before his malignant adversary, his coolness and apathy in striking contrast with the violence and clamour of the Scotch declaimer, while grave men clapped their hands in boundless amused delight at the baiting of the American.

Wedderburn said that the Hutchinson letters could not have come into Franklin's hands by fair means. There was no evidence to show that either the writers or the recipient of the correspondence had given them to him.

Nothing then will acquit Dr. Franklin of the charge of obtaining them by fraudulent or corrupt means, for the most malignant of purposes; unless he stole them from the person who stole them. This argument is irrefragable.

I hope, my Lords, you will mark and brand the man, for the honour of this country, of Europe, and of mankind. Private correspondence has hitherto been held sacred, in times of the greatest party rage, not only in politics but in religion.

Working to his climax, Wedderburn continued:

He has forfeited all the respect of societies and of men. Into what companies will he hereafter go with an unembarrassed face, or the honest intrepidity of virtue? Men will watch him with a jealous eye; they will hide their papers from him, and lock up their escritoires....

A few friends of Franklin who were present and listened to Wedderburn's tirade were shocked by his "indecency." Among them were Joseph Priestly, Jeremy Bentham, Edmund Burke, Lord Shelburne and a few Americans: Arthur Lee, Ralph Izard and Edward Bancroft. All said that Franklin received the abuse in total immobility, that not a muscle of his face changed.

Within a week after the session in the cockpit, he received notice that he had been dismissed from his office of deputy postmaster general in America.

The importance of the incident lies in its effect upon Franklin. He soon turned as bitter against England as he had once loved her. He even turned against his one-time hero, King George. From that moment, still smarting from Wedderburn's insults, he began to see that separation was inevitable and realized now the immense part he must play in his country's independence.

As Horace Walpole wrote of the effect of Wedderburn's brutal attack:

> Sarcastic Sawney, swol'n with spite and prate
> On silent Franklin poured his venal hate.
> The calm philosopher, without reply,
> Withdrew, and gave his country liberty.

CHESS

IF he felt personal bitterness, as he could scarcely have helped doing, as a result of the Solicitor General's public and vulgar attack, Franklin never showed it even to his closest friends. About a month after the session in the cockpit, he wrote to his Dutch friend Jan Ingenhousz, in reply to a letter expressing concern "on account of the late attack on my character before the Privy Council and in the papers."

> Be assured, my good friend, that I have done nothing unjustifiable, nothing but what is consistent with the man of honour and with my duty to my king and country. . . . I do not find that I have lost a single friend on the occasion. All have visited me repeatedly with affectionate assurances of their unaltered respect and affection, and many of distinction with whom I had before but slight acquaintance. You know that in England there is every day, in almost every paper, some abuse on public persons of all parties, the king himself does not always escape, and the populace who are used to it, love to have a good character cut up now and then for their entertainment. On this occasion it suited the purpose of the ministry to have me abused, as it often suits the purpose of their opposers to abuse them. And having myself been long engaged in public business, this treatment is not new to me. I am almost as much used to it as they are, themselves, and perhaps can bear it better.

Here speaks the philosophical politician which Franklin had learned, the hard way, to be. More intimately, he wrote to his sister, Jane Mecom, "intending to disgrace me, they have rather done me Honour." He was amused to see that, when the proceedings of the Privy Council were published, the quotations from Wedderburn's speech were modified. Printed were the parts of the speech that concerned Franklin's "theft" of the letters.

> This part of the speech [he wrote to Thomas Cushing] was thought so good, that they have since printed it in order to defame me everywhere, and particularly to destroy my reputation on your side of the water; but the grosser parts of the abuse are omitted, appearing, I suppose, in their own eyes, too foul to be seen on paper so that the speech, compared to what it was, is now perfectly decent.

When the cockpit episode became known in Boston, Franklin's reputation soared to new peaks; the new Committee of Correspondence broadcast the word and soon he was a hero in most of the colonies. This counteracted the impression that had been growing among the extremist patriots that he was "too much of an Englishman"—a corollary to the London comment that he was "too much of an American." His silent reception of the torrent of vilification that the ministry had poured out upon him had an impact that made persons everywhere review the whole affair of the governors' letters.

Yet it is interesting that the word and thought of independence was nowhere prevalent *except* in England. One might almost suppose that the more articulate English actually goaded the colonies into the Declaration of 1776. When, however, we examine more closely the sequence of events that led to the final separation, one becomes aware of incendiary propaganda which the public at large found emotionally irresistible.

In his speech at the session of the Privy Council, Wedderburn echoed the suspicion that had long attached to the rumors about the colonies.

> My lords, [he said] Dr. Franklin's mind may have been so possessed with the idea of a Great American Republic that he may easily slide into the language of the minister of a foreign independent state.

It was the fashion in London, however, to scoff at the suggestion that the colonies might be successful in their rebellion. Franklin had overheard an army general proclaim that with a thousand British grenadiers, he could go "from one end of America to the other, and geld all the Males, partly by force and partly by a little coaxing." He takes the Americans, said Franklin, "for a species of Animals very little superior to Brutes."

To combat some of the most arrogant notions held about America by the English, Franklin resorted to satire. It was a favorite literary instrument of his during the uncertain interval before the storm broke and, as events proved, there was much truth in his sarcasm. It is an index of the split temper of Britons as the clouds came nearer that some of his most acrid pieces were so eagerly reprinted and read in England. One, published in 1773, was "Rules by Which a Great Empire may be reduced to a Small One." In it he told how Great Britain might lose her American colonies by a continuance of the precise expedients she had already tried. The first rule, addressed "to all ministers who have the management of extensive dominions":

> In the first place, gentlemen, you are to consider that a great empire, like a great cake, is most easily diminished at the edges. Turn your attention, therefore, first to your remotest provinces; that, as you get rid of them, the next may follow in order.

Rule four states:

> However peacably your colonies have submitted to your government, shewn their affection to your interests, and patiently borne their grievances; you are to *suppose* them always inclined to revolt, and treat them accordingly. Quarter troops among them, who by their insolence may *provoke* the rising of mobs, and by their bullets and bayonets *suppress* them. By this means, like the husband who uses his wife ill *from suspicion,* you may in time convert your *suspicions* into *realities.*

Rule eleven rises to a peak of indignation:

> To make your taxes more odious, and more likely to procure resistance, send from the capital a board of officers to super-

intend the collection, composed of the most *indiscreet, ill-bred,* and *insolent* you can find. Let these have large salaries out of the extorted revenue, and live in open, grating luxury upon the sweat and blood of the industrious; whom they are to worry continually with groundless and expensive prosecutions before the abovementioned arbitrary revenue Judges; *All at the cost of the party prosecuted,* tho' acquitted, because *the King is to pay no costs.*

Thus the quiet, tolerant and calm Franklin, once he takes pen in hand. Published first in the *Public Advertiser,* it was reprinted in the *Gentleman's Magazine.* He signed it Q.E.D., but shrewd readers know that no one but Franklin could have produced it.

Whether the scene in the cockpit influenced his thought about his former hero, King George III, or whether, before this, the truth had been slowly borne in upon him, it was about this time that he lost his faith in that arbitrarily ruling monarch. An apostle of extrasensory perception might see a connection between this and a letter he wrote his son-in-law, Richard Bache, in September, 1774:

Dear Son:

The Bearer, Mr. Thomas Paine, is very well recommended to me, as an ingenious, worthy young man. He goes to Pennsylvania with a view of settling there. I request you to give him your best advice and countenance as he is quite a stranger there. If you can put him in a way of obtaining employment as a clerk, or assistant tutor in a school, or assistant surveyor, (of all of which I think him very capable,) so that he may procure a subsistence at least, till he can make acquaintance and obtain a knowledge of the country, you will do well, and much oblige your affectionate father.

Of this letter, Professor Aldridge in his *Benjamin Franklin: Philosopher and Man* has this to say:

Although Franklin had no way of knowing it at the time, perhaps the greatest service he performed for his native country in this year was to encourage the emigration to Pennsylvania of a former customs inspector, who . . . had failed in every career he had so far tried. His name was Thomas Paine, and he had been introduced to Franklin by a member of the Excise Board.

Whatever, in their brief acquaintance, Paine may have told Franklin of his opinion of kings in general and of George in particular, he was largely responsible, less than two years later, for changing the mood of a majority of the American people in relation to their sovereign.

2

In Philadelphia, meanwhile, much had happened which affected both the course of international events in general and Franklin's little family in particular. In May, 1774, the House of Burgesses in Virginia had ordained that a Congress of delegates from all the colonies should sit in Philadelphia and act for the whole of the American people. This gathering, which presently assumed the grand, if somewhat hyperbolic, name of Continental Congress, was to be a kind of super-legislature to which the provincial assemblies should send representatives. This, in a sense, made Philadelphia the capital of the united colonies. The Congress's first acts, in the autumn of 1774, were a Declaration of Rights and the creation of an association for nonimportation of British goods which would apply to all the colonies represented. It disbanded in the winter to reopen in time to welcome Franklin into its midst in the spring of 1775.

Franklin had known of his wife's decline in health since she had suffered a paralytic stroke several years before. Oddly enough, he did not take it as seriously as did his son and son-in-law, who were closer to her. Indeed, in the summer of 1774, he became irritated with her for not writing him regularly as she had used to do. One cannot avoid sympathy with him, harassed as he was by the Court, yet it seems a pity that after their long, warm, affectionate friendship, he should have turned, even momentarily, against her. Perhaps if the other members of the family had kept him better informed about her, he would have been more tolerant. In September, 1774, he complained, "Why might I not have expected the same Comfort from you, who used to be so diligent and faithful a Correspondent, as to omit scarce any Opportunity." She probably never got the letter. Another stroke on December 14 was followed by her death on the 19th.

When William wrote his father about Deborah's death, he explained that he had gone through a blizzard to be present at her funeral but had arrived just before her body had been taken to the cemetery. A few old friends had been her pall-bearers. It was a sad, dreary account. William also told of her premonition of death, saying that unless her husband should come back before the summer, she should never see him again. We have no record of Franklin's reaction to the news of her death, but it is natural that he would not write of so intimate a sorrow.

Most biographers emphasize the social gulf that grew between Benjamin and Deborah when, because of his achievements, he was received at receptions and various ceremonies of which "aristocratic" Philadelphians were the hosts, but to which Deborah was not invited.

> Class prejudice against Franklin [writes Paul Conner in his *Poor Richard's Politicks*] was for the most part eventually eradicated. An Addisonian wit, politics, Freemasonry, some experiments in natural philosophy, a bit of Latin, and chess were powerful recommendations in eighteenth-century society. There was one taint, however, that no amount of skill could fully erase—the more conspicuously lower-middle-class qualities of his wife Deborah. A carpenter's daughter, she knew her way around a shop and was a helpmate to Benjamin in his work as printer-stationer-bookseller and postmaster.... But she was plain, at times embarrassingly loud and, in short, not the sort that the wives of Franklin's more select acquaintances would welcome.... Franklin's amorous adventures in the better circles abroad proclaimed a latent yearning for a wife more genteel and witty.

More debatable is Mr. Conner's comment:

> Deborah was a constant reminder of a past Franklin did not fully relish. A humble origin looked well in an *Autobiography,* but carried a social residue which he strove to minimize.

The biographer's evidence for this seems a little far-fetched in view of Franklin's self-styled epitaph which he wished to state only his name with the word "Printer." Mr. Conner's reference to the attitude of the nobler members of Philadelphia society was undoubtedly accurate and still is.

William thought that Deborah's failure to write was because she expected Benjamin to appear any moment. Several of his letters spoke of his returning and he was constantly hoping to be able to come home. Yet this was postponed more than once, either at the request of a colonial assembly—he was now the agent for four colonies: Pennsylvania, Massachusetts, New Jersey and Georgia—or because of a sudden conviction on his part that there was still something to do in London. But, by Christmas, 1774, he had become finally convinced that he could do more good in America than in England. Deborah's prophecy that she would never see him again, however, came true.

3

Franklin's last months in England were busy enough to take his mind temporarily off the afflictions of his close personal friends. Polly's two little boys had a siege of smallpox and her worry over their sickness was aggravated by the blood poisoning of her husband, Dr. Hewson. In making a dissection, he had infected himself. He died, a martyr to his profession, in May, 1774, leaving Polly desolate from grief and pregnant for the third time. She needed what comfort her mother and Franklin could give her.

What remained of the extremely tenuous colonial politics was done by Franklin usually with the obligato of games of chess. He gave the impression of taking chess as seriously as he took impending revolution. That skill at chess and an apparently absorbing interest in it was part of his diplomatic equipment is, perhaps, only partially true; in any case it seemed to ease some otherwise difficult perplexities. It was, of course, peculiarly fortunate that his chief opponent in the game was a lady of considerable charm and wit and the sister of one who should prove himself an antagonist in other and more sanguinary competitions. In 1774, however, Richard Howe, later "Admiral Black Dick" of the British navy at New York and Newport, was extremely conciliatory.

> On Christmas-Day evening, 1774, visiting Mrs. Howe, she told me as soon as I came in, that her Brother, Lord Howe, wished to be acquainted with me; that he was a very good Man, and she was sure we should like each other....
>
> After some extremely polite Compliments as to the general Motives for his desiring an Acquaintance with me, he said he had a particular one at this time, viz. the alarming Situation of our Affairs with America, which no one, he was persuaded understood better than myself.

Lord Howe said he had disapproved of the treatment Franklin had received from the ministry and some of the ministers were ashamed of it, "and sorry it had happened." He then

> wish'd me to draw up in Writing some Propositions containing the Terms on which I conceived a good Understanding might be obtained and established, and the mode of Proceeding to accomplish it; which Propositions, as soon as prepared, we might meet to consider, either at his House, or at mine, or where I pleased; but, as his being seen at my House, or me at his, might, he thought, occasion some Speculation, it was concluded to be best to meet at his Sister's ... where there was a good Pretence with her Family and Friends for my being often seen, as it was known we play'd together at Chess.

At their next meeting, however, Howe, who in the meantime had considered a paper prepared by Franklin entitled "Hints for Conversation *upon the Subject of Terms that might probably produce a durable Union between Britain and the Colonies,*" said that he regretted that he was certain such terms would be unacceptable to the government. And no wonder, for the "Hints" were that though the tea destroyed at Boston should be paid for, yet the tea duty should be withdrawn, that the hated Navigation Acts should be reenacted, that the duties collected should be paid into the provincial treasuries, that customs officers should be Americans, not Englishmen, that no British troops be allowed to enter or be quartered in any colony except with the permission of the colonial legislature, that governors be paid by the provincial assemblies and that all powers of internal legislation be disclaimed by Parliament. In short, the "Hints" proposed to abolish all the measures dearest to king and government!

Surely it was too late for such recall of so many intolerable acts! And Franklin, Howe probably thought, should have known it. Whether, as king's pawn moved over Mrs. Howe's beautiful inlaid chessboard to king's 2nd, Franklin did indeed know it, the record does not disclose. But it is interesting and pleasant to read, in the midst of such harsh diplomacy as we see less than two hundred years later, what suave and courteous discussion took place in charming eighteenth-century parlors about the conditions of a war on which the world's greatest empire was to be split.

Between chess matches, Franklin had a more satisfactory interview with a statesman far greater than any Howe. The incomparable Pitt, Lord Chatham, after whom many an American town is named today, had made an apparently miraculous recovery from what was popularly known as insanity. He was wholly himself again and wanted to see Benjamin Franklin, the person who knew more about America than anyone then in England.

Though Chatham, in the clouded and apathetic intervals his illness had forced upon him, had let power slip from his hands, he had never repudiated his sympathy with American grievances, nor abandoned his hope that the breach might somehow be healed. In preparation for their meeting, Franklin had sent him, at his request, any important news he had received from America. This consisted of the proceedings of the

Continental Congress. To meet Chatham he went to Hayes, where the statesman was staying.

> He received me with an affectionate kind of Respect, that from so great a Man was extremely engaging; but the Opinion he expressed of the Congress was still more so. They had acted, he said, with so much Temper, Moderation and Wisdom, that he thought it the most honourable Assembly of Statesmen since those of the ancient Greeks and Romans, in the most virtuous Times. That there were not in their whole Proceedings above one or two things he could have wished otherwise; perhaps but one, and that was, their Assertion, that the keeping up a standing Army in the Colonies in time of Peace without Consent of their Legislature was against Law; he doubted that was not well founded.... The rest he admired and honoured. He thought the Petition decent, manly, and properly express'd.

Together, Franklin and Chatham drew up a "Plan" which was the final attempt at healing the breach. They were assisted by various friends of Franklin's, including Lord Howe, Dr. John Fothergill, who had attended Franklin in his various illnesses, David Barclay and others. Howe even went so far in his effort to get a proposition that would not be rejected as to promise Franklin emoluments in the form of important government positions in compensation for certain concessions. Such an offer was entirely in accord with the corrupt conventions of the time but, naturally, it was instantly refused.

In the end, however, a stubborn ministry, afraid at this point of showing any weakness toward the colonies, rejected all conciliatory "plans." There was, to be sure, what was called a "wild debate" in Parliament, resulting from an accommodating motion introduced by Chatham, showing that, to the end, there were responsible Members who entirely sympathized with the Americans even after, and in spite of, the Boston Tea Party.

It was now February, 1775, and the gods, seeking whom they would destroy continued to grind slowly. Franklin made plans to go home in the near future. Meanwhile, he continued his friendly games of chess.

INDEPENDENCE

IF, as he prepared to leave England, he had looked down the vista of scenes since his arrival in London in 1757, Franklin would have observed a sequence of changes that had occurred, not in circumstance, but only in his own mind and mood. His very first encounters with official England reflected the corruption that underlay the gaiety, the wit, the refinements of London society that had so impressed the Philadelphian and blinded him to the sinister erosion. He saw it now; rather he seemed to smell it—a sense he expressed in a letter to Joseph Galloway in February, 1775, in which he finally abandoned the hope that he had so long held:

> I have not heard what Objections were made to the Plan in the Congress, nor would I make more than this one, that, when I consider the extreme Corruption prevalent among all Orders of Men in this old rotten State, and the glorious publick Virtue so predominant in our rising Country, I cannot but apprehend more Mischief than Benefit from a closer Union....
>
> Here Numberless and needless Places, enormous Salaries, Pensions, Perquisites, Bribes, groundless Quarrels, foolish Expeditions, false Accounts or no Accounts, Contracts and Jobbs, devour all Revenue, and produce continual Necessity in the Midst of natural Plenty. I apprehend, therefore, that to unite us intimately will only be to corrupt and poison us.

Could the Franklin of 1757, exuberant about everything English—the people, the physical country and the king—ever call Great Britain "this old rotten state"? Yet one of the things we must admire about this strange and often unorthodox genius was his refusal to be consistent if consistency should be in conflict with changing convictions; another, his capacity, even after middle life, for growth. It is true that for long he resisted change, hoping that his world would come true according to his happy creation of it, but he was eventually content to see his prejudices dissolve without a trace of residue.

Abroad, his native sensitiveness, escaping from Puritan crudities, quickly responded to the amenities of the English nobility or the more delicate perfume of Paris, yet, when he slept, tired at last of a world so largely artificial, his dreams were of a cleaner, franker land where the values of virtue were higher than those of place. Sure enough, his vanity was tickled by the respect, often adulation, of men accounted—and sometimes truly—great, yet he learned a shrewd appraisal, separating the real from the pretended.

For his inconsistencies, especially of political beliefs, he has been abundantly criticized. Yet the economic conditions of the world changed so rapidly that an opinion held in 1750 was hardly tenable in 1775. Thus, with the burgeoning of the British industrial revolution, which had got under way in these years, it could no longer be argued, as Franklin had often declared, that the only real source of wealth is agriculture. Also, as an expanding America continued to refuse to import manufactured goods from Britain, it could not be reasonable to tell the colonists in their growing independence of the evils of the manufacturing industry. Thus, in the critical years he spent in London, Franklin's economic creed had, like that of every other wise and aware person, to be in a continual state of flux.

His private life in this time was, as we have seen, quite at variance with his moral preachments. For example, from his visit to France, he brought back, concealed in a wig, some presents of French lace for Margaret Stevenson at the very moment when he was framing the diatribe against smuggling which was published on his return. At the very time, too, when he was warning his wife against extravagance because of his diminishing fortune, he ordered, within four months, according to bills now in the American Philosophical Society, ten and a half barrels of beer at a cost of some seven pounds. Nor did he at any time in his life abroad follow the habits of health or temperance in eating and drinking prescribed by Poor Richard.

Later biographers, following the fashion of the times in which they wrote, placed an exaggerated emphasis on his amorous impulses in London and, especially, in Paris. That in his sixties and seventies he constantly, or even frequently, gratified those impulses except in a sublimated way is exceedingly improbable. And, compared with the robust men in a licentious era and in morally tolerant societies, Franklin's life was an uncommonly temperate one. It is important, therefore, to see his personal behavior in a context of contemporary time and place, not against a post-Freudian backdrop with sex dominating the literary scene.

Undoubtedly, as we gather from his letters, many of the light and witty exchanges with women in which he engaged merged in his imagination into "affairs," but in the salon atmosphere in which this "badinage," as it was called, was usual, men and women in the upper echelons of intellect often went close to the edge without going over. The impression sometimes given, therefore, that Franklin was an "old lecher" or more than momentarily preoccupied with physical sex is grossly false. He was worldly, yes, even "earthy," as some have said; in the course of an incredibly full and varied career, he touched every phase of life but his abundantly recorded relations with women reflect a richness of thought and a philosophical depth unmarred by a flicker of evil.

In the public realm, he accomplished more than could be known at the time; perhaps, indeed, his influence there altered the history of the world. No estimate or even guess is possible of the change he brought about in the English attitude toward America and Americans. Through his talk, his writing, even his presence, in the transitional unease of London he turned the view of many a stubborn Briton toward that overseas society of other Britons, almost, if not quite, as English. Franklin could never stomach the prevailing ignorance of that other England, the nauseating superiority that looked on those American fellows as a lesser breed. And he never lost an opportunity to inform, to enlighten, to clarify. Did this weaken the English will to resist, so that, at last, the thirteen colonies won their independence against otherwise overwhelming odds?

Yet all this propaganda that he pushed so assiduously was not in the interest of independence. On the contrary, he did it in the effort to bring about unity within the empire, directly opposed to the separation that was taking place nearly all the time he was in London, and apparently in ignorance of the dangerously widening gulf. Looking back from a telegraphic age it is easy to accuse Franklin of a stupidity unworthy of so shrewd a statesman. The fact is that he was as ignorant of America as the English, though the circumstances were wholly different: they thinking of the colonists as an inferior and perhaps a barbaric race of men; he of their being on too high a level for their explosions of rage and, finally, for their rebellion against their mother country. But the cause of both ignorances was the same: the physical apartness, for by the time the news of a particular incident got to England such progress had been made that the incident had faded in its significance. For example, by the time the humble petition to the king requesting the removal of the Massachusetts governors reached the Privy Council in London, the Boston Tea Party had already taken place and it was this news—nearly two months old—that so inflamed the ministers against Franklin.

So, against all the inconsistencies that marked Franklin's conduct during the eighteen years—interrupted by one Philadelphia interval—of his English mission, we have the one stubborn consistency: his belief that the empire, a beautiful and invaluable "China vase," must never break. As late as February, 1775, when he finally saw the tottering of that vase on the edge of its destruction, he said:

> I cannot but lament... the impending Calamities, Britain and her Colonies are about to suffer, from great Imprudencies on both Sides—Passion governs, and she never governs wisely—Anxiety begins to disturb my Rest....

A month later, he left England forever. While he was in mid-ocean, the Lexington farmers clashed with uniformed English and the point had been reached of no return.

2

Franklin's last days in London were harrowing indeed. The failure of his last unofficial negotiations with Chatham, Barclay and Fothergill had piled frustration on frustration. He had lost his temper at last and written an insulting note to Dartmouth but he was dissuaded from sending it. What had driven him to the peak of his anger was the continual effort, even on the part of those who considered themselves his friends, to induce him to accept bribes for concessions by the colonies he represented. In Britain's state of corruption, it seemed inconceivable to English politicians that peace with America could not be bought. At the same time, Franklin was sure, because of the prevailing commercialism, that if the colonies could hold out for a year in their boycott of English imports the North ministry, which had been so stubborn in its rejection of conciliatory proposals, would be overthrown. With this conviction, he had written to James Bowdoin in February, 1775:

> The eyes of all Christendom are upon us, and our honour as a people is become a matter of the utmost consequence to be taken care of. If we tamely give up our rights in this contest, a century to come will not restore us in the opinion of the world; we shall be stamped with the character of dastards, poltroons, and fools; and be despised and trampled upon, not by this haughty, insolent nation only but by all mankind. . . .

His last day was spent with Joseph Priestley reading over the American newspapers and deciding on what should be reprinted in the London journals. According to the biography of Priestley by J. T. Rutt, Franklin was unable to control his emotions and the tears rolled down his cheeks. Though Franklin said America would win in the end, what he justly called a "civil war" would probably last ten years.

He boarded a Pennsylvania packet at Portsmouth on the 21st of March and, after a voyage so calm that "a London wherry might have accompanied us all the way," he arrived on May 2 and was in Philadelphia on the 5th. The journey cooled him and gave him a long rest, though he was working most of the time. For his son, he wrote a detailed account of the last secret negotiations and, when they met the Gulf Stream, he became completely engrossed in experiments with a thermometer which confirmed some of his theories about the warm current.

In Philadelphia, the Continental Congress was about to meet and there was a universal clamor for his attendance at the first session. So, forgetting his sixty-nine years, he spent, in the summer and fall of 1775, what were, in many ways, the most strenuous months of his life.

3

Though the word "independence" was still spoken in the American provinces with bated breath and so remained all through the year 1775, abundant preparations for the war which would become "The War of Independence" were being made from Maine to Georgia. The skirmishes at Lexington and Concord, the besieging of the British in Boston, the Battle of Bunker Hill, the burning of Boston's neighbor, Charlestown, the recruiting of volunteer soldiers for General George Washington's "continental army," the training of backwoods riflemen, the drilling of raw but patriotic soldiers and, of paramount importance, the manufacture, assembling and secret importation of every sort of matériel—all these were hardly characteristic of a community at peace. To deal directly with these activities, Congress appointed a Committee of Safety to which, in the summer and autumn of 1775, Franklin devoted most of his energies.

Much of this committee's work was congenial to Franklin's experience. His brilliant contributions years before to the Braddock expedition probably made that disaster less devastating than it would have been without them. His studies in chemistry helped in the uses of saltpeter in explosives. His inventive flair was responsible for a pike that the American soldiers found effective against the British bayonets and aided in the design and construction of the cheval de frise, which blocked the passage of the British ships up the rivers. His many hours of work each day on such projects were a vigorous sequence to his long, slow, London efforts.

Yet Franklin did not neglect the secret diplomatic preliminaries to foreign aid in matters of finance, contraband trade and moral support against Britain, the hated potential enemy of most of Europe. Following the procession of French spies which had, for several years, been infiltrating the colonies, came the undercover agent Achard de Bonvouloir, who was in unofficial communication with France's foreign minister, the Comte de Vergennes. Night after night, he and Franklin kept rendezvous in the dark and successfully eluded British spies. The French government, de Bonvouloir told him, dared not openly come to the support of the revolutionaries as long as there remained the possibility of reconciliation with England. In other words, until the colonies declared their independence, no frank aid and comfort could come from France. But a vicious circle resulted from the apprehension in Congress that independence could not be declared until there was the promise of foreign aid. The French agent was able, however, to give the sort of encouragement that fitted into the sequence of events that followed.

In October, Congress appointed Franklin to head a delegation to confer with Washington at Cambridge, where the general had gone to take official command of the Continental Army. There Franklin was able to see the difficulties under which Washington labored trying to inject discipline into raw troops—mainly farmers—who were averse to having their personal liberties curtailed and were determined to leave the army and go home at harvest time to take care of their crops.

On the way back from Massachusetts, Franklin, having heard that his beloved sister, Jane Mecom, was visiting his old friends the Greenes at Warwick, in Rhode Island, stopped off there for a brief, happy reunion. Perhaps because the disabilities of old age were beginning to afflict him, he needed female comfort and a degree of nursing. He was having swellings of the legs which he tried to dismiss as "dropsy" and occasional attacks of his old enemy, gout.

Though his extremely active work may have diverted his fluid mind from sadness, he must have felt through all this time a sense of personal tragedy. Though he kept it to himself, the house minus Deborah must have held its lonely hours. The house itself was new to him; most of it had been constructed in his absence and though the misspelled, ungrammatical and often incoherent correspondence of his wife had told him a few details, the new structure in Market Street was too strange to be a real home. But the poignancy here came with memories of the past on which it was not his habit to dwell; far more immediately disturbing was the alienation of his son.

Perhaps the split with William was one of the things that made Franklin call the revolution a "civil war." That, of course, was what it was, a fact which most Americans have forgotten. Although the Declaration of Independence and other more flamboyant documents suggest that a united people opposed the British, such was far from the case. It has never been accurately determined whether loyalists or patriots were in the majority and, in the pre-Declaration year even families were divided. On Franklin's last visit to the governor's residence in Amboy, he and William agreed to go their separate ways. Not long after, William was arrested and imprisoned for his Tory sympathies.

Another disappointment was the defection from the American cause of Franklin's close friend and frequent collaborator Joseph Galloway. Galloway eventually escaped the fate of many other loyalists by moving to England, where he spent the rest of his life. It is probable that some of the escaped American loyalists found that Great Britain was not all they expected, but it is true that many of the patriots deeply regretted the breach—perhaps from the same ignorance of conditions in Britain. It is certain, too, that there was wide apprehension among

Americans who stuck to the cause of liberty that they would find that along with the freedom they desired would come dangerous insecurity.

4

As the new year dawned, there came a phenomenon so startling that, in many parts of the country, deep-held convictions were reversed overnight. It had become in the colonies a generally accepted view that however intolerable the conduct of the British Parliament, the king could do no wrong. He was the anchor that would draw us all back to safety, once our petitions should be allowed to reach him; it was only because he had been kept in ignorance of true American conditions that he had permitted this tyranny by the ministers and the legislature. Now, on the 10th of January, 1776, came a book which attacked all monarchy and the sacred, by the Grace of God sovereign, George Hanover the Third, in particular! Moreover, the book made sense—*Common Sense,* as its title proclaimed.

Perhaps never had a piece of propaganda been more adroitly composed. Abundantly it cited scripture to bring to conviction the masses who had never wavered in their implicit faith in revealed religion. It must have surprised the few intimates of Tom Paine that so irreligious a writer should have been so familiar with Biblical injunctions. With devilish cunning, Paine held the hated popery responsible for our faith in kings. "For monarchy," he wrote, "in every instance is the popery of government." In a summary of parts of the Book of Samuel, he stated:

> Government by kings was first introduced into the world by heathens, from whom the children of Israel copied the custom. It was the most prosperous invention the devil ever set on foot for the promotion of idolatry.... Monarchy is ranked in Scripture as one of the sins of the Jews, for which a curse in reserve is denounced against them.

Then the author (later called an atheist) rose to a height of eloquence in his specific attack:

But where; say some, is the King of America? I'll tell you, friend, he reigns above, and doth not make havoc of mankind, like the royal brute of Great Britain.

Was this blasphemy or common sense? Some readers were not, at once, sure but in any case there was scarcely paper or pressmen enough to satisfy the fanatic demand for copies of Thomas Paine's book. Within three months, in a population of three million, including illiterates, 120,000 copies had been sold. In every corner of the country, in crowded urban coffee-houses and on the loneliest frontiers, men asked each other: "Have we then been worshipping false gods? Have we been practicing idolatry? Is this sacred person really a royal brute?" In the Declaration that followed six months later there was reflection of *Common Sense,* for in the twenty-eight paragraphs of complaint, the king is the only target, Parliament and the ministries are ignored.

Paine, in gratitude to Franklin, sent him the first copy of *Common Sense* off the press.

5

As the winter drew into the cold spring of 1776, the Continental Congress made one of its many colossal blunders. It would have cost the life of one of America's greatest statesmen but for the iron constitution which had saved him before and was to save him again. It was decided to explore the sentiment in Canada toward the now united colonies with the view to requesting Canadian aid in the war. The lack of what has since become known as "intelligence" about this near neighbor seems to us scarcely credible till we remember both the defective communications and the complacent self-sufficiency of the thirteen colonies.

The French Canadians were naturally hostile to the solidly anti-Catholic northern colonials. The abortive attack of Benedict Arnold on Quebec, with the consequent letting loose of his discontented forces on the countryside, had turned general Canadian sentiment against the colonials. There were many other causes of hostility, as the commission appointed by the Congress was soon to discover.

Perhaps the cruelest move—as it turned out—was the appointment of the seventy-year-old Benjamin Franklin to head the commission. Nevertheless, he accepted the appointment, ignoring the perils of the journey.

In March, then, the commission proceeded by frail riverboats, calèches, sleds over deep snow and other precarious means of transportation, plus long portages between lakes and rivers. After twenty-seven days of such travel the group reached Montreal, where their attempted negotiations met a total rebuff. After a two-week stay which took them into early May, Franklin returned with Dr. John Carroll, chosen because he was a Catholic, whose tender care of the old man was thought to have saved his life.

Back in Philadelphia, almost more dead than alive after his sufferings on the Canadian expedition, Franklin was in time to participate in the conference which resulted in Jefferson's Declaration. He was asked to read and criticize the draft and offered only two minor amendments. He suggested changing Jefferson's "We hold these truths to be sacred and undeniable" to "We hold these truths to be self-evident"; and, where Jefferson had accused the king of sending mercenaries to "deluge us in blood" to the briefer and less histrionic "destroy us." The few other corrections were merely verbal in the interest of exactness.

Part of the legend that has grown up round the Declaration has it that John Hancock, president of the Congress, said as he signed his name, "We must all be unanimous; there must be no pulling different ways; we must all hang together"; to which Franklin is supposed to have replied, "Yes, we must indeed hang together, or, most assuredly we shall all hang separately," but, though the sentiment has passed into the language, precise historians are agreed that the story is apocryphal. Such purists have dented most of the myths that the American people lives by.

Second only in importance to the signing of the Declaration was the concern of Congress with the hope of a foreign alliance against England. Drafts were made of possible treaties with France and Spain. In September, Congress, behind closed doors, agreed to send commissioners to the Court of France to work toward an alliance. Franklin, Jefferson and Silas Deane were named. Jefferson, because of his wife's illness, could not accept and Arthur Lee, with whom Franklin had occasionally tangled in England, was chosen to replace him. Deane was already in France.

There was a last-ditch interview with Richard Howe, who had come to New York to offer final terms of reconciliation. Anticipating American rejection, Franklin sent his former friend Howe a letter which Howe received on his arrival at Staten Island. The irony with which he regarded Howe's intended offer of Britain's "pardons" for colonial misbehavior presents Franklin at his shrewdest as well as his most candid:

> Directing Pardons to be offered to the Colonies who are the very Parties injured, expresses indeed that Opinion of our Ignorance, Baseness, and Insensibility which your uninformed and proud Nation has long been pleased to entertain of us; but it can have no other effect than that of increasing our Resentments. It is impossible we should think of Submission to a Government that has with the most wanton Barbarity and Cruelty burnt our defenceless Towns in the midst of Winter, excited the Savages to massacre our Peaceful Farmers and our Slaves to murder their Masters, and is even now bringing foreign Mercenaries to deluge our Settlements with Blood. These atrocious Injuries have extinguished every remaining Spark of Affection for that Parent Country we once held so dear; but, were it possible for *us* to forget and forgive them, it is not possible for *you* (I mean the British Nation) to forgive the People you have so heavily injured.

Franklin then met Howe, for whom, personally, he felt respect and even affection, at Staten Island but the meeting came to nothing, though there were refreshments in the form of "good claret, good bread, cold ham, tongues and mutton." Franklin left Howe to his prepared collusion with his brother William in the attack by sea and land on Manhattan.

After he had begun his preparations for the journey to France, Franklin sent word to his grandson, Temple, who was at his father's house in Amboy, to come to Philadelphia at once. He wanted the boy to go with him, though secrecy prevented his saying so in the message. He wanted, partly to get Temple away from his father's influence, but he also wanted his companionship and the secretarial assistance which Temple in his seventeenth year was amply able to furnish. His decision to take Richard Bache's son, aged seven, is less understandable but the courage of the child's parents, who were willing to trust the boy to his septuagenarian grandpa on so perilous a voyage, is characteristic, not only of their faith in the old man but of the brave spirit of the time. The trio left on the 27th of October on the armed ship *Reprisal*, which sailed, so it seemed, into the very teeth of the enemy. Had she been captured by the British, there is little doubt that Franklin would have been hanged for treason. What would have happened to the boys is a matter of grim conjecture. That they arrived safely some thirty days later after an uncommonly rough voyage was due to the combination of luck and skill which seemed to follow Benjamin Franklin wherever he went.

❧ XII ❧

PASSY—PEACE AND WAR

WHAT, then, was this land to which the envoys from a nation in the perils of childbirth so hopefully came? What was the background against which Silas Deane, Arthur Lee and Benjamin Franklin must perform? Was French society a stable structure in which all classes were at peace with one another or was all France a mere tottering frame, waiting only for the deluge that legend said a dying Bourbon monarch had predicted would sweep it away?

Already a mob of the poor had stood outside the gates of Versailles presenting a list of grievances inspired by hunger. Inside the walls of the palace, the extravaganza initiated by the fifteenth Louis continued; its cost alarmed certain ministers who had one eye on an angry *petite bourgeoisie* and the other on the precarious balance sheets that were kept in balance only by an intolerable tax increase.

But 1776 was too soon for the activities of the Tiers État, far too soon for the meetings of the States General in the Salle des Menus Plaisirs. A skilled locksmith had already been lost to trade in the person of Louis XVI, but Marie Antoinette, his wife in the time he had left after his tinkering, kept up the gaiety of ladies- and gentlemen-in-waiting and the nobles who attended her champagne suppers. To the outside world, therefore, France presented a proud and still formidable front.

Perhaps the arrival of Benjamin Franklin helped save her for a time. Surely, no greater contrast can be imagined than that of this simple, unwigged American with the powdered and perfumed courtiers who were gorging themselves on the people's bread. Immediately the bourgoisie saw it with relief and gathered round this apostle of nature who seemed, indeed, to be another Jean-Jacques Rousseau, adored by those who were, or pretended to be, nostalgic for the simple life. Even the queen, playing at milkmaid in her Petit Trianon, seemed friendly to that image.

Furthermore, he was to present a heroic view—that of a fight for liberty—to a people urgently in need of heroic victuals. Liberty, bright avatar of folk on the verge of insurgency against a stifling rule, was brought alive by this *Bonhomme Richard,* this man of the people, this champion of democracy.

So a welcome awaited Benjamin Franklin in France.

Beneath the round cap of marten fur and the simple, Quaker-like brown clothes, there was, of course, another truth not visible to the crowds in the streets. The chemist Lavoisier, the revolutionary skeptic Voltaire, the scientific experimenter La-Place, and the philosophical group that called themselves physiocrats knew well enough that a man who had disclosed the giant potential of electricity was no simpleton. Statesmen such as Turgot and Vergennes and Caron de Beaumarchais, talented in both drama and intrigue, would soon discover the shrewdness beneath the artless appearance. And the British ambassador to Paris, Lord Stormont, knew that the man who had for years twisted the tail of the British lion was at large among the French enemies.

In the first weeks of December, 1776, the rumor ran through the streets of Paris that the apostle of liberty was already at Nantes. Soon, with his two American boys, he would be among them.

2

Franklin, though so exhausted from the voyage that he could hardly stand, insisted on being put ashore at Auray, up a little inlet from Quiberon Bay in Brittany. From the long shipboard diet of salt meat he had a bad case of scurvy; the marten cap, in addition to being a symbol of simplicity, was convenient for covering the scorbutic rash on his broad forehead. He seems to have been in a hurry to get to Nantes, though, because of the great secrecy of his moves at this time, he was careful to leave little written record. There is every reason to believe, however, that he wished to confer with Sieur Montaudouin, an important merchant of the city, who later played such a vital part in getting contraband arms, munitions and other supplies to the embattled American colonies and who had already shipped some forbidden commodities to the Caribbean with directions to forward them to the ports of New England, to Philadelphia and to the southern coast of America. There was every reason for confidential exchange with Montaudouin; a fellow member of the Royal Academy of Sciences, a fellow Mason and a physiocrat—he was congenial indeed to Franklin. We know that Franklin dined with him at Nantes, and his letter from Nantes to the Committee of Secret Correspondence has a P.S., dated December 10 stating:

> I have just learned that eighty pieces of cannon, all brass, with carriages, braces and everything fit for immediate service, were embarked in a frigate from Havre, which is sailed; the rest were to go in another frigate of thirty-six guns.

The British spy system seems to have got immediate word to the British ambassador, Lord Stormont, of Franklin's arrival, for Stormont wrote, on December 11, 1776, to his chief, Lord Weymouth, in London:

> I learnt yesterday evening that the famous Doctor Franklin is arrived at Nantes, with his two grandchildren. They came on an American privateer, which took several [two] English vessels in her passage. . . . I cannot but suspect that he comes charged with a secret commission from the Congress, and as he is a subtle artful man, and void of all truth, he will in that case use every means to deceive, and will avail himself of the general ignorance of the French, to paint the situation of the rebels in the falsest colours, and hold out every lure to the ministers, to draw them into an open support of that cause. He has the advantage of several intimate connexions here, and stands high

in the general opinion. In a word, my Lord, I look upon him as a dangerous engine, and am very sorry that some English frigate did not meet with him by the way.

Lord Stormont's informant then seems to have let his imagination take control, for the next day, December 12, the ambassador wrote again to Weymouth, Franklin's purpose, in the meantime, having been greatly favored by the fanciful spy:

> My suspicions with regard to Franklin are confirmed. He came over in a Forty Gun Ship [!] to give more Eclat to his Mission and was at Versailles last night as I am positively assured.... He talks the Language I expected, represents the Affairs of the Rebels as being in the most flourishing Condition, says that General Howe never will dare attack Washington and adds that the Hessians who were advanced before the Main Army had attacked, and had been repulsed with loss. It is not to be doubted that he will make France the most insidious and tempting offers, and there is, I think, but too much Reason to fear that he will draw her into the Snare.

If Franklin had waylaid Stormont's agent, given him a drink and imparted this magnificent piece of misinformation it could not have had a more desirable effect. For, in fact, Franklin had never left Nantes.

3

Those biographers who imply that Franklin remained in Nantes for two weeks merely for a rest after his tiring voyage underestimate the speed with which he recovered his energy. In fact, he was extremely busy during that stay. He was elaborately entertained at an official reception arranged by the mayor of Nantes. He wrote letters to the people he was to meet at the earliest opportunity, telling them the latest news from America and explaining his own plans. The letters are packed with information and waste no words. He wrote to Thomas Morris, brother of Robert Morris, of the Committee of Secret Correspondence, saying he had letters he would soon deliver and sent it "by express" to Paris. He wrote his co-commissioner Silas

Deane, who was in Paris, telling him to find Arthur Lee, who had not yet heard of his appointment. "I shall endeavor to join you as soon as possible. I propose to retain my incognito until I ascertain whether the court will receive ministers from the United States." The incognito was, of course, entirely a matter of protocol as there was no possibility of a true incognito for a man everyone was expecting and wanting to see. He wrote, before he left Auray, to his friend Dubourg, telling him the bad news he had probably heard from America was not true. This, of course, was a case of Franklin whistling to keep up his spirits. And he wrote an extremely important letter to John Hancock, president of the Continental Congress.

Evidently, in his first two days at Nantes, he received vital information from Paris. Presumably this came in the post which he picked up as soon as he got to the Loire port. Writing Hancock, he said:

> I understand that ... an underhand supply is obtained from the government of two hundred brass field pieces, thirty thousand firelocks, and some other military stores, which are now shipping for America, and will be convoyed by a ship of war. ... I find several vessels here laden with military stores for America, just ready to sail. On the whole, there is the greatest prospect that we shall be well provided for another campaign, and much stronger than we were last.

This must have been heartening to the Congress, which had hardly recovered from the news that the Howes had captured Long Island and New York, forcing the retreat of Washington. Hancock, perhaps, did not entirely realize that Franklin's incorrigible optimism gave him occasional delusions of grandeur about America's part in the war.

4

Meanwhile, in Paris, rumors were constant. Madame du Deffand, the elderly gossip of the salons, wrote Horace Walpole that "what is the most singular of all is that no one can tell whether he is actually in Paris or not. For three or four days it has been said in the morning that he had arrived and in the evening that he had not yet come." There was much speculation about *why* he had come to France. The British embassy spread the propaganda that Franklin was discouraged and in flight from his native land. But Burke and Rockingham in England scorned this story. "I never can believe," wrote Burke to a correspondent in Paris, "that he is come thither as a fugitive from his cause in the hour of its distress, or that he is going to conclude a long life, which has brightened every hour it has continued, with so foul and dishonourable flight."

Rockingham, remembering the cockpit, wrote:

> The horrid scene at a Privy Council is in my memory, though perhaps not in his. It may not excite his conduct. It certainly deters him not.—He boldly ventures to cross the Atlantic in an American little frigate, and risk the dangers of being taken, and once more brought before an implacable tribunal. The sight of Banquo's ghost could not more offend the eyes of Macbeth, than the knowledge of this old man being at Versailles, should affect the minds of those who were principals in that horrid scene.

But the men who were in the secret had made practical preparations. Dubourg had circulated cards among all his circle announcing Franklin's approach. Caron de Beaumarchais had interspersed work on his operas with the affairs of the dummy firm he had established to carry on the secret business of supplying the new United States with arms. "Roderigue Hortalez et Compagnie" appeared to be just another of the mysterious financial operators with whom Paris abounded.

When, on the afternoon of December 21, Franklin finally arrived, Parisians were glad but not surprised. He went first to Silas Deane's Hôtel d'Hambourg in the rue de l'Université. The street was packed with curious, admiring crowds, waiting for him to show himself, to come out so that they might look at him, follow him, see if the stories about him were really true. Women, as if he had been a Messiah, wanted to touch his coat, to look into his face. He knew that if this adulation continued he would be unable to go about his business. Fortunately an escape was offered when Donatien le Ray de Chaumont persuaded him to settle on his estate in Passy.

The village of Passy (as it then was) is just across the Seine, northwest of Paris. Away from the smoke and noise of the city and on ground that rises rapidly from the Seine, it has long been the home of the *grand monde* and for Franklin's purposes it was ideal. Chaumont turned over to him a wing of the large mansion which seems to have been complete in itself with all the facilities of a comfortable, indeed a luxurious, home. Round this "Hôtel Valentinois" was a garden in which, when the weather was appropriate, Franklin could entertain his visitors and, especially, his neighbors the Brillons, with whom he soon became intimate. Whatever the burdens of his business, his diplomacy or his conspiracies, two things he always found: a chess partner and a lovely lady; in Madame Brillon, half his age, he found both. Their relations did not pass the "Dear Papa" and "Dear Child" stage, though he made other suggestions which she rejected.

In the healthy atmosphere of the heights of Passy, Franklin quite recovered from his fatigue and his bodily vigor returned. His new home was particularly convenient for his favorite exercise as, by descending a few steps, he was at the river and he was able to take a long, daily swim in which his grandson often joined him. An objective was a bathhouse on a barge, opposite the Tuileries. This was a public facility and though Franklin was well known by sight to the attendants there, they had no idea that he was the famous *Bonhomme Richard*.

He was able, therefore, to use this bathhouse as a secret rendezvous with persons not supposed to be acquainted with him. Benjamin Vaughan told a story about this. Vaughan had met Franklin in London and had an admiration for him and for the American cause. In September, 1777, he came to Paris and was extremely anxious to meet Franklin and give him certain intelligence from the Whigs in Parliament and also to promote various commercial ventures which defined British wartime statutes.

Vaughan was therefore desirous that there be no publicity about the meeting and it was also impolitic for Franklin to be known to have any intercourse with Englishmen. It was therefore arranged that Vaughan should go to the bathhouse on the Seine and ask for a stout, elderly gentleman known to be a strong swimmer. The unwitting attendant immediately produced Franklin and the two had a long clandestine conference.

5

For his first year in France, Franklin led the sort of double life in which he had acquired great skill. At Passy, he appeared genial, unhurried, willing and able to sit for hours engaged in a game or in conversation. He seemed not to have a care in the world. Yet at the same time he was obliged to juggle in his mind the most secret commercial negotiations, by which the fighting American army could be kept in the field, the extremely delicate, undercover relations with the French king and court, and applications from young French soldiers of fortune who wanted commissions as officers in Washington's army.

It was true that the three American "commissioners," Franklin, Deane and Lee, had communicated with Comte de Vergennes, Louis's foreign minister, informing him officially that Congress had sent them to negotiate treaties of commerce and, if possible, of military alliance. Vergennes, however, hearing nothing but bad news about the American conduct of the revolution, was not willing to make official commitments. He and the king were naturally afraid of a British victory, in which case the fighters for independence would be obliged to capitulate. This would leave France at war with England without the support of the American colonies. Furthermore, after a forced reconciliation, France would have their hostility. It was a risk the French government could hardly afford to take.

On the other hand, hatred of England was extremely bitter throughout France. Virtually all the French people were emotionally in favor of colonial independence and certain firebrands like Beaumarchais were constantly urging an alliance or, failing that, all possible *sub rosa* aid. Already, Beaumarchais, through his fictitious firm of Roderigue Hortalez & Company, had secured loans of two million francs from the French and Spanish governments and had arranged for the shipment of large cargoes of war matériel. But neither Franklin nor the other commissioners were invited to the French court at Versailles, and the communications with Vergennes were largely clandestine. Franklin understood this and bided his time. He agreed that he was not to have public appearances in Paris and the people were to believe that no commitment had been made.

Meanwhile, turning from the harassing business of his office which had become, in fact, the United States embassy, Franklin provided himself with a *maître d'hôtel* who, in turn, supplied an efficient staff of servants. Franklin stocked his cellar with some two hundred and sixty bottles of red Bordeaux, more than a hundred red Burgundy, four hundred of various white wines including champagne, two hundred *vin ordinaire* for the servants and forty-five of rum. In the matter of food, he lived well. For dinner, there was a joint of beef, veal or mutton followed by poultry or game, two dishes of vegetables, two of sweets and one of pastry, two kinds of fruit in winter and four in summer, a platter of cheese, one of biscuits, one of bonbons, ices once a week in winter and twice in summer.

In the morning, the callers became a real annoyance. Most of their requests had to be refused since Franklin had no blanket authority from Congress to give military commissions. Then there was an immense mass of correspondence, including numerous requests from authors to read and criticize their manuscripts. A vast quantity of paper work was handled by grandson Temple; John Adams's son, John Quincy Adams, sometimes volunteered his clerical services. There was also the confidential secretary, Edward Bancroft, trusted by Franklin although he was, in reality, an agent of the British government and sent copies of many of Franklin's letters to the London office of information.

But Franklin's attitude about spies was surprisingly careless. When Juliana Ritchie, the wife of a Philadelphia merchant who had come to live in France, wrote him on January 12, 1777, warning him that he was surrounded by spies, he replied:

> I have long observ'd one Rule which prevents any Inconvenience from such Practices. It is simply this, to be concern'd in no Affairs that I should blush to have made publick, and to do nothing but what Spies may see & welcome. When a Man's Actions are just and honourable, the more they are known, the more his Reputation is increas'd and establish'd. If I was sure therefore that my Valet de Place was a Spy, as probably he is, I think I should not discharge him for that, if in other Respects I lik'd him.

The Paris police, however, took another view. In the paper, *Nouvelles de Divers Endroits* for August 20, 1777, this notice appeared:

> Certain sinister-looking persons, seen lurking around Dr. Franklin's lodging at Passy, and others no less suspected, who have even penetrated to his presence upon different pretexts, have led the government to give positive orders to the Lieutenant General of Police to watch over the safety of this respectable old man, and take all the precautions to this end that prudence could suggest.

Nevertheless, the British ambassador, Lord Stormont, received plenty of information. A tree in the Tuileries gardens served as the spy post office. Communications were to be put in a bottle placed near the tree's roots. "The bottle to be sealed —and tyed by the Neck with a common twyne, about half a Yard in length—the other end of which to be fastened to a peg of wood split at the top to receive a very small piece of Cord— the bottle to be thrust under the Tree, & the Peg into the Ground on the west side."

All communications were to be written in invisible ink, which should become visible only when the paper was warmed before a fire. Undoubtedly information about ships with cargoes destined for America was sent to Stormont from Franklin's office by Edward Bancroft, whom Franklin continued to trust. Many of these communications have been found and preserved.

One such document gives instructions on the subjects that Lord Stormont and the British spy, Paul Wentworth, wished to know about. The communication was to be carried on by a "Doctor Edwards," which name biographer Albert Smyth believes to have been a thin disguise for Edward Bancroft:

> The progress of the Treaty with France & of the Assistance expected, or Commerce carryed on in any of the ports of that Kingdom,—The Same with Spain, & of every other Court in Europe. The Agents in ye foreign Islands in America, & the means of carrying on the Commerce with the Northern Colonys. . . .
>
> Franklin's & Dean's Correspondence with the Congress, & their Agents: and the secret as well as the ostensible Letters from the Congress to them. Copys of any transactions committed to Paper, & an exact account of all intercourse & the subject matter treated of, between the Courts of Versailles & Madrid, and the Agents from Congress.

Lord Stormont was particularly anxious to know:

> Names of the two Carolina Ships, Masters both English and French, descriptions of the Ships, & Cargoes: the time of sailing, & the port bound to—
>
> The same Circumstances respecting all equipments in any port in Europe: together with the names of the Agents imployed.
>
> The intelligence that may arrive from America, the Captures made by their privateers, & the instructions they receive from the deputys.
>
> How the Captures are disposed of.

Much of this information passed through Franklin's office. He was concerned not only with the purchase of ships and the commissioning of their captains, but also with cargoes they were to pick up at the various ports of France, Spain and Holland, where they were to carry them, how they were to avoid capture by British warships and much similar business. Yet we know that a large part of the contraband commerce was successful. There are good reasons for this. Franklin's original letters got

through to captains, merchants, American spies and Congress
before Bancroft's copies could be evaluated and acted upon.
And there was need for quick action and adroit dodging by
American, French and Dutch sea captains. The sea story of the
war is full of narrow escapes, fraudulent ship registries and flags,
and ships hiding in the many coves of the Caribbean islands.
To be sure, the merchants involved were not trying to carry
on a patriotic trade but to make a good thing of it for themselves. War, in the eighteenth century, was an exceedingly prof-
itable business for most of the background figures. While soldiers were dying on the battlefields, businessmen *on all sides*
were amassing fortunes. There were few exceptions; even the
extremely zealous and often self-sacrificing Beaumarchais was
not above making shrewd deals in captured prizes and the
American Morrises, notwithstanding their immense financial
help to the patriot cause, emerged richer than ever.

Though Franklin was harassed by Frenchmen who wanted to
fight against Britain in America, he was able to suggest a number of valuable men to Washington. Thus he arranged for the
commissioning of the brilliant boy, Lafayette, whom he personally consigned to Washington's care and for whom he made a
careful financial provision, and the German, Steuben, in whom
he recognized a high military potential.

In general, the year 1777 was a difficult and puzzling one for
Franklin and those who most intimately supported him. The
hesitation by the French court made all calculations difficult
for him. Then, in October, something happened at Saratoga,
New York, which, when it became known in Paris, changed
everything. Parisians have often danced in the streets, but seldom with more abandoned enthusiasm than then, in December,
1777, when the news from across the Atlantic was proclaimed.

❦ XIII ❦

VICTORY AND ALLIANCE

AMONG the many things that were said in Paris about Saratoga that first week in December, 1777, there was little about the arrogance or the reckless stupidity of General John Burgoyne. That his movement from Quebec to the Hudson was slowed by a gigantic baggage train and by some female camp followers who had to be driven in comfortable calèches, that the savagery of his Indian allies had roused the rage of his Yankee enemies to a pitch never before reached in the Revolutionary War and had insured his defeat, or that the fatigue and homesickness of his large numbers of Hessian mercenaries had rendered them almost useless—these and other contributing factors to the total victory of the Americans at Saratoga were not mentioned in Paris, even by the undercover British contingent. To the Parisians, Burgoyne's defeat was due entirely to the heroism of the liberty-seeking colonials, who probably fought against overwhelming odds. In fact, Burgoyne's army was heavily outnumbered.

A new word entered the French language: *burgoinissé*, meaning disastrously defeated; it was used about the losers either at cards or in *l'amour*. Franklin, naturally—the nearest available American—became the center of a new hero-worship. There was no more need for discretion: now the alliance was inevitable; the ministers, even the king himself, must agree to what the people had urged all along. Now, surely, there would be war with England: a sacred war of revenge and a war, too, in the great cause of liberty!

Caron de Beaumarchais, in a characteristic frenzy of excitement, drove to Passy to bring Franklin the news of Saratoga which he had just heard; apparently his horses caught his near-hysteria, for on the way back they ran away and threw him from his carriage with a result which his surgeon said had almost proved fatal. He soon recovered, however, sufficiently to write Vergennes a letter not distinguished by the restraint with which one usually addresses a royal minister.

> This propitious event is balm to my wounds. Some god has whispered in my ear that King Louis will not disappoint the hopes of the faithful friends whom America has acquired for herself in France. It is my voice which calls out on their behalf from beneath my blankets: "Out of the depths have I cried unto thee, Oh Lord! Lord, hear my prayer!"

The Comte de Vergennes, however, did not need the playwright's prayer to urge him. When he communicated his own hitherto frustrated desire to the king, Louis met him halfway. His majesty, indeed, was so anxious to have the credit for an American alliance that he let it be known that it was really his idea in the first place.

It was suggested, therefore, to Franklin, that if the American commissioners would repeat their original offers they might well get a warmer response than that of the year before. How much better, thought the sly, quiet American, to have the request for an alliance come from France than from the new nation scarcely out of the perils of childbirth! It was a reward, was it not, for his long restraint?

The negotiations took a while: Spain, which had been approached, must be consulted, or at least, informed, and the details of the treaty worked out. However, as Trevelyan records,

> on the sixth of February 1778 the signatures were affixed to a Treaty of Commerce, and Treaty of Amity and Alliance, between France and the United States. The French Government, paying a tribute by anticipation to the principle of the Monroe Doctrine, solemnly disclaimed all intention to re-conquer Canada. No condition whatever was exacted from America,

except a promise that she would never purchase peace with Great Britain by consenting to resume her subjection to the British crown.

Meanwhile, however, during the delay over the signing, peace feelers came from England. Lord North, alarmed at the way the war was going in America, believed that a last attempt at reconciliation might be worthwhile, and planned a series of bills to be introduced in Parliament repealing the objectionable statutes. They adopted, indeed, the plans proposed by Franklin before the Declaration, minus independence. Although news of the proposed treaty with France had already been brought by spies to England, it was decided to send Paul Wentworth, the British master spy, to Paris to talk, if possible, with Franklin himself.

Franklin was delighted at the prospect. As soon as it should become known to Vergennes that Franklin was talking to an English agent, the French minister would become fearful that America would accept peace terms and so leave France exposed to war with England without American support and, perhaps, with American hostility. This fear would hurry the negotiations. Thus, if Franklin played his cards right, he would accomplish two purposes: encourage the English into thinking there was still a hope of retaining the colonies and, by introducing panic into the French court, rush the final signing.

It was a game much to the fancy of the American diplomat. Whether or not Wentworth knew that Franklin was playing with him, he went back to England with an empty briefcase. The commissioner, he reported, had said he could make no commitment without instructions from the American Congress; that he had referred to the British conduct of the war as "savage," that the American patriots would find this hard to forgive, but as to an eventual reconciliation, he could say neither yes nor no.

In England, nevertheless, the North ministry was quite serious. Indeed, they appointed three envoys: Lord Carlisle, George Johnstone and William Eden, supposed friends of the colonies, to go to America and confer with the Congress. These "Commissioners for Restoring Peace" sent ahead copies of the bills of reconciliation, which assured that every colonial grievance should be met, provided only that the idea of independence be abandoned.

As it turned out, due largely to Franklin's adroit diplomacy, the treaty with France was signed and sent across the Atlantic at about the same time that the bills were dispatched to Congress with the notice that the commissioners would follow. The British message got to Philadelphia first and the few conservative members who were always advising caution to the Congress were already telling the majority that it might be wise to receive the commissioners. But when the signed treaties arrived with a request for ratification, the voices of the doubting Thomases were drowned in the general jubilation.

2

At the ceremony of the signing and at the later court presentation, Franklin showed that sense of the theater which had dictated much of his conduct in Paris. To the signing, he wore the faded but still elegant costume he had worn in the Whitehall cockpit the day that Wedderburn had insulted him. "But why?" asked Silas Deane. "To give it a little revenge," Franklin replied.

The signing was followed by Franklin's presentation at court. As the representative of a republic, he scorned the formal dress, complete with wig and sword, that protocol required. According to the gossip Madame du Deffand, for whom the occasion offered an uncommon opportunity,

> Mr. Franklin has been presented to the King. He was accompanied by some twenty insurgents, three or four of whom wore a uniform. Franklin wore a dress of reddish brown velvet, white hose, his hair hanging loose, his spectacles on his nose, and a white hat under his arm. I do not know what he said, but the reply of the king was very gracious, as well towards the

United States as towards Franklin their deputy. He praised his conduct and that of all his compatriots. . . .

"The courtiers in the corridors and the antechamber," writes biographer Carl Van Doren, "many brilliant shows as they had seen, thought they had never seen anything as striking as this republican simplicity in such a place. (Franklin had known what they would think.)"

A witness reports that Louis said to Franklin:

> Firmly assure Congress of my friendship. I hope this will be for the good of the two nations.

Later Franklin was presented to Marie Antoinette, who was so charmed by him that she interrupted a game which she was playing for high stakes. After talking to him a while, she asked that he stand by her side while she resumed her play. These things, which may appear trivial to later readers, were reported with awe by contemporaries. To the historian who must report the rolling of the queen's pretty head in the Place de la Concorde some twenty years later, both the trivia and the awe are important.

3

The first policy of the American Congress in 1776 of sending three commissioners to negotiate for the treaty with France was obsolete in 1778. Then the treaty had been signed and Conrad Alexandre Gérard had been sent as minister plenipotentiary from France to the United States. Gérard made it clear to the Congress that the French court would prefer to deal with one official envoy rather than with a group. Gérard knew also that Arthur Lee had become unpopular in France, that he was widely regarded as a troublemaker. There was thinly veiled hostility between Lee and Silas Deane because Lee had accused Deane of what we now call war profiteering. In addition, Lee, who had an almost pathological ambition and a definite paranoid tendency, was intensely jealous of Franklin.

On September 14, 1778, therefore, Congress revoked the tri

partite commission and named Franklin as sole plenipotentiary. The Marquis de Lafayette, who had just passed his twentieth birthday and was a major-general on Washington's staff, was given a leave of absence to carry Franklin's commission to France. It was a belated move but a wholly necessary one.

Lee's characteristic anger at the change must have marred Franklin's enjoyment of the smoothness with which the transactions were proceeding. Nonetheless, he made a gentle reply to the insolent letter in which Lee refused to turn over his papers as commissioner.

Inevitably Franklin's growing power and popularity made him enemies among some of his jealous colleagues. John Adams, later the republic's second president, was evidently envious when he wrote that

> He loves his ease, hates to offend, and seldom gives any opinion till obliged to do it. . . . Although he has as determined a soul as any man, yet it is his constant policy never to say yes or no decidedly but when he cannot avoid it.

Adams also deplored Franklin's friendly relations with women, which he thought dangerous for a diplomat. That the Puritan Abigail shared her husband's feelings is evident from a description she wrote of Franklin's friend, Madame Helvétius:

> Her hair was frizzled; over it she had a small straw hat, with a dirty gauze half-handkerchief round it, and a bit of dirtier gauze than ever my maids wore was bowed on behind. . . . I own I was highly disgusted, and never wish for an acquaintance with any ladies of this cast. . . . She had a little lap-dog, who was, next to the Doctor, her favourite. This she kissed, and when he wet the floor, she wiped it up with her chemise.

Abigail added that "manners differ exceedingly in different countries," though she left it unsaid that Boston, in this respect, was superior to Paris.

In Philadelphia, the hostility of Franklin's old enemies increased with his growing power. There was still a hangover from the quarrels over the proprietary government, now, of course, a thing of the past, and the hostile group still believed that he had gained his influence by corrupt means. It is significant that, of all the colonies, Pennsylvania alone refused to approve his election as plenipotentiary.

4

Though in his new position his labors were augmented, his pleasures were not reduced. As his biographer and editor Albert Smyth explains at the beginning of the chapter in the tenth volume of *Writings,* entitled "Social Life in France":

> With no assistance, save the slight help furnished by his grandson—an inexperienced boy who was more familiar than he with the French language,—surrounded by spies and beset by jealous and malicious foes, Franklin performed alone the varied duties of merchant, consul, commissioner, and plenipotentiary. He bought and sold ships, adjusted difficulties between rival commanders, pacified mutinous crews clamouring for prizes, purchased arms and clothing for the Continentals, recommended soldiers and sailors for the army and navy in America, made treaties with the farmers-general, influenced the policy of foreign newspapers, honoured the large and constant drafts of the Congress, and persuaded the French government to advance large sums of money to relieve the desperate necessities of America.

Smyth then goes on to tell of the good times Franklin had in Passy and Paris, for "his life was not all toil." This narrator, however, gives too little credit to Temple. In addition to acting as interpreter when Franklin's linguistic talents failed him, the boy performed the Herculean job of keeping the legation's papers in order—a duty which his grandfather notoriously neglected. Then, too, he was chosen to present the sword Congress awarded to Lafayette and, in 1779, the marquis appointed him his aide. The functions of courier, which sometimes required great discretion, he meticulously carried out. Finally, we owe gratitude to Temple for his faithful record of the sequence of events in this critical phase of Franklin's career.

When Franklin first came to Paris, a friend, William Alex-

ander, visited him at the Hôtel d'Hambourg and noticed the
disorder in his quarters there.

> Will you forgive me my Dear Sir [Alexander wrote him on
> March 1, 1777] for noticing, that your Papers seem to me to
> lye a little loosely about your hands—you are to consider your-
> self as surrounded by spies and amongst people who can make
> a cable from a thread; would not a spare half hour per day
> enable your [grand]son to arrange all your papers, useless or not,
> so that you could come at them sooner, and not one be visible to
> a prying eye?

That Temple took this rebuke seriously is evident from
the fact that his grandfather eventually bequeathed to him a
large number of documents. Yet at first the boy—then only sixteen—quailed before the job Alexander recommended and it is
not surprising that some vitally important letters got diverted
into hostile hands. It is even more surprising that so little evil
resulted from the accidents. Of course even Benjamin Franklin's greatest admirer must admit that the goddess Luck was a
mistress who seldom left his side.

5

Nearly twenty years before (they must have seemed centuries
as he looked back at them from 1778), Franklin had written a
piece entitled "The Interest of Great Britain considered with
Regard to her Colonies" in which he recommended certain
proposals for settlement of the Seven Years' War with France.
One of them was that Britain should certainly take Canada
rather than any French sugar islands in the West Indies. This
was to counteract a then popular move to profit from the sugar
plantations. Naturally, at the time Franklin was wholly concerned with the British interest and it did not occur to him
that West Indies islands in French hands would one day be
extremely useful to America in winning her independence.

When, however, the French decided to aid the North American colonies the islands became essential, first to the clandestine

enterprise before the treaties were signed, then to the open commerce which made success possible for the joint armies on the continent.

Caron de Beaumarchais, the brilliant cloak-and-dagger operator, sitting in the office of his dummy Hortalez and Company in Paris, was constantly fingering his map of the archipelago south and southeast of Florida. He was almost as familiar with the islands as the sea captains whose ships moved in and out of their countless coves and harbors. He could order a ship laden with a cargo of arms and munitions from L'Orient in France to say, St. Pierre in Martinique with the certainty that when that cargo was unloaded there, it would be picked up by an American merchantman and carried north to Charleston or New Haven or Boston. Meanwhile, the imaginative Beaumarchais devised many tricks of sleight of hand by which a ship's registry or flag or inventory might be changed en route if there was any danger of pursuit or detection. Thus, in pre-Treaty days, several million francs' worth of supplies had been stored in the arsenals of the thirteen colonies.

The money which Beaumarchais used to buy the supplies was, after all, only a loan from the French and Spanish governments. But the colonial merchants, who were slowly enriching themselves by the clandestine transactions, were scrupulous about paying for the goods. Thus, ships carrying lumber from New England, rice and indigo from the Carolinas and, especially, Virginia tobacco were continuously moving by the same circuitous routes into the ports of France, and Beaumarchais's agents arranged for the sale of their cargoes at exceedingly lucrative prices. Thus, as all was fair in eighteenth-century war, both the trade and the traders prospered and, eventually, success in the field came to Washington's armies.

Once France was in the war, however, there were new hazards to Franco-American intercourse. As long as she had remained technically neutral, international law gave a certain protection to her operations. But once France became an enemy, Britain could exercise a close scrutiny over her naval intrigues, and occasionally forged ships' papers and tricks with flags and registries were discovered. Also, British ships stood outside the harbors of the French islands and seized the vessels bound for North American ports. On the other hand, American privateers became active in West Indian waters and took many British prizes. Here the French islands offered a useful convenience to the Americans, who could take their prizes into a French island port and sell their cargoes there, thus avoiding long and dangerous voyages.

Both Guadeloupe and Martinique did a thriving business throughout the war to supplement the sugar-plantation prosperity. American merchants from Massachusetts and Connecticut established branch mercantile houses on Martinique and sent agents there to manage them. Another exceedingly active French port with which Hortalez and Company did much business was Cap François on the north coast of the island of Santo Domingo. But none of the French islands was more deeply involved in the gunrunning than the Dutch St. Eustatius, commonly known as Statia. Though Holland was officially neutral, the Dutch were friendly to the American "rebels" and, like most of the people in continental Europe, hostile to Britain.

Charles Dumas, a Swiss living in Holland, was deep in the Statia conspiracy. From his first acquaintance with Franklin, he was zealous for the cause of the North American colonies. Throughout the Revolution he was the secret agent in Holland for the colonies and for the United States. Like so many of the men, especially the Europeans, who acted as secret conspirators in these times, Dumas was a scholar and a man of letters. More than two hundred and fifty notes written by him to Franklin have been preserved and they reveal much of the commerce that was carried on via the Dutch island of Statia. A good portion of this correspondence passed through Statia, managed by the brave and faithful courier Thomas Story.

Franklin wrote Dumas in September, 1778, when there had been negotiations for an alliance with Holland—negotiations which Franklin had given up because the Dutch terms seemed unacceptable. The letter shows Franklin's opinion of what should be the proud attitude of the United States, young as that nation then was:

> I think that a young State like a young Virgin, should modestly stay at home, & wait the Application of Suitors for an alliance with her; and not run about offering her Amity to all the World; and hazarding their Refusal. My Colleagues have this day proposed to me to go to Holland on this Business; but tho I honour that nation, having been frequently there, and much esteeming the People, and wishing for a firm Union between the two Republicks, I cannot think of Undertaking such a Journey without some assurances of being properly received as a Minister of the United States of America. Our Virgin is a jolly one; and tho at present not very rich, will in time be a great Fortune, & where she has a favourable Predisposition, it seems to me to be well forth cultivating.

Though Franklin was skeptical of the Dutch alliance, especially in view of the apparently patronizing attitude of what he called the "high and mighty ministers" at The Hague, he welcomed any material assistance they might render in their West Indies island. Like many of the undercover operations that were carried on with European nations, this one was very largely a one-man performance by the supposedly quiet and scholarly Dumas.

Among the other valuable helps that Dumas gave was his invention of a cipher, pronounced almost unbreakable by cryptographers, which he and Franklin were to use in their letters.

In all the dealings for supplying the American armies from abroad, Franklin, living quietly and pleasurably at Passy, had either an active hand or at least full cognizance. He was instrumental, too, in buying ships, commissioning their captains, supervising their registries and their cargoes through a large number of secret agents in the French ports. Much of his communication with such persons was in code and their itineraries were carefully planned.

In addition to his frequent conversations with Beaumarchais and communications with such large-scale French merchants as Montaudouin and Penet, Franklin kept himself informed as to the privateering and the sea battles of the war. The intrepid John Paul Jones gave him news of his adventures with his *Bonhomme Richard,* named, of course, from the almanac character; and Captain Lambert Wickes of the *Reprisal,* who had brought Franklin and the two boys safely to France in 1776, gave him the details of the large number of British prizes he took.

One concern which occupied much of his thought was the fate of American prisoners of war in English prisons. His humane feelings about the probable mistreatment they received led to strenuous efforts for their exchange. His fears for their sufferings may have been exaggerated but he had known of accredited examples of enemy cruelties in other directions and he was entitled to lively misgivings. Through some of his old friends in England, he was able to reach the authorities there and to arrange for the return of English prisoners taken from prizes or sea combat in exchange for British-held Americans. In this work, David Hartley was especially instrumental.

That Franklin was able to do these things and at the same time to continue his full enjoyment of life was due to personal qualities which, in his time at least, were unique.

XIV

"DEAR PAPA"

THIS," wrote Franklin from Paris to his niece Elizabeth Partridge, "is the civilest nation upon Earth." He felt that he owed her an explanation of the rumors about "the Kindness of the French Ladies to me."

> Your first Acquaintances endeavour to find out what you like, and they tell others. If 'tis understood that you like Mutton, dine where you will you find Mutton. Somebody, it seems, gave it out that I lov'd Ladies; and then every body presented me their Ladies (or the Ladies presented themselves) to be *embraced*, that is to have their Necks kiss'd. For as to kissing of Lips or Cheeks it is not the Mode here, the first, is reckon'd rude, & the other may rub off the Paint. The French Ladies have however 1000 other ways of rendering themselves agreeable; by their various Attentions and Civilities, & their sensible Conversation. 'Tis a delightful People to live with.

Arriving in the colder and less "civil" Boston, this letter may have aroused speculation as to what might have been the thousand "other ways" in which the Parisiennes rendered themselves agreeable to Uncle Benjamin. Whether Betsey showed this letter to Captain Partridge, superintendent of the Boston almshouse, is not recorded. In any case, the daughter of John Franklin was one of Benjamin's favorite nieces and he undoubtedly enjoyed writing her as he did.

This and other letters of his voluminous correspondence of the period suggest the wisdom of Smyth's judgment that the life of the plenipotentiary in France was "not all toil."

He lightened the burden [writes Smyth] and forgot his wor-
ries by social diversions. He was admired by philosophers and
petted by society; and he found himself as much at home in the
salon of Madame d'Houdetot or Madame Helvétius as in the
laboratory of Lavoisier, the clinic of Vicq d'Asyr, or the cabinet
of Vergennes. Never lived a man more idolized. Curious crowds
followed him with applause when he walked abroad; men carried their canes and their snuff-boxes *à la Franklin,* fair women
crowned him with flowers, and wrote him roguish letters af-
fectionately addressed "dear amiable Papa."

"Amiable" in English is weaker than the French *aimable,*
which should be translated "lovable" and coupled with the
affection form of "father" seems to imply that these women felt
the sort of love one felt for an adored parent rather than a sexual infatuation. That Benjamin occasionally felt otherwise is
obvious from the correspondence, but it is doubtful that he ever
expected a fulfillment other than the indulgence of a nostalgic
fancy. Certain it is, however, that the "sensible conversation"
of these worshipping women was not an adequate consum-
mation.

Revelations of this kind of devotion reflect the mood of
French feminine society in the eighteenth century. The *fin de
siècle* women of the upper classes evidently felt an urgency for
something different from the fatiguing practice of *l'amour.* As did
their husbands, married women often had separate affairs and
these, in time, became tedious, as such things usually do. The
desire for this less physical but equally intense love was part of
the trend toward freshness, toward simplicity and away from
passion tired from repetition, that must come to a sated society.
It was all of a piece with the attachment to Rousseau, specious
as that commonly was; of the gasping for a breath of fresh air
from across the Atlantic that all Paris had come to know since
it knew that the fight for freedom was there.

And Franklin, after all, was nearing seventy-four when he
wrote to Betsey Partridge. Given his superb constitution and
his great physical strength, it is still unlikely that he was assailed
by the same "ungovernable passion" as he was when, at nine-

teen, he stole his friend's mistress in London. Yet, however
sublimated such a passion may be, it never quite vanishes. So,
though the most inquisitive biographer may not uncover an
authentic Parisian bedroom scene, he cannot dissolve the charm
which this aspect of the Franklin story must eternally present.

There are men, of course, of any age who might lose their
peace of mind when a beautiful woman made sensible conversation while sitting on their lap but not Benjamin Franklin.
Perhaps, on the contrary, such diversions in the late afternoons
stopped the escape of that peace which must have threatened
after a hard day of complex mental work. For some of us, the
immense mutative possibilities in a game of chess will produce
agitations which prevent sleep, but Franklin, after half a night
of this tense play, slept like a baby. Whether, without these
means of relief, he would still have retained his peace is a sense-
less question, for if neither had been present, he would have
invented others.

2

A short walk brought him from the Hôtel Valentinois to
the home of the Brillons. Madame d'Hardancourt Brillon
was often relieved of the presence of her husband, who was
waited upon by another lady, and Franklin assuaged her lone-
liness. He rarely found her alone, however; her daughters were
usually present. Their evenings were gay, spiced by chess and
music, as we learn from the letters they wrote each other recalling those pleasures. What unrecorded incidents took place we
may only guess at but their letters were intimate. It was in the
letters that a closer relation was discussed: total love proposed
by Franklin and consistently rejected by her. It would *spoil*,
she thought, the beautiful father-daughter make-believe.

Further, she resented any who suggested that their friendship was anything but what might exist between parent and
child:

> Do you know, my dear Papa, that people have the audacity
> to criticise my pleasant habit of sitting upon your knees....

I despise slanderers and am at peace with myself, but that is not enough, one must submit to what is called *propriety* [the word varies in each century in each country], to sit less often on your knees. I shall certainly love you none the less, nor will our hearts be more or less pure; but we shall close the mouths of the malicious and it is no slight thing even for the secure to silence them.

Yet a stranger to the circumstances coming suddenly on these letters in, say, the mid-twentieth century would believe them to be communications between lovers. "I shall count the days, the hours, the minutes," she wrote when she was away from home, "each minute passed brings me nearer to you. We like to watch when it is the only means of uniting us to those whom we love." Again, "Will you not write me a word? a word from you gives me so much pleasure. It is always good French to say *'je vous aime.'* My heart always goes out to meet this word when you say it to me."

That there should have been so many letters between friends who were such close neighbors suggests that there was much these two had to say to each other that could only be expressed in written form. And this, of course, was Franklin's way. He was not a talker. He was accused, by many who knew him, of being taciturn. His presence at any official gathering, such as a session of Congress, was marked by long silences. We who have met him lately are glad of this; his habit of subjective writing has given us the best of him.

Franklin's letters to Madame Brillon were in French. His biographers have made haste to tell us how bad his French was lest knowledgeable readers detect an error here and there, but to the ordinary American it seems, in the letters at least, fluent and colloquial. It delighted the Frenchwomen to whom he wrote; they found it picturesque and far more "from the heart" than if it had had academic correctness. The chances are that, when he spoke it, his accent was not good but this, in an English-speaking person, is so generally expected that to a Frenchman, a perfect accent in a foreigner is often disappointing and sometimes suspicious.

3

A walk of something more than a mile would bring Franklin to the village of Auteuil and the home of the widow of the celebrated philosopher Claude Arien Helvétius. It was his habit to dine twice a week with Madame Brillon and on Saturdays with Madame Helvétius, a woman nearer his own age. Once beautiful, she was now, at sixty, compared by catty Frenchwomen to "the ruins of Palmyra." According to Abigail Adams, she gloried in demonstrations of magnificent vulgarity, but to Franklin, she was still so attractive that he proposed marriage to her. Her rejection of him as a potential second husband was due, she said, to her eternal attachment to the memory of her first, which gave rise to Franklin's famous dream. The story has been retold so many times that it has become an accepted literary fact that no Franklin biography is complete without it. The tale of the dream that he told the widow Helvétius is so contrived that it may be doubted that he ever dreamed it, but it is a tribute to his creative fancy.

No sooner, he wrote to the lady whom he called "Notre Dame d'Auteuil," had she declined his proposal, than he went home and, in despair, threw himself on his bed and, suddenly, he was in Paradise. There, he inquired at once for M. Helvétius and the philosopher appeared before him. The letter—the translation from Franklin's halting French we owe to Carl Van Doren—goes on from there:

> He received me with much courtesy, having known me by reputation, he said, for some time. He asked me many things about the war and about the present state of religion, liberty, and government in France. "You ask nothing then," I said to him, "about your dear friend, Madame Helvétius; and yet she still loves you to excess. I was with her less than an hour ago." "Ah!" he said, "you remind me of my former happiness. But we must forget if we are to be happy here. For several years at first I thought of nothing but her. At last I am consoled. I have taken another wife; the most like her I could find. She is not, it is true, altogether so beautiful, but she has as much good sense and plenty of wit, and she loves me infinitely. She studies

continually to please me, and she has just now gone out to search for the best nectar and ambrosia to regale me with this evening. Stay with me and you will see her." "I perceive," I said, "that your former friend is more faithful than you; she has had several good offers and has refused them all. I confess to you that I have loved her, to madness; but she was cruel to me and rejected me for love of you."

Helvétius commiserated with him and advised him to persist in his suit. At this point:

the new Madame Helvétius came in with the nectar; immediately I recognized her as Madame Franklin, my former friend. I claimed her again, but she said coldly: "I was a good wife to you for forty-nine years and four months, almost half a century. Be content with that. I have formed a new connexion here which will last for eternity."

Indignant at this refusal from my Euridice, I at once resolved to quit those ungrateful shades, return to this good world, and see again the sun and you. Here I am. Let us avenge ourselves."

4

One whom he saw less frequently was the Comtesse d'Houdetot, at Sannois near Argenteuil. The countess's *salon* would have been famous even had she not been the object of one of Jean Jacques Rousseau's mad passions, for her wit had attracted many men of letters and her beauty had made an impact on Parisian society. She was an accomplished writer of verse, and at one of those large outdoor affairs known as a *fête champêtre,* which she put on for Franklin at her Sannois estate, she produced a dozen or so stanzas in his praise, each of which was recited by a guest as a kind of toast along with a glass of wine. When he drove to her château, she and her family walked half a mile to meet him, made him dismiss his carriage and walk back with them. At the end of the evening, she bade him farewell with this verse:

Législateur d'un monde, et bienfaiteur des deux,
L'homme dans tous les temps te devra ses hommages;

Et je m'acquite dans ces lieux
Da la déité de tous les ages.

Later, he wrote her from Philadelphia, recalling the pleasure
she had given him:

> The Memory of your Friendship, & of the happy hours I
> passed in your sweet Society at Sanois, has often made me regret
> the Distance, that makes our ever meeting again impossible.

5

Soon after he had become settled in Passy in 1777, he installed there a small printing press. Perhaps he had wished for
a press of his own in London, for he always itched to get his
hands into a font of type, but there, through his friend Strahan,
he had been able to get anything he wanted printed, either in
the newspaper for which Strahan did the printing or published
by his friend in pamphlet form. In Passy, however, many official
forms had to be printed quickly so there was an excuse for
setting up a press on the premises. After he had used it for
official business, however, it became a recreation or, as we
should say, a hobby.

Being an expert printer and a perfectionist in the art, he
worked over every detail with his own hands, making a type
foundry and casting his own type. He had some assistance from
a foreman and several other people, including a girl. These
persons had other household duties when they were not engaged
with printing.

Soon the need for forms and other official items was filled but
there stood the press, a constant temptation. What better use for
it than to print satires and what Franklin called "bagatelles,"
such as his account of the dream of paradise? These writings
had become popular among his constantly increasing circle of
friends. To entertain these folk with manuscript copies would
have been impossible. Nor was there an English-language newspaper to which he could send the satires as he had done in
London.

The bagatelles were light essays, usually in the form of parables or fables with morals, such as the story of "The Whistle." This was a lesson in the value of money and the stupidity of extravagance which he learned at the age of seven when he paid four times its worth for a toy whistle. "The Deform'd and Handsome Leg" is the brief tale of a man who had both and who gauged potential friends by whether they stared at the good or the bad leg when first they met him. One of the most celebrated was the "Dialogue Between Franklin and the Gout." In it the Gout scolds and intends to punish him for sins of which he knows he is guilty.

> What have I done [he asks] to merit these cruel sufferings?
> GOUT: Many things; you have ate and drank too freely, and too much indulged those legs of yours in their indolence.

Franklin denies that he is a "glutton and a tippler," to which Madame Gout (for she is, apparently, a lady) replies:

> ... I very well know that the quantity of meat and drink proper for a man, who takes a reasonable amount of exercise, would be too much for another who never takes any.

Madame Gout stresses exercise more than anything else: this, of course, reflects precisely what Franklin knows about himself. This piece was written in October, 1780, and it reveals how subtly, in less than four years, the man has surrendered to his age. In 1777, the year after he had come to France, he did much swimming and walking, but in 1780, though he exaggerates the accusations of "Gout," he has depended very largely on his carriage to take him to visit his friends.

Franklin sent a copy of this "bagatelle" to his young friend Georgianna Shipley, in England, and distributed other copies abundantly in Paris. Madame Brillon agreed with Madame Gout and lectured him anew on his habits as soon as she read the Dialogue. To this he replied that when he had been young and enjoyed more favors from the opposite sex than he got from the ladies of Passy he had no gout; therefore, if they would be kind and Christian enough to give him what he asked, the gout

BENJAMIN FRANKLIN : 164

would disappear. In a letter to Madame Brillon about sin in general, he wrote:

> And now I am Consulting you upon a Case of Conscience I will mention the Opinion of a certain Father of the church which I find myself willing to adopt though I am not sure it is orthodox. It is this, that the most effectual way to get rid of a certain Temptation is, as often as it returns, to comply with and satisfy it.

The bitterest satire which came off the press was the fictitious "Supplement to the Boston *Independent Chronicle*." Franklin loved a "hoax," something that happily has gone out of fashion, though in the eighteenth century it was often used in order to make a point. Temple tells us with regard to this one:

> The deception intended by this supposed "Supplement," (which was very accurately imitated with respect to printing, paper, the insertion of advertisements &c) was, that, by transmitting it to England, it might actually be taken for what it purported to be.

The main story in the paper was an account of American scalps taken by Indians and sent as a present to Governor Haldimand of Canada "in order to be by him transmitted to England." There were gruesome details about the scalps of women and children. All these scalps were packed in boxes according to the age and sex of the victims and listed as if the list were a genuine invoice. Franklin distributed this "satire" widely both in England and on the Continent and had the satisfaction of learning that it was generally believed. This phase of Franklin's literary activity seems to later readers rather juvenile but he had evidence that it was effective.

Many of the products of the Passy press have been lost; the French Revolution, with its widespread chaos, followed, after all, soon after Franklin's departure from France. But enough remains to give us a pleasant picture of the good times and happy recreations that provided an antidote to the grueling work of the legation. The surviving bits of correspondence produced in this time show what a host of happy memories Franklin was able to take home with him to regale his last years.

XV

PRISONERS AND PRIVATEERS

WHETHER or not concern for prisoners of war is the duty of a minister plenipotentiary of a nation deep in conflict, it engaged much of Franklin's attention and more of his worry than anything else in the Passy phase. His distress came from his humanitarian apprehensions about the sufferings of his unlucky fellow countrymen and from the frustrations of his attempts to interest the British in the business of exchange. Stories of the conditions in British prisons, especially in prison ships such as the notorious *Jersey,* had come to Franklin's ears and he made many fruitless attempts to persuade British authorities to release Americans and accept English prisoners in return. But there were endless delays: his communications were ignored or insultingly rejected.

Franklin's fears for the safety and welfare of Americans captured by the British appeared soon after his establishment at Passy—six months before the treaty with France when the French still pretended to be neutral—in a letter to Lord Stormont, British ambassador at Paris.

> We did ourselves the Honour of writing some time since to your Lordship on the subject of Exchanging Prisoners. You did not condescend to give us any Answer, and therefore we expect none to this. We however take the Liberty of sending you Copies of certain Depositions which we shall transmit to Congress whereby it will be known to your Court that the United States are not unacquainted with the barbarous Treatment their People receive when they have the Misfortune of being your Prisoners here in Europe. And that if your Conduct towards

us is not altered it is not unlikely that severe Reprisals may be thought justifiable from the Necessity of putting some Check to such abominable Practices. For the sake of Humanity it is to be wish'd that Men would endeavour to alleviate as much as possible the unavoidable Miseries attending a State of War. It has been said that among the civilized Nations of Europe the ancient Horrors of that State are much diminished. But the Compelling Men by Chains, Stripes & Famine to fight against their Friends and Relations, is a new Mode of Barbarity which your Nation alone has the Honour of inventing. And the sending American Prisoners of War to Africa and Asia remote from all Probability of Exchange and where they can scarce hope ever to hear from their Families even if the Unwholesomeness of the Climate does not put a speedy End to their Lives, is a manner of treating Captives that you can justify by no Precedent or Custom except that of the black Savages of Guinea.

This letter was signed by Franklin and his co-commissioner Silas Deane and is indorsed by Franklin, "return'd with insult." Though Stormont evidently believed that he had deceived Franklin into thinking that the letter had not been opened and read, evidence later discovered shows that he not only read the letter but had it copied and sent the copy to his superior, Lord Weymouth, with this note:

I send your Lordship a Copy of a very Extraordinary, and Insolent Letter, that has just been left at my House, by a Person who called himself an English Gentleman; I thought it by no means Proper to appear to have received, and kept such a Letter, and therefore my Lord, instantly sent it Back, by a Savoyard, seemingly unopened, under Cover to Mr. Carmichal who I discovered to be the Person that had brought the Letter, I added the following short unsigned Note. "The King's Ambassador receives no Letters from Rebels but when they come to implore His Majesty's Mercy."

Thus thwarted in his efforts to deal directly with the British ambassador, Franklin turned to an English friend. David Hartley was the son of the English philosopher of that name; a person of education in his own right, he was a Bachelor of Corpus

Christi at Oxford and a Fellow of Merton College, a member of Parliament from Hull and a close friend of Lord Rockingham. He was a friend of America and an intimate of Franklin's. He hated the war and constantly sought a means of reconciliation between England and the colonies, though he knew that nothing could be done in the face of American insistence on independence. He had carried on a lengthy correspondence with Franklin on this subject; Franklin kept assuring him that the Americans were becoming more and more obdurate the longer the war went on.

Even so, Franklin thought, here was a humane fellow who deplored the British acts of tyranny and especially the atrocities which public opinion in his country apparently justified. After Franklin had taken up his residence in France, communication between these friends became difficult. So many of their letters miscarried either by accident or due to interception that to obtain a continuous story we must put together the pieces of a picture puzzle, guessing at the ones that are lost. Fortunately, it was Franklin's practice to make a copy of everything he wrote.

> Fill'd tho' our letters have always been [he wrote to Hartley in October 1777] with sentiments of good will to both countries, and earnest desires of preventing their ruin and promoting their mutual felicity, I have been apprehensive, that, if it were known that a correspondence subsisted between us, it might be attended with inconvenience to you. I have therefore been backward in writing, not caring to trust the post, and not well knowing whom else to trust with my letters. But being now assured of a safe conveyance, I venture to write to you, especially as I think the subject such an one as you may receive a letter upon without censure.

It is probable, however, that Franklin did not greatly care about the safety of the letter—that he might well have been glad to have it read by a British interceptor. This is evident from parts of its contents.

> Happy I should have been, [the letter went on] if the honest warnings I gave . . . had been attended to, and the horrid mis-

chief of this abominable war been thereby prevented. I should still be happy in any successful endeavours for restoring peace, consistent with the liberties, the safety, and honour of America. As to our submitting to the government of Great Britain, it is vain to think of it. She has given us, by her numberless barbarities in the prosecution of the war, and in the treatment of prisoners, by her malice in bribing slaves to murder their masters, and savages to massacre the families of farmers, with her baseness in rewarding the unfaithfulness of servants, and debauching the virtue of honest seamen, intrusted with our property, so deep an impression of her depravity, that we never again can trust her in the management of our affairs and interests. It is now impossible to persuade our people, as I long endeavoured, that the war was merely ministerial, and that the nation bore still a good will to us. The infinite number of addresses printed in your gazettes, all approving this conduct of your government towards us . . . and the popular rejoicings on occasions of any news of the slaughter of an innocent and virtuous people, fighting only in defense of their just rights . . . all join in convincing us that you are no longer the magnanimous and enlightened nation, we once esteemed you, and that you are unfit and unworthy to govern us. . . .

Having thus expressed himself in eloquent and uncommonly strong language, Franklin came to the point of his letter. Even if peace should be impossible, there could be "some act of generosity and kindness towards prisoners."

I can assure you from my own certain knowledge, that your people, prisoners in America, have been treated with great kindness; they have been served with the same rations of wholesome provisions with our own troops, comfortable lodgings have been provided for them, and they have been allowed large bounds of villages in a healthy air, to walk and amuse themselves with on their parole. . . . Some considerable act of kindness towards our people would take off the reproach of inhumanity in that respect from the nation. . . . This I hint to you, out of some remaining good will to a nation I once sincerely loved. But, as things are . . . I shall content myself with proposing, that your government would allow us to send or employ a commissary to take some care of those unfortunate people. Perhaps on your representations this might speedily be obtained in England, though it was refused most inhumanely in New York.

He hoped that David Hartley himself might visit the prisons, assure himself of the truth of ill treatment and distribute two or three hundred pounds among the prisoners "for which your drafts on me here shall be punctually honour'd." And, perhaps he could say something in Parliament.

If you cannot obtain for us permission to send a commissary, possibly you may find a trusty, humane, discreet person at Plymouth, and another at Portsmouth, who would undertake to communicate what relief we may be able to afford those unhappy, brave men, martyrs to the cause of liberty.

American captains, Franklin explained, had set free in France hundreds of prisoners they had taken from English ships and even dismissed a great number "at sea on your coasts, to whom vessels were given to carry them in: But you have not returned us a man in exchange."

Franklin's persistent concern with the welfare of his imprisoned countrymen is evident from a letter he wrote some weeks later to Sir Grey Cooper, a secretary of the British treasury and an old acquaintance, asking that the bearer of the letter be allowed to visit the prisons and distribute some perquisites among the prisoners. That he chose as the messenger a man he had just met, who represented himself as deeply sympathetic with the captives, shows Franklin's curious gullibility—the reluctance to suspect the good faith of anyone. That this Major Thornton was, in fact, a British spy never occurred to him or to Arthur Lee.

Thornton, however, was so happy to ingratiate himself with Franklin that he followed to the letter Franklin's instructions in England. He delivered the letter to Sir Grey Cooper and arranged to get a similar one to Lord North; further, he himself saw many of the prisoners and gave them the money Franklin had decreed. Thus he came to be trusted, not only by Franklin, but by his co-commissioner Lee, who made Thornton his confidential secretary. So, Major John Thornton became one of the most effective links in the spy ring that surrounded the embassy of the United States in France. He not only brought to the information ministry in England many of the secrets which the commissioners shared with Vergennes and Beaumarchais, but he played the commissioners against each other, aiding Lee in his underhand dealings against Deane and Franklin and encouraging Lee's paranoia, his jealousies and his ambitions.

Nevertheless, the American prisoners benefited from Thornton's mission. A second appeal, which Franklin addressed to Hartley, reached him through Thornton, just as Hartley was setting up a committee in England to obtain subscriptions for them, to which generous Englishmen and Scots gave gladly. As Helen Augur tells us in her *The Secret War of Independence:*

> Every man received a pound of tobacco, a blanket, a suit of clothes and a greatcoat, soap and a variety of food. Officers got an allowance of five shillings a week, scaling down to two shillings for seamen. The men were now allowed to bathe, six at a time, at the pump in the jailyard and to wash their clothes in new troughs installed in the yard.

2

All this occurred before the treaty of alliance with France was signed. Whatever part "neutral" France played had, therefore, to be a clandestine one. For example, the French could not offer French prisons for British prisoners captured by the Americans. Thus, though Franklin talked continually of the "exchange" of prisoners, there could be no great accumulation of British prisoners to trade. British prisoners had either to be held on American ships, which had scant room for them, or they had to be released on French soil, an expedient that accounted for the majority. The English, of course, knew this, which was one of the reasons no great effort was made in England to comply with Franklin's request.

The main reason, however, was that in the first years of the conflict the captured American seamen were not regarded by the British authorities as prisoners of war. Rather, they were rebels, guilty of high treason, and all that kept the British from hanging them was the hope that they could be persuaded (bribed) to turn traitor to their own cause and join the king's forces.

Failing, therefore, to effect an exchange of prisoners, Franklin sought means to aid their escape. He and Deane and certain Frenchmen created an elaborate organization which has been compared to the "underground railway" of the American Civil War. As Helen Augur explains,

> they arranged by an elaborate network to get money to the officers in prison and direct them to English friends who would smuggle them across to Holland or the northern ports of France. In every port there was a designated ally who would help the escapees on their journey. Most of them wanted to go to Paris to see Franklin, who was rapidly becoming the patron saint of the prisoners, but he finally spread the word that this was a waste of time and money and the men should go direct to Nantes or other safe ports, where work was waiting for them.

In short, Franklin wanted them to get back into American ships with the least possible delay as there was a shortage of seamen to man the growing American fleet. Thus Franklin got into the business of building an American navy, an enterprise that would be openly aided by the French, once there was an official treaty of alliance.

Through the year 1778, both in England and in prison ships off the American coast, American prisoners in British hands suffered severely. There is an abundance of diaries and letters of survivors to show the details of the treatment they received in spite of all the efforts of humane and generous Englishmen and others to bring them relief. One estimate, made after long study of all these documents, states that out of every three taken captive, one died, either in captivity or later as a result of his confinement. Starvation, cold, dirt and lack of medical care were all recorded. The worst conditions were in the British prison ships off the coasts of New Jersey and New York— these for the most part were out of Franklin's reach—but the English prisons visited by Franklin's emissaries were bad enough.

There was, for instance, the notorious "Old Mill" prison at Plymouth, described in its horrible details by Charles Herbert, who managed to keep a journal from the time of his capture in 1777. In it we get a confirmation of much of Franklin's effort and its results—missing from his correspondence.

Herbert called the Old Mill prison "the black hole" and wrote in his journal in August, 1777:

> Many are strongly tempted to pick up the grass in the yard and eat it, and some pick up old bones in the yard, that have been laying in the dirt a week or ten days, and pound them to pieces and suck them. Some will pick up snails out of the holes in the wall . . . boil them and eat them and drink the broth. . . .

In February, 1778, Herbert saw a newspaper,

> wherein is an extract of a letter from Dr. Franklin, Dean and Lee, to Lord North, and to the ministry, putting them in mind of the abuse which the prisoners have received from time to time, and giving them to know that it is in the power of the Americans to make ample retaliation, but they hoped there was more humanity left in their hearts. They also wrote concerning an exchange of prisoners. . . .

Then again in February, 1778, there was a successful escape of five, who managed it by bribing two sentries and then taking the sentries with them. Among the captains who escaped was the intrepid Henry Johnson, who had already spread terror among the British with his brig, the *Lexington,* and had been finally captured by a British cutter and sent to Old Mill. Taking advantage of Franklin's underground railway, he was able to reach Passy, where he was given new orders. Silas Deane, who was sailing to America with the admiral Comte d'Estaing, took Johnson along as a pilot who knew the American coast, and could get the French fleet into the harbors and ports for its successful operations.

When, in 1778, the treaty with France was signed, French prisons could be used for British captives and they accumulated to a point at which exchanges could be made. Also the British government, having found that they could not press American prisoners into the service of George III, were more willing to let them go. On this point, we have the word of Mary L. Booth, who, in her *History of the City of New York*, quotes one of the prisoners of New York's Sugar House prison:

> Although our sufferings were intolerable, and the men were urged by those who had been their own townsmen and neighbors who had joined the British, yet the instances were rare that they could be influenced to enlist. So wedded they were to their principles, that they chose honorable death rather than to sacrifice them.

3

With the treaty of alliance signed and France in the war, Franklin's part in maritime operations became easier. Now the American privateers could bring their prizes openly into French ports. The French ministry of marine no longer had to give clandestine aid to the embryo American navy. It could procure or build ships for the American service, arrange for the refitting or overhauling of damaged American ships in the shops of L'Orient or Nantes or Brest and for the sending of French ships of the line and French officers to aid in the American naval war. British ships hovering round the French islands in the West Indies could be engaged in combat and, if possible, driven off, thus making the immense commerce between island ports and those on the North American coast less secretive and more effective.

All these matters came more and more under the scrutiny of Franklin, eventually, largely under his direction. With Ambassador Lord Stormont sent home to England and the French envoy at London recalled, with the departure of Gérard de Rayvenal as minister to the United States and finally with the elimination of Lee and Deane as commissioners and his own appointment as plenipotentiary, Franklin's task became both easier and larger.

He had at his command some courageous and experienced officers and their sturdy ships. He sent Captain Thomas Thompson and his thirty-two-gun frigate the *Raleigh* and Captain Elisha Hinman with the twenty-gun *Alfred* on a "cruise" covering the coast of Africa to plunder the "British Factories and Commerce," the West Indies and portions of the coasts of Europe, taking prizes where possible and otherwise to "annoy and distress the Enemy." One of the most reliable of the captains, Lambert Wickes, who had brought Franklin to France in the *Reprisal in* 1776 and who, in his brief career, had captured some thirty valuable prizes, perished in his sinking ship shortly before the treaty was signed, but the legend of his wide and fearless ranging inspired all later American captains. Franklin was instrumental in furnishing the hero John Paul Jones with a ship procured from the French. When in the summer of 1778, the British finally, reluctantly, agreed to an exchange of prisoners, Franklin wrote to Jones:

> As you may like to have a Number of Americans, and your own are homesick, it is proposed to give you as many as you can engage out of two hundred prisoners which the Ministry of Britain have at length agreed to give us to exchange for those you have in your hands. They propose to make the exchange at Calais, where they are to bring the Americans.

Franklin then wrote to French Minister of Marine de Sartine:

> As our People languish in their Confinement, and may, when recovered be of Use to Capt. Jones, or in some other Enterprise, we wish the Exchange may be made as soon as possible, and therefore request your Excellency would take the Affair into Consideration, and afford us your Advice and Determination upon it.

With all this preparation, the first exchange did not take place until well into 1779. We may imagine the satisfaction that must have been felt by men so long imprisoned when they were sent to serve with so just and humane a commander as John Paul Jones.

Carl Van Doren gives a summary of Franklin's part in privateering which suggests that this may have been an unwelcome task.

> Franklin commissioned the American privateers which used French ports as their base for raids against British ships. When they came back with prizes, he served—in Paris—as judge in the proceedings of condemnation and sale. This he found troublesome and exhausting, in part because he disapproved of the whole system.

This suggests that Franklin disapproved of all privateer warfare, as he may well have, for it was carried on largely for the enrichment of individuals and to some extent came under our later designation of "profiteering." It appears, however, from a letter he wrote Robert Morris, financier of the American Revolution, in June, 1780, that he was opposed to the taking of neutral ships as prizes, which of course was a step nearer piracy than the use of privateers against enemy vessels.

> Russia, Sweden, Denmark, and Holland are raising a strong naval force to establish free navigation for neutral Ships and of all their Cargoes, tho' belonging to Enemies, except contraband, that is, military stores. France and Spain have approved of it, and it is likely to become henceforth the law of Nations, that *free Ships make free Goods.* England does not like this confederacy. I wish they would extend it still further, and ordain that unarmed Trading Ships, as well as Fishermen and Farmers, should be respected, as working for the common Benefit of Mankind, and never be interrupted in their operations, even by national Enemies; but let those only fight with one another whose Trade it is, and who are arm'd and paid for that purpose.

Again, Franklin, who was given to thinking far ahead of his time, puts the interests of mankind before national interests. This was indeed the prevailing attitude among the Founding Fathers of the United States—in the eighteenth century, an advanced view.

❦XVI❦

FROM LIGHTNING RODS
TO BALLOONS

ALMOST in view of the Hôtel de Valentinois was the
Château de Passy, home of the Comte de Boulainvilliers.
His daughter, sometimes called Mademoiselle de Passy, was said
to be the most beautiful girl in France. Naturally she was one
of Franklin's favorites. Observing this, John Adams said, not
wholly approving, "at the age of seventy-odd Franklin had
neither lost his love of beauty nor his taste for it." Love of
beauty, in the Puritan view, was generally suspect.

When this girl's engagement was announced to the Comte
de Clermont-Tonnerre, Franklin's hostess, Madame de Chaumont, said to him, "Alas! All the lightning rods of Mr. Franklin
have not prevented the thunder from falling on Mademoiselle
de Passy." Following these teasing words, he wrote to the girl's
mother:

> It gives me great Pleasure Madam my respected neighbor to
> learn that our lovely Child is soon to be married with your
> Approbation & that we are not however to be deprived of her
> Company. I assure you that I shall make no Use of my Paraton-
> nerre [lightning rod] to prevent this Match. I pray God to favor
> it with his choicest blessings, and that it may afford many Occa-
> sions of Felicity to all concerned. . . .

This sort of play was in character with the period. While it
may touch no sympathetic chord in the late New York-Algon-
quin school of humor, it does reflect the sunnier and the gentler

side of a dark and cruel world. While every day the menace of total social upheaval drew nearer, this sort of thing had a place in the salons along with powdered wigs and knee breeches. And it was pleasing to Franklin, who had a dark side too.

He had by no means forgotten the serious aspect of the lightning conductor. One of his first enterprises when he was settled at Passy was to equip the Hôtel Valentinois with *paratonnerres*. He sat in the garden and watched while the workmen erected the rods and wires, talking with one of his feminine friends and occasionally shouting an order to the men. As he had done in London, he gave directions to his friends to put this kind of protection on their houses and Paris was soon bristling with lightning rods. In London, however, he had excited a royal controversy which gave him many a subsequent laugh. While King George III felt that the palace must be protected, he had insisted on conductors of his own design. A vital part of Franklin's invention was the pointed rod atop the conductor. George, however, made the workers substitute rounded ones. It was characteristic of this monarch, Franklin observed, to prefer the blunt rather than the sharp.

Nor did the busy diplomat abandon his own scientific interests. He saw much of a fellow academician, Jean-Baptiste Le Roy, and he managed to combine scientific conversations with many a social evening spent at the Le Roy house. Madame Le Roy received his especial attention. He called her his *petite femme de la poche*, which, translated into "my little pocket-wife," is meaningless but to him was a term of endearment at which Le Roy could not possibly take offense. That the evenings with the Le Roys contained other than scientific inquiries is evident from the drinking song which, we understand, was written and sung by Jean-Baptiste himself, the refrain of which may be translated as

> With the glass in hand
> Let us sing to our Benjamin.

Presumably the entire Le Roy family including the *petite femme de la poche*, and one or more of the Le Roy brothers,

Charles, David and Pierre—all men of science—held a glass in hand while they joined in the chorus.

There exists a letter from Madame Le Roy which, like so many of the missives from Franklin's admirers and his replies, suggests an intimacy that we may well doubt considering the family friendship:

> Will you, my dear friend, dine with me Wednesday; I am most desirous of seeing and embracing you.

To which he answered:

> I will certainly not fail to be at your house next Wednesday. I take too much pleasure in seeing you, in hearing you talk and too much happiness when I have you in my arms to forget an invitation so precious.

In the original French, this seems mere gallantry. In any case, she continued to call him *"mon cher bon papa."*

Again, later, just before he left Paris for the last time she wrote:

> Good bye, my dear, good friend. I promise you that as long as I continue to breathe the breath of life your little pocket-wife will love you. She embraces you with all her heart.

2

Franklin managed, with all his heavy diplomatic duties to wedge in a letter to Joseph Priestley or Jan Ingenhousz. This one to Priestley in February, 1780, reveals to what extent Franklin lived in the future:

> The rapid progress true Science now makes, occasions my regretting that I was born so soon. It is impossible to imagine the Height to which may be carried, in a thousand years, the Power of Man over Matter. We may perhaps learn to deprive large Masses of their Gravity, and give them absolute Levity, for the sake of easy Transport. Agriculture may diminish its Labour and double its Produce; all diseases may by sure means

be prevented or cured, not excepting even that of Old Age, and our Lives lengthened at pleasure even beyond the antediluvian Standard.

That so many of these dreams might come true in less than two centuries was a fact far beyond his or any other imagination in 1780. But there is something grim indeed to the twentieth-century reader about the next sentence:

> O that moral Science were in as fair a way of Improvement, that Men would cease to be Wolves to one another, and that human Beings would at length learn what they now improperly call Humanity.

The communications with Jan Ingenhousz required so much concentrated thought that it seems hardly credible that Franklin was able to find the time to write him in such detail. Ingenhousz asked him a series of questions resulting from some inexplicable experiments he had made with Leyden jars. Franklin answered each one with an assurance; it is evident from this correspondence that Franklin, in 1780, knew more about electricity than anyone who had yet published his experiments and that every scientist who was puzzled about his inquiries must turn to him for the answers. It is interesting that both Franklin and Ingenhousz referred to electricity as a "fluid," a theory that was long discarded until something very like it was postulated by the first experimenters in electronics.

Again, Franklin answered questions put by Ingenhousz about the curious effects of a stroke of lightning upon a vane on the steeple of a church in Cremona. But, in this case, he asked Ingenhousz not to publish his answers lest the publication "may occasion Disputes, and I have no time to attend to them." But how he wished for time to attend to the questions that so fascinated him! He lamented, "my Thoughts are so employ'd of a different kind, that I cannot easily fix them on philosophical Subjects." In this same letter, he wrote:

> I last year requested of Congress to release me from this Service, that I might spend the Evening of Life more agreeably in philosophic Leisure; but I was refus'd.

3

In 1780, Franklin suffered a severe attack of gout. He records a method of treating it which he says was first recommended to him by his son, William:

> You inquired about my gout, [he wrote to Alexander Small in 1780] and I forgot to acquaint you, that I treated it a little cavalierly in its last two accesses. Finding one night that my foot gave me more pain after it was covered warm in bed, I put it out of bed naked; and, perceiving it easier, I let it remain longer than I at first designed, and at length fell asleep leaving it there till morning. The pain did not return, and I grew well. Next winter, having a second attack, I repeated the experiment ... constantly with the effect of rendering it less painful, so that it permitted me to sleep every night....

Penetrating further into his life at Passy, a later reader of the record might think that a more abstemious way might have brought an even more effective cure, but the older Franklin grew, the less ready he was to make sacrifices.

Every Sunday all his more intimate friends were invited to dinner. As this custom continued, Franklin began to think of himself as a gourmet and devoted much thought to the planning of the meals. He collected menus and ordered his *maître d'hôtel* to serve the proper wine for each course. He himself was especially fond of burgundies and could not resist glass after glass of Nuits St. Georges.

His friends, in return for his hospitalities, sent him quantities of the best wine, beer, rum, and Madeira. Franklin's wing of the Hôtel de Valentinois was not a strictly temperate household, nor were its victuals wholly suited to a rheumatic cure. Franklin knew this and knew, too, that the slackening of his physical activity as his age crept up on him was not conducive to the sort of health he had enjoyed all his life.

In the later years of his seventies, he felt more keenly the approach of the shadow of death. In many of his letters, he spoke of it, cheerfully enough as one who had no doubt of a next world. He would go to sleep at night, he thought, and wake up in another place. Yet he felt that there was much to be done first; "in the little time that is left me" he must hurry. He must get home to his beloved America, which his imagination painted in warm colors. Yet his fancy never quite envisaged the work that he could and would do to finish his mission in France.

In his advanced age, he expressed a cynical view of the human race, as in this letter to his fellow "philosopher," Joseph Priestley:

> I should rejoice much, if I could once more recover the Leisure to search with you into the Works of Nature; I mean the *inanimate*, not the *animate* or moral part of them, the more I discover'd of the former, the more I admir'd them; the more I knew of the latter, the more I am disgusted with them. Man I find to be a Sort of Beings very badly constructed, as they are generally more easily provok'd than reconcil'd, more disposed to do Mischief to each other than to make Reparation, much more easily deceiv'd than undeceiv'd, and having more Pride and even Pleasure in killing than in begetting one another; for without a Blush they assemble in great armies at NoonDay to destroy, and when they have kill'd as many as they can, they exaggerate the Number to augment the fancied Glory; but they creep into Corners, or cover themselves with the Darkness of night when they mean to beget, as being asham'd of a virtuous Action. A virtuous Action it would be, and a vicious one the killing of them, if the Species were really worth producing or preserving; but of this I begin to doubt.

The letter goes on to the more congenial subject of chemical experiments discussed at the Academy of Sciences. Franklin continued, even when in great pain from the gout and from a kidney stone, to write about hygrometers and ways of measuring the humidity of the atmosphere, of the aurora borealis, of the persistence of infection in dead bodies, the dubious pathological value of mesmerism and the longevity without nourishment of toads and tortoises.

4

Franklin was seventy-seven when he was caught in the excitement which was thrilling all Paris:

> All the Conversation here at present [he wrote to Richard Price in September, 1783] turns upon the Balloons fill'd with light inflammable Air, and the means of managing them, so as to give man the Advantage of Flying. One is to be let off on Friday next at Versailles, which it is said will be able to carry up 1000 pounds weight. . . .

Illness prevented Franklin from seeing the Versailles ascension, though he had already watched one by the Montgolfiers at the Champs de Mars in August. But these were unmanned. In November, he witnessed the ascension of the first balloon to carry human beings. A Montgolfier hot-air balloon rose five hundred feet above Passy carrying Pilâtre de Rozier and the Marquis d'Arlandes and was swept by the wind across the Seine. After their safe landing in Paris, enormous crowds, which had gathered from a combination of curiosity and the veiled hope of disaster, cheered the courageous aeronauts.

There was a conflict between the Montgolfiers and Jacques-Alexandre-César Charles over the use of hot air or hydrogen gas to inflate the balloons. The Parisians, according to their tradition, passionately chose sides. But in December, Charles rose two thousand feet over the Tuileries with his hydrogen balloon.

Franklin wrote in great detail to Sir Joseph Banks of the Royal Society in London about all these experiments, explaining that the inflation by hot air was "cheap and expeditious" whereas the hydrogen method was "a tedious operation and very expensive," as well it might have been since the hydrogen gas was obtained by pouring sulphuric acid on iron filings. This would "prevent the invention being of so much use as some may expect, till chemistry can invent a cheaper light air producable with more expedition." Franklin added:

I am sorry this experiment is totally neglected in England, where mechanical genius is so strong. I wish I could see the same emulation between the two nations as I have seen the two parties here. Your philosophy seems too bashful. In this country we are not afraid of being laughed at. If we do a foolish thing, we are the first to laugh at it ourselves, and are almost as much pleased with a bonmot or a good chanson, that ridicules well the disappointment of a project, as we might have been with its success.

Had Franklin lived a little more than a century later, he would have known of the ridicule in America that broke the heart of Samuel Langley when his experiments with a heavier-than-air flying machine failed and that caused the Wright brothers to do their first flying in secret.

One of the thoughts that the balloon ascensions inspired in Franklin were of war. This was natural as his mind had been recurrently drawn toward war during the last eight years. But the balloons also brought thoughts of peace for now, in 1783, Cornwallis had surrendered to Washington and a treaty of peace with Britain had at last been ratified. Thus, he wrote to Jan Ingenhousz in January, 1784:

> Convincing Sovereigns of the Folly of wars may perhaps be one Effect of it; since it will be impracticable for the most potent of them to guard his Dominions. Five thousand Balloons, capable of raising two Men each, could not cost more than Five Ships of the Line; and where is the Prince who can afford so to cover his Country with Troops for its Defence, as that Ten Thousand Men, descending from the Clouds might not in many places do an infinite deal of mischief, before a Force could be brought together to repel them?

The French balloons, so important in the private life and thought of Benjamin Franklin, have brought us ahead of our story. In January, 1783, before the sensational performances that he witnessed in Paris, Franklin was able to write his old friend Polly Hewson:

At length we are in Peace, God be praised, and long, very long, may it continue. All Wars are Follies, very expensive, and very mischievous ones. When will Mankind be convinced of this, and agree to settle their Differences by Arbitration? Were they to do it, even by the Cast of a Dye, it would be better than by Fighting and destroying each other.

Some two hundred years later, the echo of Franklin's question still hangs in the air.

Franklin's part in the negotiations of the summer and autumn of 1782 must now engage our attention. It was the crowning work of his life.

WORLD WAR

IT is a common notion among Americans that the Revolutionary War of 1775–1783 was simply a conflict between Great Britain and her North American colonies, which hoped to secure independence from the mother country. But the more one studies the enormous ramifications, international in scope, that reached out from the Atlantic center, the more convinced one becomes that the American War of Independence was, in fact, a world war. Most of Europe was covered with a network of spy trails, secret diplomatic missions planned with intent to deceive, intrigues supported by forged documents, suspect communications between royal courts and a passionate grasping for land conquest that reached south to the Mediterranean, east to India, across Siberia to the Pacific, west to the Mississippi, north to Canada and even into Central and South America.

The belligerents, in addition to Britain and the struggling United States, were Spain and Holland and France. Active in what we might call a "cold war" were Russia, Prussia and Austria, each determined to get what it could out of an eventual peace settlement, either in power, in land or in satisfaction derived from the defeat of another national ambition. Into the complex of absolute monarchies, all more or less hostile to republican liberty, came, in the early 1780's, the peace commissioners named by the Congress of the United States. These men, fiercely independent but honest in their single motive, unfamiliar with the prevailing corruption and mendacity of Europe, were what we call the Founding Fathers, among the truly great in all American history.

This scene, obscured for nearly two centuries by the fogs of inadequate knowledge and misinterpretation, has finally been clarified by the exhaustive scholarship of Richard B. Morris in his single volume *The Peacemakers,* published in 1964. This book, based largely upon documents hitherto not examined, must, henceforth, constitute the reference point for any history of the period or the biography of any of its personages.

The so-called Continental Congress, acting under the Articles of Confederation and Perpetual Union adopted in 1781, appointed John Adams, Benjamin Franklin, John Jay, Henry Laurens and Thomas Jefferson commissioners to conduct the peace negotiations with Britain. As neither Laurens nor Jefferson was able to take an active part, the burden fell on Adams, Franklin, and Jay. It was an odd combination. Both Jay and Adams presented a sharp contrast to Franklin; Adams, as we have seen, disapproved of Franklin for his personal behavior and Jay was disturbed by Franklin's informal conversations with the temporary British peace commissioner. That they all finally agreed is a tribute to their capacity to put their patriotism on a plane above all personal considerations.

What placed Franklin apart from the others was his long experience in a world as remote from America socially and politically as it was geographically. While he was not always aware of everything that went on in the European scene, he took with equanimity the revelations of perfidy which came to him. Though the forthrightness of the Massachusetts Puritan, Adams, frequently threw him into indiscretions which horrified or irritated the old-school diplomats and ministers, and though the New Yorker, Jay, was driven distracted by the delays of the Latin courts, the serenity of Passy was seldom disturbed. Franklin was flexible—perhaps too flexible—of opinion; patient—perhaps too patient—under provocation, but the others had tempers bred of the war-heated environment of America. And it was Franklin, though he was ultimately persuaded of the diversity of French and American aims, who preserved the basic integrity of the Franco-American alliance against a destructive break. He retained also the respect of a frustrated and momentarily angered French foreign minister.

2

As early as 1778, peace feelers had come from England; they came in mysterious and clandestine ways, and they indicated that opinions in that country about the American war had become more and more sharply divided. In what is known as the Opposition in Parliament, the feeling had grown that the war was expensive, unjust and dangerous to the empire and that some sort of reconciliation was still possible and, perhaps, easily available. In spite of several British military successes, recruiting had become increasingly difficult and service in America, from which ugly stories had come home, appeared singularly unattractive.

Proposals for reconciliation, however, almost invariably stopped short of independence. A few realists were convinced that separation was inevitable—a very few radicals, such as Edmund Burke and Charles James Fox, went so far as to believe that it was desirable—and a few advanced thinkers hoped for some sort of "federal union," but the notion of independence, of the colonies becoming a different sovereign nation, of the people of America ceasing to be British subjects scared the majority. One reason—perhaps the main one—for their timidity was the obstinate stand of the king, who held to the conviction that the war must continue until all thought of independence was stamped out.

A bit of melodrama was contributed by a peace feeler addressed to Franklin in a pseudonymous letter by one who signed himself Weissenstein, suggesting a meeting in Nôtre Dame cathedral. Franklin was to go to the cathedral, where he would see a man with a rose in his hat. He was to leave his reply to the letter where the stranger could pick it up. The reply was to state Franklin's response to the propositions for compromise listed in the letter. These admitted British mistakes in dealing with the colonists and stated that everything might be evened out if only American representatives would talk to the king himself. What most angered Franklin was the suggestion that any attempt at reconciliation which might be made by such American gentlemen as John Adams, John Hancock, George Washington, Benjamin Franklin and others would be richly rewarded with money or positions of power by the British government.

Franklin wrote a furious reply which was never sent, nor was the appointment with the stranger ever kept. The Paris police, to whom he had communicated the approach, intervened, went to Nôtre Dame and kept the stranger under surveillance till he left. Franklin was convinced the messenger had come under the direct orders of King George.

After that a number of approaches showed that the British wanted peace on any "honorable" terms, meaning any terms that would satisfy their monarch. Meanwhile, France and Spain both wanted peace if it could be obtained with benefit to themselves. As time went on, it began to look as if there were two wars, one between Britain and the United States and the other, France, Spain and Holland against Britain, but with different objectives—objectives, indeed, which had little to do with the thirteen United States. It was these other wars which occasioned the international intrigues. None of the participants appeared to care what happened to the United States, provided the anti-British belligerents were satisfied.

Spain wanted the English-held Gibraltar, exclusive navigation of the Mississippi River and the Floridas. Holland wanted a commercial treaty that would protect her ships from British seizure whether they operated in the West Indies or elsewhere. France—or rather the Comte de Vergennes, who carried on all French negotiations—wanted to retain a hold on the United States and regulate her conduct in the future, establish a system of checks and balances in America, keeping the British in Canada and establishing Spanish control on the western frontier of the United States and, especially, because France was on the brink of bankruptcy, bring the war to a quick close even at the price of concessions to the British. Russia wanted to create a "league of armed neutrality," including Denmark, Norway and Sweden, to prevent seizure of ships or cargoes by a belligerent. Austria wanted a treaty which would prevent the United States from becoming a sovereign nation by partitioning what were called "the colonies" and by not recognizing national independence.

So much for the European belligerents and those European neutrals that were offering to "mediate." We have seen what Britain wanted: negation of American independence, restoration of property to the loyalists, Gibraltar, reconciliation with the "rebellious colonists" and a permanent breach between America and France.

The United States, though denying territorial ambitions, had covetous eyes on Canada—Franklin thought the cession of Canada would be a just reparation for British destruction. Free navigation of the Mississippi, not yet conceded by Spain, and universal recognition and sovereignty of the United States of America completely independent of foreign control and empowered to treat with all other nations on a plane of equality were, however, the key aims of the peace commissioners.

3

John Adams, the Yankee lawyer, encountered trouble as soon as he got to France. At their first interview, Vergennes conceived an antagonism toward this commissioner which increased with every meeting. Accustomed to the urbanity and diplomatic adaptability of Benjamin Franklin, the rigid, arrogant and outspoken conduct of this more characteristic American so jarred on the devious French aristocrat that he tried, through his minister at Philadelphia, to have Adams recalled. The Congress, however, though at times seeming like putty in the hands of the French, was so impressed with Adams's other successes in Europe that it continued to applaud him. His principal triumph in his first years in Europe was in winning the approval and even affections of the Dutch when he went, as American plenipotentiary, to Holland before the peace conferences started in

Paris. There, he paved the way for a treaty of commerce with the Netherlands and thus eased them in their discomfort over the war which England had thrust upon them.

John Jay went first to Spain. Because of Spain's participation in the alliance, he hoped to get as much as possible in loans and ships, and to appraise Spain's demands on the North American continent with intent to soften them, particularly as they concerned the Mississippi River. It was obvious to most Americans that if there was to be western expansion, navigation of the great river would be essential to the settlement of the western lands.

But Jay met with constant postponement of his interviews with the Spanish minister, Conde de José de Moñino y Redondo Floridablanca. Whenever he requested an appointment with the minister, Floridablanca sent some lesser person to act as his alter ego, with the result that the American got nowhere. What Jay did not know at first but found out later was that there was a secret treaty between Spain and France which specified that no accord should be made with Britain except jointly by the two nations and with the guaranty that British-held Gibraltar be returned to Spain. Yet France had made an open treaty with America whereby no peace with Britain would be possible except with the full collaboration of the United States, based on a recognition of American independence. "Thus," as Samuel Flagg Bemis explains, "was the cause of American independence chained to the European rock of Gibraltar."

Finally Jay made an offer to relinquish to Spain the navigation of the Mississippi south of thirty-one degrees north latitude and to guarantee all the dominions of the Spanish king in America in exchange for a recognition by Spain of independence, plus a special alliance with Spain by which she would aid in the prosecution of the War of Independence. As Richard Morris writes:

> Jay's was indeed a generous offer. The issues of the Mississippi and the boundary of West Florida, which were to plague Spanish-American relations for years to come, could have been clarified to Spain's entire satisfaction at this time. All Spain had

to do was to recognize American independence and make an alliance with her ... but the Spanish Minister preferred to fight the war without the United States as an ally, to postpone the evil day of recognition, and to leave the Mississippi and the Florida boundaries to the future.

At last, because Jay made it known in France that Spain's credit was bad, the Spanish ministry conceded a loan which came to about $150,000 and the American mission was saved from bankruptcy. This seems to have come about through the intervention of Franklin with the French ministry.

To the infinite relief of John Jay, he was ordered, in the spring of 1782, to proceed to Paris to take part in the peace negotiations for which Congress had named him commissioner. His one comfort during the Spanish ordeal had been a letter from the president of Congress approving his diplomatic conduct. No letter, he replied, ever gave him "more real pleasure" after his experience of "one continued series of painful perplexities and embarrassments."

When he got to Versailles, however, he made discoveries which shocked both him and Franklin as much as anything that had come to light even in the sequence of devious intrigues that had run through the late 1770's. Meanwhile, a significant event in America moved Britain even nearer the conference table. This was the surrender of Cornwallis to the American forces at Yorktown in October, 1781, which historians have agreed ended British adventures in the War of Independence. About a year later, Britain regained a certain prestige through the successful defense of Gibraltar in the course of which she brought disastrous defeat to a Franco-Spanish naval coalition. This, of course, removed a signal stumbling block to the peace negotiations.

4

One might suppose that Franklin, committed as he was both diplomatically and emotionally to France, would have rejected the revelations which resulted from Jay's skillful detective work at Versailles, and insisted on obeying his instructions to the letter. The instructions of Congress to the peace commissioners, revised in the early summer of 1781, under the direct, persistent influence of La Luzerne, the French minister at Philadelphia, read, in part:

> ...you are to make the most candid and confidential communications upon all subjects to the ministers of our generous ally, the King of France; to undertake nothing in the negotiations for peace or truce without their knowledge or concurrence; and ultimately to govern yourselves by their advice and opinion, endeavoring in your whole conduct to make them sensible how much we rely upon his majesty's influence for effectual aid in everything that may be necessary to the peace, security, and future prosperity of the United States of America.

As soon as Vergennes became aware of the signal service of his minister to the United States in rendering the Congress completely pliable, he knew that, if these instructions were obeyed, he would have complete control over the peacemaking. He counted, however, on the docility of the commissioners toward their Congress. His friend Franklin, for instance, who had so often expressed his devotion to the French court, would surely do nothing without consulting him. Adams, to be sure, was cantankerous, and Jay, already bitter against France's other ally, Spain, might argue and quibble, but Franklin would soon whip the others into line. Unluckily for Vergennes, he put the whip in the wrong hands.

5

Since 1779, Catherine II of Russia had hoped to mediate among the belligerents. She was intermittently friendly to both the British and the French. She got word to the British advising them to renew their efforts at reconciliation with the "colonies" but on a new basis. This would concede independence to certain groups such as New England while retaining control over the Carolinas and Georgia, which she thought were less committed to the ideal. As for New York, the British were already in control there, so they might as well remain on the basis of the rule of *uti possidetis,* which might be loosely translated into the slogan, "possession is nine points of the law."

Catherine then conferred with Joseph II, emperor of Austria. It was agreed that both Russia and Austria would participate in the mediation, that a peace conference should assemble at Vienna and, in the meantime, the Machiavellian Austrian chancellor, Prinze Wenzel Anton von Kaunitz-Rietberg, was to draw up a plan by which a complete peace settlement might be presented to the conference. In this proposal, Kaunitz collaborated with the Russian chancellor, Nikita Panin, so that it became known as the Kaunitz-Panin plan. By it, the United States should become disunited. The new American nation would be partitioned. Instead of the Continental Congress sending commissioners to the peace conference, commissioners who represented the whole United States, each "colony" was to send a separate delegate. Thus Britain would be faced at the conference with thirteen Americans, each presenting an individual desire, either to remain a British colony or to hold a separate independent sovereignty.

Though cool to this project at first, Vergennes, the French foreign minister, became more sympathetic. It would, after all, prevent the formation of a formidable and powerful nation; rather, it would create a league which would soon fall apart, thus giving both France and Spain future opportunities.

In discussing this suggestion with various interested persons, Vergennes acted with the greatest secrecy. It would spoil his plan for the partition of independence in the United States if the Americans found out about it; it would also be disastrous if the Americans uncovered the secret treaty with Spain which tied the American treaty of "alliance" to the rock of Gibraltar.

But too many people were privy to these plots for the secret to be kept. Among them was a shadowy British diplomat named Mountstuart, who, though a go-between, had sounded out the French foreign office and who also knew something of Austrian and Russian plans of mediation. He had recorded the results of his soundings in his "letterbooks," to which John Jay had indirect access and which have since found their way into the British Museum, where they were examined more than two centuries later by Richard Morris, thus clearing up a mystery which had persisted ever since the peace negotiations, and which had caused certain critics to wonder at the conduct of the American commissioners.

Both Jay and Adams became suspicious of the Comte de Vergennes the moment they met him. The indiscreet John Adams came as near an open quarrel with him as is possible in the climate of diplomacy. Jay soon smelled a conspiracy and pursued its source. He knew that the only way to scotch it was first to repudiate all outside mediation, then to negotiate directly with the British and to draw up "preliminaries" to a final settlement. This would have to be done without telling the French anything about it—a definite violation of an article in the Franco-American treaty of alliance and a disobedience to the instructions Congress had given the commissioners.

Jay's problem was to persuade Franklin of the necessity of doing this. All along, Franklin had stressed the importance of keeping faith with France in every detail of their relationship. His belief in the integrity of Vergennes had not been dented in any respect. Now he must be told that France's foreign minister had pushed American independence (possibly only partial) into the background where it must await a final peace settlement by all the warring nations. To Jay and Adams, recognition of independence must come *first* before there could be any peace negotiations whatsoever. After all, Franklin must believe this too, if only he could be induced to act without the collaboration of a minister who was betraying the whole American cause.

Moreover, Franklin had just had extended talks with an Englishman in whose honesty he had implicit faith and who suggested to him that the chief of the new British ministry, Lord Shelburne, who had succeeded the antagonistic North, was adaptable to American demands. This Richard Oswald did not even reject Franklin's "hint" that the British might cede Canada to the United States as reparation for the destruction British forces had done in American towns. And independence—total separation—that too might be agreed to in spite of the intransigence of the king. The English, after all, were thoroughly tired of the American war and the surrender of Cornwallis at Yorktown had scarcely encouraged them to go on fighting.

On the 10th of August, 1782, Jay prevailed upon Franklin to accompany him to Versailles to talk to the French foreign minister and, perhaps, detect his perfidy.

6

Vergennes received the two Americans courteously but soon began to express the cautious opinion that the demands of the United States were extravagant. One of them opposed the establishment of the Mississippi as the States' western boundary. Another insisted on possession of the "Old Northwest," which France wanted Britain to retain along with Canada as a check, Jay believed, on American ambitions. The Mississippi argument revealed, Jay was convinced, some secret arrangement with Spain.

After the unsatisfactory exchange, Jay went back to Passy with Franklin. Jay argued long and heatedly. As Richard Morris tells:

> To Jay the evidence of France's motives in backing America had been disclosed. It was apparent that the French Foreign Office had supported the Revolution for reasons of power politics, and that it considered the American War to be no different from other wars which were in the past settled by compromise lines and deals under the table.

Franklin, however, was slow to agree. He believed at first that they must follow the instructions of Congress. "Would you deliberately break Congress' instructions?" Franklin asked, according to Morris. "Unless we violate these instructions," Jay replied, "the dignity of Congress will be in the dust." Still,

Franklin persisted. "Then you are prepared to break our instructions, if you intend to take an independence course now." The story is told that Jay then threw his long clay pipe into the fireplace. "*If,*" said Jay, "the instructions conflict with America's honor and dignity I would break them—like this!"

The "preliminary articles," signed on November 30, pulled the rug out from beneath Vergennes. By them England had recognized the independence of the United States, granted American rights to the western lands and granted rights to the New Foundland fisheries, which had long been a bone of contention. Canada remained a British possession, but the United States did not engage to restore property confiscated from the loyalists.

After the signing, the signers adjourned to Passy to celebrate. They were joined by some French guests. There was a marked divergence between the French people and their foreign minister. Unaware of the intricacies of international power politics, they felt a simple, sentimental attachment to America and the principles of liberty for which she stood and this continued throughout the later general peace negotiations. As for Vergennes, he was astonished by the act of the American commissioners but he could hardly go beyond a routine protest without opening a controversy which could do little credit to his backstairs maneuvers. To the end he maintained his friendship with the old Doctor.

Why the facts behind this preliminary negotiation remained unconfirmed until 1964 is a mystery for which there must be a host of explanations. That they were guessed at is shown by this observation by Albert Henry Smyth in his "Life of Benjamin Franklin":

> It is just possible, too, that Jay and Franklin knew of the existence of a secret treaty between France and Spain in accordance with which peace with England was to depend upon her restitution of Gibraltar to Spain. . . .

The most plausible reason for the failure of historians to go further into the research of the background of the negotiations was the official denial by France through its minister Edmond Genêt of Jay's charges against Vergennes. France further denied that the secret negotiations recorded in Mountstuart's letterbooks had ever taken place. As these letterbooks were not available for checking, being locked away in the vaults of the Bute family to which Montstuart belonged, Genêt's denial was generally accepted. It has been proved false only by Professor Morris's examination of these documents after the British Museum acquired them.

In 1783, the general peace treaty was signed. By this time, the Gibraltar question had been settled by the British success there.

For the final signing, Franklin's old friend David Hartley represented Great Britain. The first article of the treaty stated that His Britannic Majesty acknowledged the United States "to be free and sovereign." Other articles specified the boundaries of the new nation, that its citizens should "continue to take fish of every kind on the Grand Bank" of New Foundland, that the navigation of the Mississippi "from its source to the Ocean shall forever remain free and open to the Subjects of Great Britain and the Citizens of the United States." Article Seven stated that "There shall be a firm and perpetual Peace between his Britannic Majesty and the said States. . . ."

Thus, through the astuteness and acumen and toughness of Adams, Jay and Franklin, the old backstairs diplomacy that had long been a tradition in Europe was defeated and the United States got most of what it wanted. It was probably the greatest diplomatic triumph in the whole of American history; indeed, it heralded a new era in the annals of the world.

Benjamin Franklin did not receive the permission of Congress to return to Philadelphia till 1785. His last years in France were painful in body, but his spirit remained brave and gay and his peace of mind never failed him.

❧ XVIII ❧

THE OLD AND THE NEW

WITH the war over and an honorable peace signed, Franklin's burden was lighter. Still Congress would not let him come home. He was too useful to the new nation in Europe. Thomas Jefferson, who was to be his successor, was not yet ready to go. There were many loose ends to be tied up and no one knew their beginnings better than Franklin. Several monarchs distrusted a people which had rebelled against its king and had established a republic without one. This upstart nation had rejected not only allegiance to royalty but the entire hierarchy of aristocracy as well. Furthermore, its endurance as a union was unlikely. It contained too many diverse elements. There seemed to be no central focus, no cynosure that might draw all eyes: Catholic, Protestant, Quaker, English, Dutch, Swedish, Spanish, Red Indian, mostly hostile to one another. Just a tenuous league of states, momentarily united for a common cause, but with no permanent basis of cohesion and the easy prey of any European power that wanted to divide and conquer.

That was the prevailing belief, at least in the higher echelons of government in the European nations, as the "definitive" treaties began to take shape. Lower down, among the merchants, there was a tendency to look across the Atlantic in a search for trade and profit. After all, here was a people that faced an almost certain prosperity. An infinity of land stretched westward from the coastal society. As that land was settled, there would come the need for an infinity of goods. With independence, with freedom from British mercantile restrictions, there would open an enormous potential market.

Whatever, therefore, might be the political future of the United States, the commercial present made treaties of commerce desirable. This being the hope of the American Congress, it became a purpose of its instrument, Benjamin Franklin, and he set about it with American propaganda or, as we should put it, "public relations." In this, he was an expert and the merchants composed an eager audience for him.

Actually the western horizon was less rose-colored than he liked to paint it. The infant nation had been exhausted by the war. Even the able and abundant financing by the wealth and genius of Robert Morris had shown signs of reaching the bottom of the barrel. The realization of the fabulous resources of the West that would occupy the minds and skills of most Americans for the next century had not yet begun.

British commercial rule had, for a long time, established a balance of power unfavorable to the colonies. There were laws against doing business with foreign nations except through Britain. There were laws against any sort of manufacture by the colonists; the pattern was that the colonies supplied the raw materials and all fabrication was done by the mother country. The result was that Americans had had to support themselves from the land, by fishing, or by extensive contraband activities. Now, in 1784, there was no establishment either of wealth or of trade, and a climate of poverty prevailed from Maine to Georgia. Finally, Britain was preparing to dump goods of every kind in the former colonial ports and with rock-bottom prices force the populace to buy.

So Franklin was obliged to work with futures—an operation which was continued through most of the nineteenth century by the majority of Americans. In the end, as we know, this policy paid off but it was Franklin who taught them how. He had a gift for hyperbole and for thinking far ahead of his time. To him, what would be true twenty years from now was true now, and he was persuasive enough to secure the belief of those we should call his "prospects." No denizens of "Madison Avenue" in the mid-twentieth century has greater "selling" skill than Franklin. However, in the very nature of things, his promises were sure of fulfilment; and he had the acumen to know it.

Franklin was aided in his propaganda by both the slowness of communication with America and the rapidity with which news traveled in Europe. Bad news from America arrived in Europe so late that it was easy to believe that there had been improvement since. On the other hand, the network of spying and diplomatic intrigue in Europe—indeed, the closeness of society in general—created channels of quick Old World communication, whether of truth or rumor. Thus hints came to Franklin that various governments, whatever they might think of the States' political stability, wanted the machinery of commercial treaties to help them to quick business. The immediate pressure, then, was from the merchants, less concerned than the international politicians with what might happen in the long run. These hints came from Sweden, Denmark, Portugal, and Prussia.

In two years, by spreading the word about American potential prosperity and responding to the resultant hints, Franklin was able to bring about definitive commercial treaties with these states and to prepare the way for others. This was so encouraging to Congress that it was reluctant to relieve him of his activities.

Far from keeping these treaties exclusively within the framework of commerce, Franklin was able, in them, to lay down certain basic maritime rules which have since been incorporated into the body of international law. One was against privateering in future war. This practice, he had long believed, must be abolished forever. Also, there must be no seizures of cargo, which are against the interests of "mankind."

> It is high time, for the sake of Humanity, [he wrote in March, 1785 to Benjamin Vaughan] that a stop be put to this Enormity. The United States of America, tho' better situated than any European Nation to make profit by Privateering (most of the Trade of Europe with the West Indies, passing before their

doors), are, as far as in them lies, endeavouring to abolish the Practice, by offering, in all their treaties with other Powers, an Article, engaging solemnly, that, in Case of future War, no Privateer shall be commission'd on either Side; and that un-arm'd Merchant-ships on both sides, shall pursue their Voyages unmolested. This will be a happy Improvement of the Law of Nations. The Humane and the Just cannot but wish general Success to the Proposition.

With all his public propaganda about America, Franklin was not without an occasional foreboding which he confessed privately to his friends. To Charles Thomson, in May, 1784, he wrote:

A few Years of Peace, will improve, will restore and encrease our strength; but our future safety will depend on our union and our virtue. Britain will be long watching for advantages, to recover what she has lost. If we do not convince the world, that we are a Nation to be depended on for fidelity in Treaties; if we appear negligent in paying our Debts, and ungrateful to those who have served and befriended us; our reputation and all the strength it is capable of procuring, will be lost, and fresh attacks upon us will be encouraged and promoted by better prospects of success. Let us therefore beware of being lulled into a dangerous security; and of being both enervated and impoverished by luxury; of being weakened by internal con-tentions and divisions....

2

Meanwhile, Franklin's private life was plagued by details which would have disturbed the peace of mind of a less serene man. In that same letter to Thomson, he wrote:

I am long kept in suspense without being able to learn the purpose of Congress respecting my request of recall, and that of some employment for my secretary, William Temple Franklin.

He had hoped to obtain a diplomatic post for Temple and had tried to train him for such a career. He would, his grandfather had suggested, be especially useful attached to the American legation in Paris as he was familiar with both the language and the ways of the court. But the lack of reply created the suspicion that Temple's relationship to his loyalist father had cast a shadow on him. Further:

> If I am kept here another winter, and as much weakened by it as by the last, I may as well resolve to spend the remainder of my days here; for I shall be hardly able to bear the fatigues of the voyage in returning. During my long absence from America, my friends are continually diminishing by death, and my inducements to return in proportion.

Another irritant was the delay of Congress in writing him about the conduct of the commissioners in violating their instructions by signing a preliminary peace negotiation with Britain without consulting the French ministry. Franklin was sure there would be repercussions from this. Meanwhile he received a letter reporting rumors that he had sold the United States short in the conference with France. He was aware, therefore, that he probably had enemies on both sides of the fence. The letter was written by Dr. Samuel Cooper of Boston.

> There is a party among us disposed to avail themselves of every incident, and of all personal resentments, to weaken and divide our public counsels, and injure the alliance.
>
> It is confidently reported, propagated, and believed by some among us, that the Court of France was at the bottom against our obtaining the fishery and territory in that great extent, in which both are secured to us by the treaty; that our minister at that court favoured, or did not oppose, this design against us; and that it was entirely owing to the firmness, sagacity, and disinterestedness of Mr. Adams, with whom Mr. Jay united, that we have obtained these important advantages.
>
> It has also been said, from the same quarter, that the court of France secretly traversed Mr. Adams's views in Holland for obtaining from the United Provinces an acknowledgement of our independence; and that the same part has been acted in Spain and Russia. All those things are incredible to me; and, though they make some impression at present, truth is great

and will prevail. Care, I hope, will be taken both at Congress and in Europe, as far as public prudence will permit, to state, as soon as may be, these matters in a just light, and to prevent the public mischiefs, as well as private injuries, that may arise from misapprehensions in matters of this moment. . . .

It was Franklin's habit to ignore such reports, especially when they seemed to be unauthenticated rumors, but this one roused him from what his critics called his "apathy." He sent a copy of Dr. Cooper's letter to Vergennes and he wrote identical letters to Jay and Adams:

> It is not my purpose to dispute any share of the honour of that treaty, which the friends of my colleagues may be disposed to give them; but having now spent fifty years of my life in public affairs and trusts, and having still one ambition left, that of carrying the character of fidelity at least to the grave with me, I cannot allow that I was behind any of them in zeal and faithfulness. I therefore think that I ought not to suffer an accusation, which falls little short of treason to my country, to pass without notice, when the means of effectual vindication are at hand. You, Sir, were a witness of my conduct in that affair. To you and my other colleagues I appeal, by sending to each a similar letter with this, and I have no doubt of your readiness to do a brother Commissioner justice, by certificates that will entirely destroy the effect of that accusation.

Copies of this letter went to Congress. Complete vindication was soon forthcoming. Having faith in their sense of truth and in his own certainty of right, he was able to dismiss the whole matter from his mind, as he had the other, lesser, charges that had been brought.

No public person can ever be immune to such attacks and Franklin knew this better than most. It hurt him personally only when he was unjustly criticized by his close colleagues. After much patience with Arthur Lee, he finally showed his anger but Lee's truly vicious calumnies seldom kept him awake. The moral censures of John Adams about his "dissipations" disturbed him less than Adams's almost pathological hatred of France, its court and its society. No doubt both these views were products of his Puritan mind, but, diverging so sharply from the sympathies of Franklin, they widened the gulf between them. Looking at Adams's antagonism with the benefit of much hindsight, we are inclined to give him credit for more reason than Franklin was willing to accord him. In July, 1783, Franklin wrote of Adams to Robert Livingston:

> He thinks the French Minister one of the greatest Enemies of our Country, that he would have straitned our Boundaries, to prevent the Growth of our People; contracted our Fishery, to obstruct the Increase of our Seamen; and retained the Royalists among us to keep us divided; that he privately opposes all our Negociations with foreign Courts, and afforded us, during the War, the Assistance we receiv'd, only to keep it alive, that we might be so much weaken'd by it; that to think of Gratitude to France is the greatest of Follies, and that to be influenc'd by it would ruin us. He makes no Secret of his having these Opinions, expresses them publicly, sometimes in presence of the English ministers. . . .

Some of these convictions are obviously absurd, even to us detached observers, but others, we know, were shared by John Jay. Jay, however, knew when to keep his counsel, and Franklin was quite right about Adams's loquacity, especially before recent enemies, and justly fearful that such attacks might get into the hands of the formidable anti-French party in America. It would, however, be unfair to appraise John Adams wholly on the basis of Franklin's judgment. There were, after all, prejudices on both sides and the many evidences history shows of Adams's later wisdom erase most of his transient hotheadedness.

Undoubtedly Franklin had traits which irritated men who had lived in the midst of continuous and perilous war for eight years and had developed a fierce idealism at variance with Franklin's pragmatic temper. His silences, his reluctance to jump impulsively at an idea or suggestion, his avoidance of quick decisions, and the obvious preference for him over his colleagues on the part of Frenchmen and Europeans generally gave the impression of a somewhat alien character.

3

In August, 1784, Franklin had received a letter from his son William, to which he replied:

> I received your letter of the 22d past, and am glad to find that you desire to revive the affectionate Intercourse, that formerly existed between us. It will be very agreable [sic] to me; indeed nothing has ever hurt me so much and affected me with such keen Sensations, as to find myself deserted in my old Age by my only Son; and not only deserted, but to find him taking up Arms against me, in a Cause, wherein my good Fame, Fortune and Life were all at Stake. You conceived, you say, that your Duty to your King and Regard for your Country requir'd this. I ought not to blame you for differing in Sentiment with me in Public Affairs. We are Men, all subject to Errors. Our Opinions are not in our own Power; they are form'd and govern'd much by Circumstances, that are often as inexplicable as they are irresistible. Your Situation was such that few would have censured your remaining Neuter, *tho' there are Natural Duties which precede political ones, and cannot be extinguished by them.*
>
> This is a disagreeable subject. I drop it. And we will endeavour, as you propose mutually to forget what has happened relating to it, as well as we can. I send your Son over to pay his Duty to you. You will find him much improv'd. He is greatly esteem'd and belov'd in this Country, and will make his way anywhere. It is my Desire that he should study the Law, as a necessary Part of Knowledge for a public Man, and profitable if he should have occasion to practise it. I would have you therefore put into his hands those Law-books you have....

He had been frustrated in his hopes for his grandson, William Temple Franklin. A glimpse of Temple and a hint as to his education is given by Luther S. Livingston in his *Franklin and His Press at Passy*, a book essential to a complete picture of Benjamin:

> From what we know of William Temple Franklin it is hardly probable that he soiled his hands with printer's ink. He was too much of a gentleman. His grandfather had brought him up to be a diplomat....

His other grandson, Benny Bache, brought him compensation. At fourteen, Benny returned from his school in Geneva, to which he had been sent because the moral climate of Switzerland was thought to be healthier than that of France. From the time he came to Passy in September, 1783, he was an immense help to his grandfather. Franklin was resolved to have him learn a trade so that he would not be at the mercy of political mutations. Benny had already shown an interest in the Passy press, and the printing trade, still so dear to Franklin, was the obvious one. He apprenticed him, therefore, to Philippe-Denis Pierres, one of the best known of the French printers. Thereafter, in his spare time the boy was of assistance with the pamphlets and brochures which came increasingly off the home press now that Franklin had time and leisure for such things.

In these later years, he was troubled by symptoms of old age other than the gout. His kidney stone gave him such pain that he had to give up using his carriage, which meant that he no longer went to Versailles to see his friend Vergennes. His eyes failed to a point at which his spectacles no longer served him. He then made one of the most useful inventions of his life, bifocal glasses. In August, 1784, he wrote of this to George Whatley:

> I cannot distinguish a Letter even of Large Print; but am happy in the invention of Double Spectacles, which, serving for distant objects as well as near ones, make my Eyes as useful to me as ever they were. If all the other Defects and Infirmities were as easily and cheaply remedied, it would be worth while for Friends to live a good deal longer, but I look upon Death to be as necessary to our Constitution as Sleep. We shall rise refreshed in the Morning.

Franklin's last winter in France—one of hard weather—was enlivened by his old friend Polly Hewson, who came to stay with her children in the house at Passy. Her husband's death had been followed by that of her mother, Margaret Stevenson, Franklin's London landlady, and to return now to her "dear Papa" was probably as great a comfort to her as it was to him.

HOME

HAD such a term been in current use in the 1780's, Franklin in his last years in France might have been called a "leftist." Against a background of authoritarian government, established aristocracy and hereditary nobility, his advanced republican notions were somewhat shocking. As the American War of Independence progressed toward its victorious close, these views became more pronounced; at least he expressed them more emphatically.

In England, the triumph of liberty brought a sort of throwback from the absolutism of George III to the philosophy of the Magna Carta. It brought an era of reform that continued through the nineteenth century. Englishmen came to believe what was so eloquently expressed by Henry Thomas Buckle in his *History of Civilization in England:*

> The opinions which it was necessary to advocate in order to justify this barbarous war, recoiled upon ourselves. In order to defend the attempt to destroy the liberties of America, principles were laid down which, if carried into effect, would have subverted the liberties of England.

And Buckle adds:

> From that risk we were saved by the Americans, who with heroic spirit resisted the royal armies, defeated them at every point. . . .

In Britain, then, the radical thoughts of Franklin received sympathetic attention, at least from many of the commoners, but in France their reception by the insurgents was dangerous. During the six years between the end of the American Revolution and the outbreak of the French one, intense fires were burning underground. Fed by Voltaire and his disciples, they grew hotter with every year Franklin continued to live at Passy. The curious fact is that he was apparently unaware of them and found it difficult to understand why his persistent attacks on institutions basic in the Bourbon regime were regarded with suspicion at the French court. Furthermore, he belonged during most of his time in France to a secret society known as "The Nine Sisters," which to him was simply a political discussion group useful as a sounding board for his advanced ideas. The Society gave Franklin the title of "Venerable" and, in 1783, after the treaty was negotiated, produced a fête to celebrate the birth of the new American republic. At it Franklin was crowned with laurels and, as usual, poems and speeches praised him.

Various reasons have been given for Franklin's membership in the group: that it was, in fact, a Masonic lodge and Franklin was a Mason; that he was an incorrigible joiner and thought of The Nine Sisters as a club like the Philadelphia Junto. But there is general agreement that he never considered it a fomenter of revolution. As David Jayne Hill has written:

> It is not credible that Franklin, as "venerable" of the "Nine Sisters," was engaged in any conspiracy, especially any secret plot against the king to whom he was accredited, or that he was in any respect disposed to encourage revolution against a government that had been so generous to his country. It is, however, certain that the society of the "Nine Sisters" was an esoteric school of political thought, in which Franklin, for every reason was esteemed the master.

Yet a list of members included Bonneville, translator of Tom Paine, Brissot de Warville, Condorcet, Danton, Desmoulins and

Lafayette, among others who played important parts in the French Revolution when it came.

One of the contributions Franklin made to the society and, indeed, to the political insurgents throughout France who constructed the background of the French Revolution was a translation into French of the book of state constitutions published in Philadelphia in 1781. It became the bible of the Society of Nine Sisters because the thirteen state constitutions which it contained declared the rights of man, the doctrine of equality and other principles contrary to the pattern of the French government. Although these ideas had been expressed and endlessly discussed by such philosophers as Voltaire, Diderot, Mably, Rousseau and John Locke in England, here, for the first time in the history of the modern world they had been taken out of the theoretical and put into actual instruments of government, doctrines which men would live by and which would form the practical foundations of a new society.

Franklin had a measure of difficulty in getting the French translation by the Keeper of the Seals before it could be published. Vergennes was instantly suspicious of it and rightly so because it became, at least for the common man in France, one of the testaments of revolution. But Franklin explained that he wished to have the book read everywhere in Europe—which it would be as soon as it was in French—because of the widespread misconceptions of America that prevailed abroad.

> The extravagant Misconceptions of our Political State in foreign Countryes, made it appear necessary to give them better Information, which I thought could not be more effectually and authentically done, than by publishing a Translation into French, now the most general Language in Europe of the Book of Constitutions which had been printed by Order of Congress. This I accordingly got well done, and presented two copies, handsomely bound, to every foreign Minister, one for himself, the other more elegant for his Sovereign.

The translation, significantly enough, was done by La Rochefoucauld. It is, therefore, possible to find this book on the path that led from the theoretical philosophers to the guillotine in the Place de la Concorde.

2

Another of Franklin's "indiscretions," if we please to call it that, was his attempt to give circulation to a letter he had written to his daughter, Sarah Bache, deploring the custom of hereditary titles. The occasion for this letter was the establishment in America of the "Society of the Cincinnati," composed of the officers of the armies that had fought in the war. Franklin's objection to the Cincinnati lay in its provision that the descendants of these officers should also be members of the society.

> My Opinion [he wrote his daughter on January 26, 1784] of the Institution cannot be of much Importance; I only wonder that, when the united Wisdom of our Nation had, in the Articles of Confederation, manifested their Dislike of establishing Ranks of Nobility . . . a Number of private Persons should think it proper to distinguish themselves and their Posterity, from their fellow citizens, and form an Order of *hereditary Knights* in direct Opposition to the solemnly declared Sense of their Country! I imagine it must be likewise contrary to the Good Sense of most of those drawn into it by the Persuasion of its Projectors, who have been too much struck with the Ribbands and Crosses they have seen among them hanging to the Buttonholes of Foreign Officers. . . .
>
> For Honour, worthily obtain'd (as for Example that of our Officers), is in its Nature a *personal* Thing and incommunicable to any but those who had some Share in obtaining it. . . .
>
> But the *descending Honour,* to Posterity who could have no Share in obtaining it, is not only groundless and absurd, but often harmful to that Posterity, since it is apt to make them proud, disdaining to be employ'd in useful Arts, and thence falling into Poverty, and all the Meannesses, Servility, and Wretchedness attending it. . . .
>
> But the Absurdity of *descending Honours* is not a mere Matter of philosophical Opinion; it is capable of mathematical Demonstration.

Franklin then proceeded to show that with the normal multiplication of generation, an original Chevalier of the Order of Cincinnatus would have only a 512th part in the making of a Chevalier three hundred years later. And, if all the persons who composed that descending line were counted, there would be "One Thousand and Twenty-two Men and Women, contributors to the formation of one Knight."

This extremely logical *reductio ad absurdum* of one of the sacred foundations of French society naturally disturbed the Frenchmen to whom Franklin gave it to read. Expanded into an essay, he wanted the letter translated and published but he was advised against it by some of his well-wishers such as his friend the Abbé Morellet, who told him that these views, when launched into circulation by a minister accredited to an hereditary Bourbon king, would be considered highly improper and would have repercussions hurtful to their author's great reputation. Franklin heeded this advice and relegated the essay to posthumous publication, but in the meantime, he lent it to the Marquis de Mirabeau, who soon embodied the subversive opinions—some of them verbatim—into a piece of his own which had wide circulation among the revolutionary conspirators. Thus, innocently and unwittingly, Franklin became a conspirator of the French Revolution as he had been eagerly and openly of the American War of Independence.

There can be no doubt, however, that the American Revolution played an early part in inspiring the French revolutionaries. In his eulogy on Franklin, pronounced after Franklin's death, Condorcet recalled the French state of mind at the time of Franklin's arrival in Paris:

> Men whom the reading of Philosophic books had disposed to a secret love of liberty were impassioned for that of a foreign people, while awaiting the occasion when they could engage in recovering their own, and were seized with joy on that occasion to avow sentiments which prudence would have obliged them to guard in silence.

3

In his new leisure Franklin naturally wrote more. And, as writing was always associated in his mind with printing, a period of great activity began for the Passy press. Now he had the assistance of his grandson, Benny Bache, and a professional press man whom he hired. But Franklin was always the master printer and did much of the work with his own hands.

> ... we may imagine [writes Luther Livingston] the old philosopher, past seventy, with glasses on his nose and a printer's stick in his hand, playing at the art which he had begun to practise as a boy of twelve in his brother's printing shop in Boston more than sixty years before.

From the moment when he began to print his own writings, he took his press very seriously and spent a relatively large proportion of his income on it. He bought much of his type from the French type-founding house of Fournier. The first order of type of which we have any record came in September, 1777. In the course of his years at Passy he bought many thousands of pounds of type in France and even from England, smuggled to him in the war time through Holland.

But Fournier not only furnished him with a variety of finished types; the house also made for him a quantity of type molds, some of them following his own design, with which he was able to cast his own types. The originals of the Passy publications which survive show the variety of type faces that Franklin favored and the art with which he used them. Unfortunately, much of this material was lost in the upheaval of the revolution which followed so soon on his departure in 1785. Perhaps the most revealing publication, and certainly the most valuable, is the little volume of *Bagatelles*, now secure in the Yale collection of Franklin papers of which Professor Leonard Labaree is the editor. The Library of Congress in Washington has the celebrated "supplement" of the *Boston Chronicle*, Franklin's most deceptive hoax, and there is a printed original, too, in the collection of the American Philosophical Society in Philadelphia. But we must remember that the editions from the Passy press were exceedingly small—limited, often, to a dozen or so copies—done for the amusement of the little circle of friends and neighbors at Passy. By good fortune, most of these were available to Temple, who copied them and gave them wide circulation.

The remarkable fact about the Passy press was that Franklin took it and all its equipment home with him to America. In these days of abundant means of transportation we are struck by the quantity of personal baggage that men loaded on the little ships then plying the ocean.

On the 2nd of May, 1785, Franklin received from Congress the long-hoped-for permission to leave France. Thomas Jefferson would succeed him as envoy plenipotentiary from the United States. Although Franklin's desire to return to his native country was as strong as ever, he had serious misgivings about his ability to stand the journey, especially the first part of it, from Passy to the coast. Once he was on the ship, he knew his troubles would be over; it was the land travel that gave him constant pain. So he had to abandon his first plan, which was to board ship at L'Orient, and go to Havre instead. Yet, as there would be no transatlantic packet at Havre until August, he must exercise his patience again.

There was plenty to do. He must arrange to give his friends the belongings that he could not take with him. He gave his armchair to his dear friend, the Abbé Morellet; to Cabanis went his cane, which had a trick interior so that he could play at magic with it; a tea table to Madame le Veillard and another table to his landlord, Chaumont, who had refused to accept a sou of rent for all the time Franklin had lived in his house. And Franklin, too, had presents given him: the most elaborate from Louis XVI, a miniature of the king set with more than four hundred diamonds. Also, for the journey the queen sent him her litter, which was borne between two large mules; this would cause him less pain than any carriage.

4

We return now to Benny Bache, on whom fell the burden of packing up the press and all the printing equipment and loading it on the barge which would carry the immense quantity of Franklin's baggage down the Seine to Havre. First it was necessary to have boxes built by "joiners," who took careful measurements of everything. Then Benny dismantled the press and it was put in one of the boxes and he saw that all the type was packed in others. From then on he told the story in an account he wrote at the end of June, 1785, which Livingston has printed in his book on the Passy press. On Tuesday, June 28, wrote Benny:

> The barge by which we are to transport the goods ... ought to have been opposite Passy and ready to be loaded very early. On this account I arose at 4 o'clock, but it was not arrived. I sent to Paris to know why. The errand boy met it in the sand bank between Paris and Passy. They were making every effort to free it and calculated to be at Passy in the evening. They said that the goods might still be carried to the water's edge, and in case they did not arrive, they would send some sails to cover them; in consequence of which we have carried a great part of the goods to the water's edge, but they are not arrived; they have sent some folded sails to secure them from the rain, and a man remained there as a sentinel all night.

On Thursday, the 30th, Benny wrote:

> It arrived and everything was loaded the same day to the number of 128 boxes.

It looked like a triumphal procession that left Passy late in the afternoon of July 12, but many mourners remained behind. Benjamin Bache wrote that the party assembled in the court-yard of the Hôtel de Valentinois "in the midst of a very great concourse of the people of Passy" and "a mournful silence ... was only interrupted by a few sobs," and Thomas Jefferson said that "When he left Passy, it seemed as if the village had lost its patriarch."

As they started, Franklin found the queen's litter surprisingly comfortable. A mule's gait causes less vertical motion than that of a horse. The litter led the procession, next to the litter was the muleteer riding another mule, behind was a two-horse coach with Le Veillard and Franklin's two grandsons. They were able to travel only about four hours that day, to St. Germain, where they arrived at eight in the evening. From then on, they moved slowly, stopping for the night at Mantes, Rouen and Bolbec. They were regaled all along the route with tea and dinner parties, and crowds turned out to see them. They arrived at Havre at five in the afternoon on the 18th, and Franklin had many visits there from various officials. The packet was delayed till the 24th by unfavorable winds, then crossed the Channel to the Isle of Wight and Franklin was entertained at Cowes by a number of his English friends who had come there for the purpose. Among them was his son William, to whom Franklin gave power of attorney to do whatever business was left behind. It is interesting that on the Channel crossing Franklin was the only one of the party who was not seasick.

At Cowes, Franklin's brief diary of his trip records:

> I went at noon to bathe in St. Martin's salt-water hot bath and, floating on my back, fell asleep and slept near an hour by my watch without sinking or turning! A thing I never did before and should hardly have thought possible. Water is the softest bed that can be.

For most persons such a feat would not have been possible. But Franklin, from his earliest Boston days, was always completely at home in the water. The experience must have restored him after the fatigue of the trip from Passy. Yet, in a letter to his friend Madame Helvétius written in Havre, he said he felt stronger than when he left Passy.

It was a short move to Southampton, where Franklin went aboard the *London Packet,* Captain Truxton, and while he was asleep on the night of July 27, it set sail.

Never, on any voyage, had Franklin's mind been so busy. Relieved from the diplomatic burden, his thought jumped eagerly to "natural philosophy"; he studied the temperature of the water at various times and made abundant notes on the setting of sails and many other shipboard operations. All this he embodied in a long letter to David Le Roy on "Maritime Operations." In it, among many other novel suggestions for safety at sea, he recommended watertight compartments to keep a ship from sinking, a device which later became a commonplace for all seagoing vessels.

He also wrote what has later been thought one of his most celebrated treatises, *On the Causes and Cure of Smoky Chimneys*, and sent it to his philosopher friend Jan Ingenhousz. He wrote, too, at length about an invention he had made in London years before: *Description of a New Stove for Burning of Pitcoal, and Consuming All Its Smoke.*

These things kept him so occupied that he forgot about the diary that he had begun in Passy and intended to continue during the voyage. Abruptly he remembered it on Tuesday, September 13th:

> The wind springing fair last evening after a gale, we found ourselves this morning, at sunrise abreast of the lighthouse, and between Capes May and Henlopen. We sail into the bay very pleasantly; water smooth, air cool, day fair and fine.
>
> We passed Newcastle about sunset, and went on near to Red Bank before the tide and wind failed; then came to an anchor.
>
> *Wednesday, September 14th.*—With the flood in the morning came a light breeze, which brought us above Glouster Point, in full view of dear Philadelphia! .... My son-in-law came with a boat for us; we landed at Market Street wharf where we were received by a crowd of people with huzzas, and accompanied with acclamations quite to my door. Found my family well.
>
> God be praised and thanked for all his mercies!

⁖ XX ⁖

PROPHET IN HIS OWN COUNTRY

IT would be many years before Benjamin Franklin would receive in the United States the esteem that was accorded him abroad. Americans were too busy consolidating the gains they had made to give much thought to either their immediate heroes or the culture they must eventually devise or assimilate.

They must exploit the vast western wilderness. They must find answers to the needs of travel. They must establish manufacture in the rear of the steadily advancing frontiers. They must construct a government to further that advance; they must secure that government against foreign encroachment and internal disruption. When these problems had been solved, there would be time to remember where they came from and how they got where they were.

Specifically, there were roads and canals to be built, ways of navigating the rivers with and against currents to be devised, eventually using steam for this and for the factories, and coal to be mined to halt the destruction of the forests. In all this there was the pressing impulse of speed; there was no time to learn and apply the scientific principles that, almost alone among his countrymen, had preoccupied Franklin. No one knew why the hurry until the job was done; then Americans realized that it had been necessary to keep the nation all of a piece and not split up into a dozen political entities as had happened in Europe.

Abroad, people had pressing concerns too, of course, but they were social or political, not geographic; more vertical than horizontal; more concerned with human beings than things or land. Europeans had the time and desire to look across the sea and admire something that seemed entirely new, something fresh and free, in contrast to the staleness that had so long oppressed them.

Too, Europeans looked upon Franklin as a bridge between their old world and his new. In so many ways he was one of them, soaked, as it were, in the culture of England and the Continent, intimate with their heroes, following their ways, exploring their learning, yet immediately aware of Nature, which underlay all being, and with a fancy and a wit that seemed to come from somewhere outside their stuffy world. When he left for home he took away something precious that he had given; yet he left them an impulse and a will to emerge from the morasses that had so long engulfed them.

In his first months in France, Thomas Jefferson noticed:

> There appeared to me more respect and veneration attached to the character of Franklin in France than to that of any other person in the same country, foreign or native. I had frequent opportunities of knowing particularly how far these sentiments were felt by the foreign ambassadors and ministers at the court of Versailles.... The succession to Dr. Franklin at the court of France was an excellent school of humility. On being presented to any one as the minister of America, the commonplace question used in such cases was, *"Il est vous, Monsieur, qui remplacez le Docteur Franklin?* [Is it you, Sir, who replace Dr. Franklin?]" I generally answered, "No one can replace him, Sir; I am only his successor."

Jefferson wrote to Congress:

> Europe fixes an attentive eye on your reception of Doctor Franklin. He is infinitely esteemed. Do not neglect any mark of your approbation that you think proper. It will honour you here.

Perhaps the most celebrated eulogy of Franklin was that pronounced by the Marquis de Mirabeau in Paris when the news came of the American's death. In moving, to the National

Assembly in Paris, that there be three days of official mourning, Mirabeau said:

> Antiquity would have raised altars to this mighty genius, who, to the advantage of mankind, compassing in his mind the heavens and the earth was able to restrain alike thunderbolts and tyrants. Europe, enlightened and free, owes at least a token of remembrance and regret to one of the greatest men who have ever been engaged in the service of philosophy and liberty.

In a letter which the Abbé Sieyès wrote to Congress, he said:

> The name of Benjamin Franklin will be immortal in the records of freedom and philosophy; but it is more particularly dear to a country, where conducted by the most sublime mission, this venerable man knew how very soon to acquire an infinite number of friends and admirers, as well by the simplicity and sweetness of his manners, as by the purity of his principles, the extent of his knowledge, and the charms of his mind.

In this time, soon after the fall of the Bastille, and before the excesses of the French Revolution had aroused the horror of the world, Sieyès could write:

> At last the hour of the French has arrived; we love to think, that the citizens of the United States have not regarded with indifference our steps toward liberty....
> We hope they will learn with interest the funeral homage which we have rendered to the Nestor of America.

After reading some of these messages from Europe, the official addresses of the Pennsylvania Assembly, the American Philosophical Society and the University of Pennsylvania which greeted Franklin on his arrival in Philadelphia seem, by contrast, cool and to have the color of routine. Yet these institutions were the ones which honored him most during his lifetime and which had the time and the learning to reflect upon his achievements after he was gone.

Meanwhile, he had a large following in America, among what we may call the "Philistines." Juvenile readers of the almanacs and the *Autobiography* were taught to repeat parrotlike the sayings of Poor Richard until they became thoroughly bored with their didactic tone, and fatigued with the emphasis on the virtue of industry and the vice of indolence. Along with all this, came the insistence upon thrift with the view to attaining wealth which called down the wrath of those who disdained the materialism of the "almighty dollar." Inevitably, the pedagogues who used the more youthful writings of Franklin as their text robbed them of all their humor and the occasional tongue-in-cheek quality which game them charm.

2

In estimating the obstacles to a true appraisal of Benjamin Franklin, we may be greatly aided by Professor Leonard Labaree's introduction to his magnificent edition of the Franklin *Autobiography*. Here he has included some of the harsher criticisms that have been based exclusively on Franklin's early writings by certain esoteric literary snobs. The most bitter is that of D. H. Lawrence, which Mr. Labaree quotes in part:

> The soul of man is a dark vast forest, with wild life in it. Think of Benjamin fencing it off! . . . He made himself a list of virtues, which he trotted inside like a grey nag in a paddock. . . . Middle-sized, sturdy, snuff-colored Doctor Franklin . . . I do not like him . . . I just utter a long loud curse against Benjamin and the American corral . . . I can't stand Benjamin. He tries to take away my wholeness and my dark forest, my freedom.

That Franklin was unsuccessful in robbing Lawrence of his dark forest or in inhibiting his examination in detail of the wild life it contained is evident from a perusal of some of Lawrence's fiction.

A more recent critic, Charles Angoff, wrote that Franklin

> was probably a colossal misfortune to the United States, for, despite his good fellowship and occasional good sense, Franklin represented the least praiseworthy qualities of the inhabitants of the New World: miserliness, fanatical practicality, and lack of interest in what are usually known as spiritual things. Bab-

bitry was not a new thing in America, but he made a religion of it, and by his tremendous success with it he grafted it upon the American people so securely that the national genius is still suffering from it.

There was, too, an angry diatribe by Mark Twain but as one reads it, one hears the submerged laughter that sweetens the echoes of Clemens's sourest moments. If readers confine themselves to Franklin's didactic writings, especially when these have been selected with an eye to the asepsis of any germ of humor, the criticisms are not altogether unjust.

If, in his early efforts to emerge from an environment which even the socially ambitious Americans of the day considered lowly, if, with the strong will to develop his uncommon talents, he worked to establish security for himself, he lapsed occasionally into vulgarity and offended the sensibilities of those who had borrowed their refinement from abroad, he may surely be forgiven the moment we examine his more mature achievement. But the carping critics, disgusted by their first look into the abundant record of an entire life, have refused to pursue further the fascinating story of a man's intellectual growth and of his emotional maturity.

It is uncommon to meet with a character which has undergone so profound a change in thought and temper. In a sense, his life presents a microcosm of the life of the United States. From a crude, materialistic and occasionally vulgar beginning, dominated largely by land and farming, the American culture has progressed into urbane sensitivity to the arts and literature, to an understanding of science in its outmost reaches and even, though less positively, perhaps, to a political maturity. (American grasp of political science may have attained its peak in the Franklin era, but the grasp then was far easier to attain.)

Only a fraction of this American progress occurred during Franklin's life, but as we examine that life more closely, we may see the pattern that he laid down and which has been followed ever since. Specifically, the Constitution which in his last years he helped frame, and which embodied many of his principles, though amended more than twenty times, has in its fundamentals endured from his day to ours and promises a long future. Perhaps it would be hyperbole to give Franklin credit for the actual construction of this immortal document but those we are pleased to call the Founding Fathers were, every one, influenced by him.

And there can be little doubt that Franklin gave the first impetus to the scientific inquiry that has so distinguished the later United States. There was a long interval in which the work in this field that he began was neglected by succeeding Americans in favor of borrowing from abroad the laws that governed applied science, but the Philosophical Society he founded kept alive the impulse toward research and for many years investigators had to go back to the questions Franklin asked and to seek the answers.

3

Not for many years did Americans realize what a prophet Founder Franklin had been. Yet, all that time, a sequence of biographers, from Temple Franklin and James Parton to Carl Van Doren, insisted upon his importance to American history, philosophy and science until, at last, the whole Franklin was recognized in his native country, in the United States, which he designed and which was the greatest of his inventions. As historians began to turn their attention to American history as something other than a patriotic exercise, and, especially, when the War of Independence, that unexplored acre in the field of United States history, began to attract their mature and even objective interest, Franklin's part in the creation of a nation separated itself from the schoolteachery tradition. The appraisals of Lecky and Trevelyan in England, with their praise of Franklin as the very god of the machine of independence, and the work of such American historians as Charles Andrews, Moses Tyler, Carl Van Doren in his *Secret History,* Samuel Bemis Flagg and, finally, the beloved Sam Morison, have raised Franklin to the high place he holds today in the American estimation.

He was a great ambassador [wrote Trevelyan] of a type which the world had never seen before, and will never see again until it contains another Benjamin Franklin. Tried by the searching test of practical performance, he takes high rank among the diplomatists of history. His claims to that position have been vindicated, in a manner worthy of the subject by an eminent American publicist.

Trevelyan then quotes this "publicist," Francis Wharton, as writing in the tenth chapter of his "Introduction" to *Digest of International Law:*

There were conspicuous statesmen at the Congress of Vienna; but the imposing fabric constructed by Metternich, and Nesselrode, and Talleyrand, with such lofty disregard for national liberties and popular rights, has long ago perished, while Franklin's work endures to this hour.

It seems curious to us of a later day that Americans so often failed to give full recognition to their own heroes until they were reintroduced to them from abroad. But this was characteristic of nineteenth-century American opinion, before the people of the United States had time to catch up with their own culture and needed this outside stimulus. In the relative calm that followed the closing of the last frontiers, when the golden spike had been driven into the transcontinental railroad and gossip came through the transatlantic cable from another continent, it was usual for Americans to think, "If Europeans say an American is great, he *must* be great." But in the next century, when at last Americans became self-conscious and began to believe in their native culture, this attitude changed and Franklin was revealed as on a level with Washington and Jefferson and Adams and Hamilton and Madison and was, perhaps, in some ways, greatest of them all.

4

While we may find areas of disagreement, there are few analyses of Franklin's character that are more penetrating or, indeed, more exact than that of Carl Becker in his biographical sketch in the *Dictionary of American Biography*.

> He was a true child of the Enlightenment, not indeed of the school of Rousseau, but of Defoe and Pope and Swift, of Fontenelle and Montesquieu and Voltaire. He spoke their language, although with a homely accent, a tang of the soil, that bears witness to his lowly and provincial origin. His wit and humor, lacking indeed the cool, quivering brilliance of Voltaire or the corrosive bitterness of Pope and Swift, were all the more effective and humane for their dash of genial and kindly cynicism. He accepted without question and expressed without effort all the characteristic ideas and prepossessions of the century—its aversion to "superstitions" and "enthusiasms" and mystery; its contempt for hocus-pocus and its dislike of dim perspectives; its healthy, clarifying scepticism; its passion for freedom and its humane sympathies; its preoccupation with the world that is evident to the senses; its profound faith in common sense, in the efficacy of Reason for the solution of human problems and the advancement of human welfare....
>
> His mind, essentially pragmatic and realistic, by preference occupied itself with what was before it, with the present rather than with the past or the future, with the best of possible rather than with the best of conceivable worlds. He accepted men and things, including himself, as they were, with a grain of salt indeed but with insatiable curiosity, with irrepressible zest and good humor.

Becker reflects some of the comment of certain of Franklin's contemporaries in a more compact and comprehensive presentation than theirs:

> In all of Franklin's dealings with men and affairs, genuine, sincere, loyal as he surely was, one feels that he is nevertheless not wholly committed; some penetrating observation is held in reserve. In spite of his ready attention to the business in hand, there is something casual about his efficient dispatch of it; he manages somehow to remain aloof, a spectator still, with amiable curiosity watching himself functioning effectively in the world.

But Becker makes an exception; in science Franklin was always explicitly committed. In his experimental work, he was wholly immersed, there was nothing casual about his observations of nature. He has truly tried to remove all obscurity and mystery from whatever scientific subject he has portrayed in the record of his experiments. As Sir Humphrey Davy—quoted by Becker—said, "Science appears in his language in a dress wonderfully decorous, the best adapted to display her native loveliness."

5

Although Franklin, on his return, was honored in his home state of Pennsylvania, which made him president of its Assembly, it appeared that he had enemies aplenty in his native state of Massachusetts. Rumors had been spread by Arthur Lee, who cherished a genuine hatred for him, and by John Adams, who had generally looked upon him with suspicion. He had, it was said, become a Francophile, not precisely a compliment among a people which had always taken a dark view of Gallic morality; it was said that he was, really, an expatriate who had never understood American purposes, but worse than all these was the innuendo that he had spent the public moneys without a due accounting. For Franklin, to whom large sums were still owing, this was an unkind cut indeed. And he soon learned that these libels were listened to in the Congress, especially by those who held political views opposite to his.

I have not [he wrote to Charles Thomson in 1788], nor ever shall, make any public complaint; and even if I could have foreseen such unkind treatment from Congress as their refusing me their thanks would not in the least have abated my zeal for the Cause, and ardour in support of it. For I know something of the nature of such changeable Assemblies, and how little successors are inform'd of the services that have been rendered ... and what effect in obliterating a sense of them, during the absence of the servant in a distant Country, the artful and reiterated malevolent insinuations of one or two envious and malicious persons may have on the minds of members, even of the most equitable, candid and honourable dispositions. Therefore I would pass these reflections into oblivion.

It is only in the private letters to friends, which Franklin never supposed would be seen by other eyes, that he mentioned these hostile communications. But upon the State of Pennsylvania in its Assembly and among the Pennsylvania delegates to the Congress, they had little effect. For the Assembly made it possible for Franklin, in the very last years of his life, to perform the crowning act of his career.

For some time, there had been general discontent with the Articles of Confederation and Perpetual Union, by which, since the end of the war, the nation had been governed. Their inadequacy was the reason for the calling of a convention to meet in Philadelphia in May, 1787, to draw up a complete and final constitution for the United States. Among its eight delegates to this convention, Pennsylvania insisted on including Benjamin Franklin.

Major William Pierce, of Georgia, took notes of the meetings of the constitutional convention and, though there are inaccuracies in his record, they give the color of the proceedings with vividness. For one thing, he wrote a character sketch of all the delegates valuable for its detail and amusing for its personal opinions and prejudices. Of Franklin, he wrote:

> Dr. Franklin is well known to be the greatest phylosopher of the present age;—all the operations of nature he seems to understand, the very heavens obey him, and the Clouds yield up their Lightning to be imprisoned in his rod. It is certain that he does not shine much in public Council,—he is no Speaker, nor does he seem to let politics engage his attention. He is, however, a most extraordinary Man, and tells a story in a style more engaging than anything I have ever heard.... He is 82 years old, and possesses an activity of mind equal to a youth of 25 years of age.

On the second of June, 1787, Franklin, physically unable to speak at length, obtained permission for James Wilson of Pennsylvania to read his speech on the Executive. The speech is significant in view of some of the criticisms of his supposed materialism and preoccupation with wealth. The speech disapproved of the payment of salaries to those in the Executive Branch:

> *Sir,* there are two passions which have a powerful influence on the affairs of men. These are ambition and avarice; the love of power and the love of money. Separately each of these has great force in prompting men to action; but when united in view of the same object, they have in many minds the most violent effects. Place before the eyes of such men, a post of *honour* that shall be at the same time a place of *profit,* and they will move heaven and earth to obtain it....
>
> And of what kind are the men that will strive for this profitable pre-eminence, through all the bustle of cabal, the heat of contention, the infinite mutual abuse of parties, tearing to pieces the best of characters? It will not be the wise and moderate; the lovers of peace and good order, the men fittest for the trust. It will be the bold and the violent, the men of strong passions and indefatigable activity in their selfish pursuits.

It is not difficult to see in these opinions the effects of long exposure to the corruptions of government abroad, but they are interesting in view of estimates of the materialism, the "miserliness" and the preoccupation with money that have been made by Franklin's critics.

He continued to attend the sessions of the convention as long as he was able, but in his last year, after the Constitution had been ratified, he announced that he was through with public affairs.

Death released him from his bodily pain on April 17, 1790. He had lived through all but sixteen years of the eighteenth century. It will be impossible ever to think of that century without him.

FRANKLIN IN THE 1960's

O F THE Founding Fathers of the United States, Franklin seems most alive today. After a century or more of needlessly lost lives, physicians have come to accept Franklin's rules of health. Psychologists, in this restless age, have come to understand what Franklin meant by "peace of mind." Theologians have moved away from Calvinism and biblical revelation toward Franklin's concepts of God and immortality. Students of international politics have come to the conclusion reached by Franklin nearly two centuries before the nuclear age that "there never was a good war or a bad peace." Military strategists recognize what Franklin foresaw in aerial warfare. Franklin is present in every classroom where physics, biology, chemistry or meteorology is taught.

If he could return to us, he would be at home in our paved and lighted cities with their police protection; he would approve the proliferation of the public library he invented; he would understand the problem of air pollution; he would adjust easily to daylight saving time, for it was his invention; he would have millions of companions in the use of his bifocal glasses. In every American city he might visit, he would see Franklin savings banks and Franklin lightning rods and Franklin stoves—changed, to be sure, almost beyond recognition. Abroad he would recognize the British Commonwealth of Nations; "I told them so," perhaps he would say, "two hundred years ago."

Franklin would be alarmed at the momentum the years have given to his advocacy of equality until at last we have attained an exaggerated democracy. Democracy was a dirty word in Franklin's day; he and others of the Founders believed in a hierarchy of intelligence and he would be shocked to see certain senators and congressmen who have been chosen by the people to represent them in the national legislature. Yet he would be happy to see the flexibility of the written Constitution he helped frame in the growth of the nation, permitting the constant addition of new territory, new climates and new or changed people and adjustment to the immense immigrant inundation. He knew that people from the old world would swarm to the new but he could not have known how quickly this foreign horde could be assimilated into the American culture and, indeed, enrich it. Yet Franklin was seldom surprised by the unprecedented or, indeed, the illogical.

2

The twentieth century, in America at least, resembles the eighteenth more than it does the nineteenth. What has become known as the Enlightenment, of which Franklin was so avid a proponent, was darkened with the progress of the 1800's. The religious throwback, the militant morality, the intemperate temperance movement, the covering up, by conventions of dress and manners, of vice and corruption, the educational hypocrisies that characterized what we are pleased to call the Victorian era, would have been anathema to Franklin and his enlightened, liberal contemporaries.

In those years between, when the moral growth of youth was in the hands of stern pedagogues, as much effort went into protecting youth from Franklin as indoctrinating them with his virtuous preachings. Boys and girls were made to learn by heart, "Sloth consumes faster than Labour wears: The used Key is always bright"; "Time is Money"; "The sleeping Fox catches no Poultry"; "Early to Bed and early to Rise...." and many others concerned with thrift, frugality and industry, but passages about "ungovernable passions," "low women" and various weaknesses were deleted from school versions of his autobiography, and youngsters were kept in ignorance of gay and prodigal years in London and Paris.

This attitude is reflected in a passage in the chapter "Satires and Bagatelles" in Volume I of Albert Henry Smyth's *The Writings of Benjamin Franklin* in which he deplores Franklin's taste for ribaldry and scatology.

> Unfortunately it is impossible without offense to quote many of his briefer paragraphs. We may track him through the thirty years of the *Gazette* by the smudgy trail he leaves behind him. His humour is coarse and his mood of mind Rabelaisian. His "salt imagination" delights in greasy jests and tales of bawdry. He came of a grimy race of hard-handed blacksmiths, and they had set their mark on him. With all his astonishing quickness and astuteness of intellect and his marvellous faculty of adaptation, he remained to the end of life the proletarian, taking an unclean pleasure in rude speech and coarse innuendo. He out-Smolletts Smollett in his letters to young women at home and experienced matrons abroad. Among the manuscripts in the Library of Congress ... [etc.] ... are productions of his pen, the printing of which would not be tolerated by the public sentiment of the present [1907] age. It is no use blinking the fact that Franklin's animal instincts and passions were strong and rank, that they led him to the commission of many deplorable *errata* in his life, and that the taint of an irredeemable vulgarity is upon much of his conduct.

Perhaps if biographer Smyth had written later in the twentieth century, he would have modified this attack or, at least, have been more lenient toward the time in which his subject lived and the society in which he moved. As for his "coarseness" deriving from his grimy blacksmith ancestry, Smyth ignores the fact that Smollett, Fielding, Defoe, Swift and an entire coterie of more or less contemporary writers had no blacksmith alibi to fall back on and, indeed, the sort of humorous, satirical treatment of ribald themes these writers engaged in is anything but proletarian. In twentieth-century coffeehouses and other gathering places of intellectuals this sort of thing is an exercise of comic relief from the intensely serious pornography of this post-Freudian age. If Franklin should come into any sophisticated New York or San Francisco club today, he would be welcomed, told to sit right down and "tell us a story," with the certainty that it would be both bawdy and funny.

Indeed, there are versions of the *Autobiography* which show the desire on the part of editors—perhaps Franklin's grandsons, Temple and Benny Bache—to purge some of the "coarseness" from Franklin's original manuscript. According to Professor Labaree, who has familiarized himself with all editions:

> Some were obvious efforts on somebody's part to correct awkwardly phrased or clumsy sentences; others substituted more "dignified" language for the manuscript's colloquial or inelegant expressions. For example, Watt's printers, who in the manuscript were described as "great Guzzlers of Beer," had become, merely, "great drinkers of beer"; Collins' explanation to the ship's captain that "Franklin wished to leave Boston because he had got a naughty girl with Child" read in Temple's version that he "had had an intrigue with a girl of bad character."

The teenagers of the 1960's need no protection from the earthiness of Benjamin Franklin. Having moved from the back-fence writings of the 1800's to the earnest perusal of *Lolita, Peyton Place, Sexus, Tropic of Cancer,* they might well look upon the ribald jocosity of Franklin as a relief, providing they retained some humorous sensibility.

3

Although Franklin saw the wealth of America and the contentment of Americans as products of agriculture, he was an inveterate city dweller himself. Boston, Philadelphia, London and Paris had none of the rural virtues he constantly extolled; it was pavements, not rich loam, that wore out his shoes. Brought up by manufacturers, educated in an artisan's trade, he nevertheless rated agriculture above manufacturing. He said that "the true source of riches is husbandry. Only agriculture is truly productive of new wealth." He wrote, too, of the vice that infested manufacturing centers. What he might have thought of the late movement of population away from the farms and into the urban centers is a matter of surmise; in any case he would have felt more at home in an urban rather than an agrarian culture. "As a citizen," writes Labaree, "of a rapidly growing urban community, he had much in common with a majority of present day Americans."

Labaree also sees Franklin content in "an age of voluntary cooperation and organization."

> Our community chests, the Red Cross, the associations to alleviate various diseases, and the countless other undertakings for civic welfare are modern expressions of the same sense of community responsibility that influenced Franklin and his associates. Far from killing the human spirit, his accounts of founding the Library, the Academy, and the Hospital, for example, and of raising funds for them, reflect an attitude toward society in full harmony with the most altruistic undertakings of our times.

As the years go by and the United States comes, culturally, more and more into its own, we turn back to Benjamin Franklin more than to the other great men who attended our birth. The others *were* great, Franklin *is* great. He walks among us always, deeply interested in everything we do, or say or think. He attends our conferences, our cabinet meetings, the signing of our treaties. He watches serenely as our new rockets carry our spacecraft into orbit, nodding his head as he understands their mission.

In our moments of panic, his hand is on our shoulder. Don't lose, he seems to say, your peace of mind.

SOURCES

Until the project now in progress under the direction of Leonard W. Labaree of the Yale University Library, entitled "The Papers of Benjamin Franklin," the most complete collection of Franklin's works was that edited by Albert Henry Smyth and published in ten volumes by the Macmillan Company of New York in 1907. The set is entitled *The Writings of Benjamin Franklin*. It also contains essays on the writings and a life of Franklin. It will be referred to hereafter as "Smyth." There is an earlier collection, *The Complete Works of Benjamin Franklin*, edited by John Bigelow and published in ten volumes by G. P. Putnam's Sons of New York in 1887. This will be referred to as "Bigelow." All other collections are specialized, *e.g., Benjamin Franklin's Letters to the Press*, etc., and the titles will be given in full.

CHAPTER I

Franklin's England

The Trevelyan quotation on corruption in England is from George Otto Trevelyan, *The Early History of Charles James Fox*, New York: Harper & Bros., 1899, p. 64. The Franklin quotations on his voyage and his arrival in London are from Smyth, Vol. III, p. 409. See also *The Autobiography of Benjamin Franklin*, edited by Leonard W. Larabee, et al., New Haven: Yale University Press, 1964, p. 259, hereafter referred to as *Autobiography*. Strahan's letter is in Jared Sparks, *The Works of Benjamin Franklin*, Boston, 1840, Vol. III, pp. 157–158. The Granville quotation is from *Autobiography*, pp. 261–262. So, too, the narrative of the interview at the Penns' house.

CHAPTER II

Interval of Pain and Pleasure

The quotation from the letter to Deborah, November 22, 1757, Smyth, Vol. III, pp. 420–421. The letter to Deborah about the carriage, February

19, 1758, Smyth, Vol. III, p. 411. Franklin was obviously worried lest Deborah think he was having too good a time in London, hence his assurance, "The agreeable conversation I met with," etc.; also the letter of November 22, 1757, Smyth, Vol. III, p. 424. The long letter about the gifts he has bought and sent to her is dated February 19, 1758. In this letter, too, is the charming account of the "large fine Jugg for Beer" which "looked like a fat jolly Dame ... and put me in mind of—Somebody." Smyth, Vol. III, p. 435 gives the letter of April 28, 1758, to Thomas Hubbard at Boston, listing Franklin's gifts to Harvard College. The letter to John Lining at Charleston, June 17, 1758, was first published in Franklin's *Experiments and Observations on Electricity,* London, 1769, p. 363. The quotations here are mainly about evaporation with the usual applications to bodily health. The letter about Franklin's good time in Cambridge and his trip to the ancestral homes of the Franklins is in a letter to Deborah, September 6, 1758, Smyth, Vol. III, p. 453.

CHAPTER III

Many Inventions

The letter to Lord Kames, January 3, 1760, is in Smyth, Vol. IV, pp. 3–7. A little "homesick" for England, he wrote to Mary Stevenson from Philadelphia March 25, 1763, about his beloved English people, Smyth, Vol. IV, pp. 191–196. The letter about George III to Strahan was written from Philadelphia, December 19, 1763, and is in Smyth, Vol. IV, p. 212. Despite the speculation by Paul Leicester Ford, *Who Is the Mother of Franklin's Son?,* which Mr. Ford admits is only a partial answer, the question remains a mystery. See Carl Van Doren, *Benjamin Franklin,* New York: The Viking Press, 1938, on "the Franklin line of illegitimacy," p. 645. The celebrated letter to Mary Stevenson about the effect of heat on colored cloth is dated September 20, 1761, and is given in full in Smyth, Vol. IV, p. 111. For comment on James Hutton's snobbish dictum, see Lancelot Hogben, *Science for the Citizen,* New York: Alfred A. Knopf, 1938, p. 584. The word on keeping rooms warm with less fuel is from a letter to James Bowdoin, from London, December 2, 1758, published in the American Philosophical Society's *transactions,* 1786. The letter to Beccaria about the harmonica, July 13, 1762, is from Smyth, Vol. IV, p. 163. Franklin's correspondence with the London newspapers is found in *Benjamin Franklin's Letters to the Press,* edited by Verner W. Crane, Chapel Hill: University of North Carolina Press, 1950. For the correspondence about Maryland, see Maryland *Archives,* Vol. XXXI, p. 507. The St. Andrews degree is recorded in the university records of the Senatus Academicus, for February 12, 1759.

CHAPTER IV

War and Peace

Franklin's fifteen-month tour is described in J. Bennett Nolan, *Benjamin Franklin in Scotland and Ireland, 1759 and 1771,* Philadelphia: University of Pennsylvania Press, 1938. Letter to Sir Alexander Dick ("many Civilities," etc.) January 3, 1760, Smyth, Vol. IV, p. 1. To Lord Kames, *ibid.,* p. 3, same date. On authorship of *Historical Review of ... Pennsylvania,* see Smyth, Vol. I, pp. 137–138. On Gov. Denny, see "Preface to the Speech of Joseph Galloway, Esq.," Philadelphia: W. Dunlap, 1764. Franklin recalled his triumph at the hearing of the Privy Council at which Lord Mansfield and various lawyers for the proprietaries conceded to his opinion of the Taxation Act, at the close of his *Autobiography.* Franklin's statement about the improbability of the colonies uniting against Britain is in the pamphlet *The Interest of Great Britain Considered,* published in London in 1760. The quotation is from Smyth, Vol. IV, pp. 71–72. In this same pamphlet is Franklin's argument for the retaining of Canada by Great Britain. Franklin tells of his arrival in America in a letter to William Strahan dated December 2, 1762, Smyth, Vol. IV, p. 179.

CHAPTER V

Philadelphia Interlude

In Chapter 13 of his biography, *Benjamin Franklin,* Carl Van Doren gives a good account of Franklin's busy and difficult time in Philadelphia. The letter about his expenses in England is to Isaac Norris, dated February 15, 1763, Smyth, Vol. IV, p. 189. To Mary Stevenson, Smyth, Vol. IV, p. 195. On the Greenes, Van Doren biography, p. 304. Franklin's most important writings during this period were *A Narrative of the Late Massacres in Lancaster County,* Smyth, Vol. IV, p. 289, a pamphlet which made him enemies among the Penn supporters, and *Cool Thoughts on the Present Situation of our Public Affairs,* Smyth, Vol. IV, p. 226—both published in Philadelphia in 1764. Mr. Julian P. Boyd gives an account of the Paxton Boys in *Dictionary of American History,* New York: Charles Scribner's Sons, 1940, Vol. IV, p. 229. An appraisal of Deborah is given by Paul W. Conner in *Poor Richard's Politics,* New York: Oxford University Press, 1963, p. 215 and note 13 on the same page. Incidentally, this little book is as well documented and has as good a bibliography as any recent secondary source. Letter to Sally, November 8, 1764, Smyth, Vol. IV, pp. 286–287. From Cadwallader Evans, Smyth, Vol. I, p. 219. Letter from William Franklin to William Strahan, Smyth, Vol. I. pp. 219–220. The resolution of the Pennsylvania Assembly, Smyth, Vol. I, pp. 221–222.

CHAPTER VI

Storm Clouds Over the Atlantic

Letter to Percival about fresh air, Smyth, Vol. VI, p. 140. Van Doren biography gives an animated account of life in Craven Street in Chapter 16, section 2, pp. 403 ff. On the Stamp Act, its repeal and the consequences in the colonies, an English historian's point of view is given in Chapter One of the one-volume edition of *The American Revolution* by George Otto Trevelyan, New York: David McKay Company, Inc., 1964. (Condensation made by Richard B. Morris.) See also Samuel E. Morrison, *The Oxford History of the American People,* New York: Oxford University Press, 1965, pp. 185–190; Roger Burlingame, *The American Conscience,* New York: Alfred A. Knopf, 1957, pp. 143 ff.; *Gentleman's Magazine,* London, Vol. XXXVI, p. 341. Van Doren's comment on Franklin going "underground" is on page 332 of his biography. Letter to John Hughes, August 9, 1785, Smyth, Vol. IV, p. 392. On "whispering campaign in Philadelphia by Franklin's enemies," Van Doren, biography, p. 330. *The Examination of Doctor Benjamin Franklin, Etc., Relative to the Repeal of the Stamp Act* is reprinted in full by Smyth, Vol. IV, pp. 412–448 from the first edition, published in London, 1766. Comment on questions and answers, Van Doren, biography, Chapter 14, section 2. Letter to Charles Thomson, February 27, 1766, Smyth, Vol. IV, p. 411, original in New York Historical Society. Letter to Deborah about her new gown, April 6, 1766, Smyth, Vol. IV, p. 449.

CHAPTER VII

Traveling Philosopher

Letter to Thomas Ronayne, April 20, 1766, Smyth, Vol. IV, p. 451. To Lord Kames, April 11, 1767, Smyth, Vol. V, pp. 17 ff. The quotation from Parton is from *Life and Times of Benjamin Franklin* by James Parton, New York: Mason Brothers, 1864, Vol. I, p. 481. Parton quotes John F. Watson, *Annals of Philadelphia,* 1857, Vol. II, p. 270 and the excerpts from Sally's letter. To Cadwallader Evans, May 9, 1766, Smyth, Vol. IV, p. 456. The letter to Deborah telling about the projected journey with Dr. Pringle, June 13, 1766, Smyth, Vol. IV, p. 459. On the illness of Lord Chatham (William Pitt the elder) Trevelyan gives a graphic account in *The American Revolution* (edition *cit.*) p. 109. Something of the antagonism to Franklin in England is told in a confidential letter to his son, July 2, 1768, Smyth, Vol. V, p. 142. Among other things was the threat to remove Franklin from his postmaster's office. This alarmed him and brought him as close as he ever came to panic when he wrote to Deborah to cut down expenses. Letters, June 22, 1767, Smyth, Vol. V, pp. 31 ff, also about Sally's match and about the house, and August 5, 1767, Smyth, Vol. V, p. 37. The letter to Polly Stevenson from Paris, Smyth, Vol. V, pp. 48 ff.

CHAPTER VIII

New Friends, New Enemies

Quotation from Parton, James Parton *op. cit.,* Vol. I, pp. 399–400. Trevelyan (edition *cit.*) p. 5. British ships to Boston, *ibid.,* p. 8. Description of the "Boston massacre," *The American Heritage Book of the Revolution,* by the editors of *American Heritage,* pp. 64–65. This book is remarkable for its illustrations, the best that have been published. The "olive branch petition," which has been curiously ignored by American historians, is described in detail by Randolph G. Adams, "The Olive Branch Petition," in *Magazine of History,* Vol. 44, No. 4, Extra Number 176, 1932. See also, the *Diary and Autobiography of John Adams,* Cambridge: Harvard University Press, 1861, Vol. II, p. 411. Letter from Franklin to Thomas Cushing, Samuel Adams, John Hancock and William Phillips on the Boston tea party, February 2, 1774, in reply to letter from them; both letters in Smyth, Vol. VI, pp. 176–180. The letter of Charles Thomson, November 1, 1774, is given in a footnote, Smyth, Vol. X, pp. 282–283. The original of the final plan of conciliation presented to Earl of Chatham, February 1, 1775, is in the Library of Congress, see Smyth, Vol. X, p. 284. To Samuel Cooper, February 5, 1771, and enclosed minutes of the conference with Lord Hillsborough on January 16, Smyth, Vol. V, pp. 300 ff. Smyth gives the "Scheme for a New Alphabet and Reformed Mode of Spelling" in full, Vol. V, pp. 169–178. Quotation from Alfred Owen Aldridge, *Benjamin Franklin: Philosopher and Man,* Philadelphia: J. B. Lippincott Co., 1965, p. 189. The epitaph for Mungo, the squirrel, is given in full in Smyth, Vol. V, p. 439. Franklin's relations with American sea captains are described by Helen Augur in *The Secret War of Independence,* New York: Duell, Sloan and Pearce, 1955, p. 13. The British navigation acts are given in Henry Steele Commager (editor), *Documents of American History,* New York: F. S. Crofts & Co., 1947, pp. 38, 42. On summons to appear before Privy Council, January 11, 1774, Smyth, Vol. X, p. 263.

CHAPTER IX

Meeting With Hate

Franklin's version of the *cause célèbre* of the Hutchinson letters is given in full in Smyth, Vol. VI, pp. 258–259. For the scene in the "cockpit," see the anonymous *Franklin Before the Privy Council,* published in Philadelphia by John W. Butler in 1860. This publication contains the Hutchinson-Oliver letters. Quotation from the petition to the king, Smyth, Vol. VI, p. 280. Quotation from Helen Augur, *op. cit.*, p. 5. All other quotations in this chapter are from Franklin's own "Tract" or from Smyth's biography, Chapter V, "The Scene in the Cockpit," Smyth, Vol. X, pp. 240 ff. Walpole verse, Smyth, Vol. X, p. 271 n. See also Van Doren, *Benjamin Franklin,* Chapter 17.

CHAPTER X

Chess

Letter to Jan Ingenhousz, March 18, 1774, Bigelow, Vol. X, p. 337. To Thomas Cushing about Wedderburn's speech, Smyth, Vol. VI, pp. 189–190. Letter to sister Jane, A. O. Aldridge, *Benjamin Franklin,* Philadelphia: J. B. Lippincott Co., 1965, p. 238. Wedderburn's speech about "Great American Republic," Van Doren, *Benjamin Franklin,* p. 471. Overheard remark by an army general, Smyth, Vol. IX, p. 261. "Rules by which," etc., *The Gentleman's Magazine,* Vol. XLIII, September, 1773; Smyth, Vol. VI, pp. 127–137. Letter to Richard Bache, September 30, 1774, introducing Thomas Paine, Smyth, Vol. VI, pp. 248–249. Aldridge comment, *op. cit.,* p. 243. Virginia and Continental Congress, Commager, *op. cit.,* Document No. 53, pp. 78 ff. On death of Deborah, Van Doren, biography, p. 503; William Duane (editor), *Letters to Benjamin Franklin, from his Family and Friends,* New York, 1859, pp. 57–60. Quotations from Paul Conner, *op. cit.,* pp. 215–216. Conversations with William about Deborah's expected death, Van Doren, biography, p. 503. Dr. Hewson's death, *ibid.,* p. 412; Smyth, Vol. VI, p. 230 n. Introduction to Lord Howe, Smyth, Vol. VI, p. 345. Franklin's "Hints" are given in full, Smyth, Vol. VI, 328 ff. For Howe's reaction, *ibid.,* p. 353. Franklin's account of his reception by Lord Chatham, Smyth, Vol. VI, p. 350. All of these conferences are given in detail in his "Negotiations in London," written on board the *Pennsylvania Packet,* Captain Osborne, and addressed to his son. This is published in its entirety in Smyth, Vol. VI, pp. 318–398. It is a primary source and fascinating reading to anyone interested in the extraordinary efforts that were made behind the scenes to avoid the separation. Included here are Chatham's motion and the "wild" parliamentary debate that followed.

CHAPTER XI

Independence

Letter to Galloway, Smyth, Vol. VI, pp. 311–312. For Franklin's inconsistencies, see, *passim,* Gerald Stourzh, *Benjamin Franklin and American Foreign Policy,* Chicago: University of Chicago Press, 1954. Almost all

Franklin's biographers emphasize the fact that, notwithstanding his extremely affectionate letters to the women who were his friends, he did not, in his elderly years in London and Paris, engage in the physical "errata" which resulted from his youthful "ungovernable passions." If he had indulged in such intimacies, it is almost certain that some hint of them would have appeared in some of his voluminous writing, as it did in the early portions of the *Autobiography*. The China vase simile was a favorite of Franklin's, see letter to Lord Howe, July 30, 1776, Smyth, Vol. VI, p. 460. Letter to Bowdoin, Smyth, Vol. VI, p. 310. On last day with Priestley, J. T. Rutt, *Life and Correspondence of Joseph Priestley*, London, 1831–1832, Vol. I, p. 212. Description of his voyage to Priestley, from Philadelphia, May 16, 1775, Smyth, Vol. VI, p. 400. Negotiations with Bonvouloir, Augur, *op. cit.*, pp. 77–79. *Chevaux de frises* and other war devices, Van Doren, biography, p. 534; appointment to meet Washington in Cambridge, *ibid.*, p. 536; visit to sister and Greenes, *ibid.*, p. 537. Quotation from Thomas Paine's *Common Sense*, "Government by Kings," etc., edition with preface by William M. Van Weiden, New York: Rimington and Hooper, 1928, pp. 17–18. On the "Brute of Great Britain," *ibid.*, p. 69. See comment by Carl Van Doren, *Secret History of the American Revolution*, New York: The Viking Press, 1941, pp. 8–9. Van Doren, biography, p. 543 ff gives a detailed description of the abortive mission to Canada. Franklin's corrections of Jefferson's draft of the Declaration, *ibid.*, p. 550. On apocryphal story, *ibid.*, p. 551. On treaties with France and Spain debated in Congress, *ibid.*, p. 553. On feelings toward France, see Burlingame, *op. cit.*, p. 167. Letter to Howe, Smyth, Vol. VI, p. 459. On voyage to France, Smyth, Vol. VI, p. 469. On appointment to go to France, *Journals of the Continental Congress*, September 26, 1776.

CHAPTER XII

Passy—Peace and War

Something of the feeling of France on the eve of revolution is given in *The Diary and Letters of Gouverneur Morris*, New York: Charles Scribner's Sons, 1888, Vol. I, pp. 22 ff. In spite of the contemptuous attitude of some revisionist historians toward Carlyle's *French Revolution* much of the color of the disorder in France may be gained from it. On Franklin's popularity in France, see *Works of John Adams*, Boston: Little, Brown & Co., 1856, Vol. I, p. 660; Carl Becker, "Benjamin Franklin" in *Dictionary of American Biography*, New York: Charles Scribner's Sons, 1943, Vol. VI, p. 592. Edward E. Hale and Edward E. Hale, Jr., *Franklin in France* (*passim*), Boston: Roberts Bros., 1887. On landing at Auray in Brittany, letter to Barbeu Dubourg December 4, 1776, Smyth, Vol. VI, pp. 472–473; and letter to John Hancock, December 8, 1776, Smyth, Vol. VI, pp.

473–475. P.S., to letter to Committee of Secret Correspondence, dated December 10, 1776, Smyth, Vol. VI, p. 477. Letter from Stormont, Smyth, Vol. X, p. 302; second letter, *ibid.*, Vol. X, pp. 302–303. Information about Franklin's official activities during first two weeks in Paris, letter to Committee of Secret Correspondence, Paris, January 4, 1777, Smyth, Vol. VII, p. 9. To Silas Deane, Smyth, Vol. VI, p. 470; to Thomas Morris, *ibid.*, pp. 469–470. Quotation from letter to John Hancock about "underhand supply," Smyth, Vol. VI, p. 474. Letters from Burke and Rockingham, Smyth, Vol. X, pp. 303–304. These quotations occur in Smyth's "The Life of Benjamin Franklin" in Vol. X of his collection. In the following pages is the account of Franklin's first business in Paris. Chapter XI of this "Life," entitled "Social Life in France," gives many informal incidents at Passy and contains much of the correspondence with Madame Brillon. For secret rendezvous with Vaughan, see Aldridge, *Benjamin Franklin*, p. 277. On activities of Beaumarchais and "Hortalez," see Augur, *op. cit.*, pp. 122 ff. On wine, food, etc., at Passy, Smyth, Vol. X, p. 316. On business of "embassy" *ibid.*, Vol. X, p. 315. Letter to Juliana Ritchie, January 19, 1777, Smyth, Vol. VII, p. 11. We are indebted to Professor Smyth for the translation of the paragraph in *Nouvelles de Divers Endroits*. Account of tree in Tuileries as hiding place for secret information, Augur, *op. cit.*, p. 157. Instructions to Bancroft and on means of secret communication, Smyth, Vol. X, pp. 311 ff.

Chapter XIII

Victory and Alliance

On the Battle of Saratoga, see Samuel Eliot Morison, *The Oxford History of the American People*, New York: Oxford University Press, 1965, p. 247. *Ibid.*, pp. 251 ff on reception of the news of the battle in France. On *"burgoinissé,"* see *Diary . . . of John Adams, op. cit.*, entry, April 29, 1779. Letter from Beaumarchais to Vergennes, Trevelyan, *The American Revolution*, Morris edition, p. 358. On relations of Franklin with Wentworth, see Van Doren, *Benjamin Franklin*, pp. 589 ff. Signing of Treaty of Alliance, *ibid.*, p. 594; Smyth, Vol. X, p. 329; Stourzh, *op. cit.*, pp. 141–144. See also, letter to Thomas Cushing, February 27, 1778, Smyth, Vol. VII, pp. 110–111. Dialogue with Deane, Van Doren, p. 594. Deffand on Franklin's dress, Van Doren, p. 595; Marquise du Deffand *Lettres (1766–80)*, London, 1912, Vol. III, p. 423. For appointment as plenipotentiary, *Journals of the Continental Congress*, September 14, 1778. Louis XVI to Franklin, Van Doren, p. 595. John Adams's comment on Franklin, *Warren-Adams Letters*, Boston, 1817–25, Vol. II, p. 74. Abigail Adams's comment on Madame Helvétius, Smyth, Vol. X, pp. 439–440. Labors as plenipotentiary, Smyth, Vol. X, p. 405. Letter from Alexander, Smyth, Vol. I, p. 2. Smyth gives *The Interest of Great Britain* in full, Vol. IV, pp. 32 ff. Helen Augur, in *The Secret War of Independence,* devotes considerable space to the doings of Beaumarchais; see Chapter VII, "Hortalez and Company," p. 114. There is also much of interest in Trevelyan, *The American Revolution,* Morris edition, pp. 322–328. On Charles Dumas, see Augur, pp. 75–77. Letter to Dumas, September 22, 1778, Smyth, Vol. VII, pp. 189–190.

CHAPTER XIV

"Dear Papa"

To Elizabeth Partridge, October 11, 1779, Smyth, Vol. VII, pp. 395–396. "Not all toil," Smyth, Vol. X, pp. 405–406. For map of environment of Passy, see *Plan de Paris Par Arrondissements,* Paris; Maison Guilman, 16th Arrondissement, *Partie Nord;* Auteuil, 16 *Partie Sud.* Though these maps were made long afterward there have been no major changes in the streets, squares, etc. At the corner of rue Singer and rue Raymond is a plaque stating that Franklin lived there and placed a lightning rod on the house. The correspondence with Madame Brillon is in the chapter "Social Life in France" in Smyth's "Life of Benjamin Franklin," Vol. X, pp. 405 ff. These include Franklin's letters to her, written in his picturesque French. Van Doren in his biography tells much about Madame Helvétius, pp. 646 ff and gives the story of the dream in full on pp. 651–652. Glimpses of the Comtesse d'Houdetot are given in Gouverneur Morris, *op. cit.,* Vol. I, pp. 251, 258, and Smyth in his biography tells the story of the fête champêtre at Sannois in detail, Smyth, Vol. X, pp. 445 ff. The letter to her from Philadelphia, undated, is in the Library of Congress. See her reply in Smyth, Vol. X, p. 449. The full story of the Passy press is told in the excellent little volume by Luther S. Livingston, *Franklin and His Press at Passy,* New York: The Grolier Club, 1914. The only known copy of *Bagatelles* printed on the press is in the collection of Franklin Papers in the Yale University Library. Smyth reprints also "Dialogue Between Franklin and the Gout," Vol. VIII, p. 154, and "The Handsome and Deformed Leg," Vol. VIII, p. 162. The letter to Madame Brillon about a "Case of Conscience," Smyth, Vol. X, p. 438. "Supplement" and Temple's comment, Smyth, Vol. VIII, pp. 437 ff.

CHAPTER XV

Prisoners and Privateers

The little book by William Bell Clark, *Ben Franklin's Privateers,* Baton Rouge: Louisiana State University Press, 1956, is instructive on both prisoners and privateers. On prisoners see pp. 9, 11. Letter to Stormont, Smyth,

Vol. VII, pp. 36–37; to Weymouth, p. 36 n. The Library of Congress has original of letter to Stormont with Franklin's notation "return'd with insult." On Hartley, see Stourzh, *op. cit.*, pp. 148–149. Also *ibid.*, pp. 191–192. Letter to Hartley, October 14, 1777, Smyth, Vol. VII, p. 68, 68 n. To Gray Cooper, *ibid.*, p. 76, to Thornton, *ibid.*, p. 75. Comment on Thornton, Augur, *op. cit.*, p. 272. On benefits to prisoners, *ibid.*, p. 245. Also on underground railway, *ibid.*, p. 245. The Rev. R. Livesey compiled from the *Journal of Charles Herbert*, Boston: George C. Rand, 1854, the harrowing story of the sufferings of this young man from Newburyport, Mass., during his confinement in Old Mill Prison in Plymouth, England. Item, August 27, 1777, on food; also February, 1778. For the escape of officers, item February 1, 1778. Quotations from Mary L. Booth, *History of the City of New York*, 1867, Vol. II, p. 512. For statistics on British prisons in America, see New Jersey Historical Society, Proceedings, Vol. 78, no. 4, October, 1960. On Lambert Wickes, see Louis H. Bolander, "Lambert Wickes" in *Dictionary of American Biography*, Vol. XX, p. 180. Franklin to John Paul Jones, Smyth, Vol. VII, p. 159. To de Sartine, Smyth, Vol. VII, p. 185. Van Doren's comment on Franklin's work with privateers, *op. cit.*, p. 617.

Chapter XVI

From Lightning Rods to Balloons

Adams's comment and letter, Franklin to Madame de Boulainvilliers, Smyth, Vol. X, p. 453. George III on lightning rods, Van Doren, *op. cit.*, p. 58. On the Le Roys, Smyth, Vol. X, pp. 453–454. Invitation from Madame Le Roy to dine and Franklin's acceptance, both in French, translation, R. Burlingame. Franklin's farewell from Philadelphia, *ibid.*, p. 455. To Joseph Priestley, Smyth, Vol. VIII, p. 10. To Ingenhousz, October 2, 1781, Smyth, Vol. VIII, p. 309, Library of Congress. To Alexander Small, Smyth, Vol. VIII, pp. 120–121. On meals at Hôtel de Valentinois, Smyth, Vol. X, pp. 406–407. Letter to Priestley, June 7, 1782, Smyth, Vol. VIII, pp. 451–452. To Richard Price, *ibid.*, Vol. II, p. 99. Letters to Banks, Smyth, Vol. IX, p. 83; Vol. IX, p. 114. R. Burlingame, *Engines of Democracy*, New York: Charles Scribner's Sons, 1940, pp. 409–410. The celebrated letter with its prophecy of air war to Jan Ingenhousz, Smyth, Vol. IX, p. 156. To Mary Hewson, *ibid.*, p. 12.

Chapter XVII

World War

Complete understanding of the complicated negotiations of the peace treaty which followed the close of the war for American independence is not possible without a careful reading of the recent volume *The Peace-makers*, by Richard B. Morris, Gouverneur Morris Professor of History at Columbia University, New York: Harper & Row, 1964. Much of the material in this chapter is based on a reading of this book. The Notre Dame incident, along with Franklin's reaction to it, is described in the Van Doren biography, pp. 604–606. For John Adams as peacemaker and his hostility toward Franklin, see A. O. Aldridge, *Benjamin Franklin*, pp. 353 ff. On Jay's difficulties in Spain, see Morris, *op. cit.*, pp. 223 ff. Quotations from Morris by arrangement with Harper and Row. Meeting of Jay and Franklin with Vergennes, Morris, pp. 307 ff. Quotations from "Life," Smyth, Vol. X, p. 395. Terms of the Definitive Treaty of Peace, Samuel Flagg Bemis, *Dictionary of American History*, Vol. II, p. 128 (brief summary); in full, Document No. 4, Commager, *Documents of American History*, pp. 117 ff. Permission from Congress to come home, Van Doren, p. 722, Smyth, Vol. X, p. 456.

Chapter XVIII

The Old and the New

To Benjamin Vaughan, March 14, 1785, Smyth, Vol. IX, p. 299. To Charles Thomson, May 13, 1784, Smyth, Vol. IX, p. 213. From Dr. Cooper, Smyth, Vol. IX, p. 91 n. Copy of the full letter sent by Franklin to Vergennes is in American Papers of *Archives des Affaires Étrangères*, Paris. To Jay and Adams on Cooper letter, *ibid.*, p. 91. To Robert R. Livingston, July 22, 1783, Smyth, Vol. IX, p. 61. To Williams, August 16, 1784, Smyth, Vol. IX, p. 252. Quotation from Luther Livingston, *op. cit.*, p. 110. To George Whatley, August 21, 1784, Smyth, Vol. XI, pp. 265–266. Death of Margaret Stevenson, Smyth, Vol. X, p. 200.

Chapter XIX

Home

Quotations from Buckle, Henry Thomas Buckle, *History of Civilization in England*. Second Edition, New York: D. Appleton & Company, 1924, Vol. I, p. 345. On the "Nine Sisters," David Jayne Hill, "A Missing Chapter of Franco-American History," in *American Historical Review*, New York: The Macmillan Co., Vol. XXI, p. 709, serial, October 1915–July 1916; quotation, "It is not credible ... the master," p. 714. On *Book of State Constitutions*, see letter to Vergennes, March 24, 1783, Smyth, Vol. IX, p. 27. "The extravagant Misconceptions" letter to Thomas Mifflin, December 25, 1783, Smyth, Vol. IX, pp. 131–132. To Sarah Bache, Smyth, Vol. IX, pp. 161 ff. Morrelet's advice about Cincinnati essay, Van Doren biography, p. 709. Excerpt from Marquis de Condorcet, *Éloge de M. Franklin,* Paris, 1791. Quotation, Luther Livingston, *op. cit.,* p. 8. Other material about Passy press also from Livingston. For Benny Bache's narrative, Livingston, p. 127. Excerpt from Franklin diary, July 25, 1785, about hot bath, Smyth, Vol. X, p. 469. Excerpts September 13 and 14, Smyth, Vol. X, pp. 470–471.

CHAPTER XX

Prophet in His Own Country

Quotation from Jefferson, Andrew A. Lipscomb, editor, *The Writings of Thomas Jefferson,* Washington, D.C., 1903–4, Vol. VIII, p. 129. See also, Smyth, Vol. X, p. 460, 460 n. For French tributes to Franklin, see A. O. Aldridge, *Franklin and His French Contemporaries,* pp. 212–234. Criticisms: by Lawrence, D. H. Lawrence, *Studies in Classic American Literature,* New York: T. Seltzer, 1923, pp. 16, 19–20, 21, 27; *Autobiography,* Introduction by L. W. Labaree, p. 15; by Angoff, Charles Angoff, "Benjamin Franklin" in Charles G. Sanford, editor, *Benjamin Franklin and the American Character,* Boston, 1955, pp. 53–54; Labaree, pp. 15–16. On scientific achievements see R. Burlingame, "Franklin and the American Culture," Chapter V of *March of the Iron Men,* New York: Charles Scribner's Sons, 1938, pp. 68 ff. Trevelyan, *The American Revolution,* Morris Edition, pp. 353–354, p. 353 note on Wharton. Carl Becker, "Benjamin Franklin" in *History of American Biography,* New York: Charles Scribner's Sons, 1943, Vol. VI, pp. 585 ff. To Charles Thomson, Smyth, Vol. IX, p. 694. Character sketch of Franklin by Major William Pierce of Georgia in the Federal Convention of 1787, *Documents Illustrative of the Formation of the Union of the American States,* House Document No. 398, 69th Congress, 1st Session, Washington: Government Printing Office, 1927, p. 100. Franklin's speech to the convention, June 2, 1787, *ibid.,* p. 138. On Franklin's death, Van Doren, pp. 775–80.

CHAPTER XXI

Franklin in the 1960's

"Good war or bad peace," letter to Josiah Quincy September 11, 1783, Smyth, Vol. IX, p. 96. On daylight saving, Van Doren, p. 710; on bifocals, *ibid.,* p. 637. Quotation from Smyth, Vol. I, p. 171. Quotation from Labaree introduction to *Autobiography* on changes of original manuscript, *Autobiography, op. cit.,* p. 33. On manufactures and agriculture, Smyth, Vol. I, p. 149. Labaree "as a citizen," *Autobiography,* p. 20. "Our community chests," etc., pp. 20–21. All quotations from Labaree introduction to *Autobiography* by arrangement with Yale University Press.

SELECTED BIBLIOGRAPHY

Books

Adams, John, *Diary and Autobiography of John Adams.* Lyman H. Butterfield, ed. 4 vols. Cambridge, Mass., Harvard University Press, 1961.

Alden, John Richard, *The American Revolution 1775–1783.* New American Nation Series, Henry Steele Commager and Richard B. Morris, eds. New York, Harper & Brothers, 1954.

Aldridge, Alfred Owen, *Franklin and His French Contemporaries.* New York, New York University Press, 1957.

———— *Benjamin Franklin: Philosopher and Man.* Philadelphia, J. B. Lippincott Company, 1965.

The American Heritage Book of the Revolution, the editors of *American Heritage.* New York, American Heritage Publishing Company, Inc., 1958.

Augur, Helen, *The Secret War of Independence.* New York, Duell, Sloan and Pearce, 1955.

Becker, Carl L., "Benjamin Franklin" in *Dictionary of American Biography,* New York, Charles Scribner's Sons, 1931, Vol. VI, p. 585.

Bemis, Samuel Flagg, *The Diplomacy of the American Revolution.* New York, Appleton, Century Company, 1935.

Bigelow, John, ed., *The Complete Works of Benjamin Franklin,* 10 volumes. New York, G. P. Putnam's Sons, 1887.

Buckle, Henry Thomas, *History of Civilization in England.* 2 vols. New York, D. Appleton and Company, 1924.

Burlingame, Roger, *Benjamin Franklin, The First Mr. American.* New York, New American Library of World Literature, 1955.

Chaumont, Vincent Le Roy de, *Souvenirs des États Unis.* Paris, Jacques Lecoffre et Cie., 1859.

Churchill, Winston S., *A History of the English-Speaking Peoples,* Vol. 3, *The Age of Revolution.* New York, Dodd, Mead and Company, 1957.

Clark, William Bell, *Ben Franklin's Privateers.* Baton Rouge, Louisiana State University Press, 1956.

Conner, Paul W., *Poor Richard's Politics,* Benjamin Franklin and His New American Order. New York, Oxford University Press, 1965.

Crane, Verner W., *Benjamin Franklin and a Rising People*. Boston, Little, Brown & Company, 1954.

——— *Benjamin Franklin, Englishman and American*. Vol. 19 of the Colver Lectures delivered at Brown University. Baltimore, Published for Brown University, Providence, R.I., by William and Wilkins Co., 1936.

——— *Benjamin Franklin's Letters to the Press (1758–1775)*. Chapel Hill, University of North Carolina Press, 1950.

Deane, Silas, *The Silas Deane Papers*. 5 vols. Hartford, Connecticut Historical Society, 1930.

Doniol, Henri, *La Participation de la France a l'Établissement des États Unis*. Vol. I. Paris, Imprimerie Nationale, 1886.

Einstein, Lewis, *Divided Loyalties*, Americans in England During the War of Independence. Boston, Houghton Mifflin Company, 1933.

Fisher, Sydney George, *The True Benjamin Franklin*. Philadelphia, The J. B. Lippincott Company, 1899.

Franklin before the Privy Council, including the Hutchinson-Oliver Letters. Philadelphia, John W. Butler, 1860.

Franklin, Benjamin, *The Autobiography of Benjamin Franklin*. Leonard W. Labaree, Ralph L. Ketcham, Helen C. Boatfield and Helene H. Fineman, eds. New Haven, Yale University Press, 1964.

Franklin, William Temple, *The Private Correspondence of Benjamin Franklin 1753–1790*. 2 vols. London, Henry Colburn, 1817.

Hale, Edward E. and Edward E. Hale, Jr., *Franklin in France*. From Original Documents, most of which are now published for the first time. Boston, Roberts Brothers, 1887.

Keyes, Nelson Beecher, *Benjamin Franklin. An Affectionate Portrait*. Garden City, N.Y., Hanover House, 1956.

Labaree, Leonard W. et al., eds. *The Papers of Benjamin Franklin*. Vol. I–VII (in progress). New Haven, Yale University Press, 1959–1963.

Livesey, Rev. R., *The Prisoners of 1776*. Compiled from the Journal of Charles Herbert of Newburyport ... confined in the "Old Mill Prison," Plymouth, England. Boston, George C. Rand, 1854.

Livingston, Luther S., *Franklin and His Press at Passy*. An Account of the Books, Pamphlets, and Leaflets Printed There. Including the Long Lost "Bagatelles." New York, The Grolier Club, 1914.

Moore, Frank, *Diary of the American Revolution*. 2 vols. New York, Charles Scribner's Sons, 1860.

Morison, Samuel Eliot, *The Oxford History of the American People*. New York, Oxford University Press, 1965.

Morris, Richard B., *The Peacemakers*, The Great Powers and American Independence. New York, Harper and Row, 1965.

Paine, Thomas, *Common Sense*. With a Preface by William M. Van der Weyde. New York, Rimington and Hooper, 1928.

Parrington, Vernon Louis, *The Colonial Mind.* Vol. I in *Main Currents in American Thought*, 3 vols. New York, Harcourt, Brace and Company, Inc., 1927, Part I, Chapter III.

Parton, James, *Life and Times of Benjamin Franklin.* 2 vols. New York, Mason Brothers, 1864.

Russell, Phillips, *Benjamin Franklin: The First Civilized American.* New York: Brentano's, 1926.

Sellers, Charles Coleman, *Benjamin Franklin in Portraiture.* New Haven, Yale University Press, 1962.

Smyth, Albert Henry, ed., *The Writings of Benjamin Franklin.* New York, The Macmillan Company, 1905–1907.

Steell, Willis, *Benjamin Franklin of Paris, 1776–1783.* New York, Minton, Balch & Co., 1928.

Stourzh, Gerald, *Benjamin Franklin and American Foreign Policy.* Chicago, University of Chicago Press, 1954.

Trevelyan, George Otto, *The American Revolution.* Condensed into One Volume, Edited and Arranged by Robert B. Morris. New York, David McKay Company, Inc., 1964.

—— *The Early History of Charles James Fox.* New York, Harper and Brothers, 1899.

Van Doren, Carl, *Benjamin Franklin.* New York, The Viking Press, 1938.

—— ed., *Benjamin Franklin's Autobiographical Writings.* New York, The Viking Press, 1945.

—— *Secret History of the American Revolution.* New York, The Viking Press, 1941.

Watson, J. S., *The Reign of George III, 1760–1815.* Oxford, Clarendon Press, 1960.

Articles

Adams, Randolph G., "The 'Passyports,'" *American Collector,* Vol. 4, 1927.

"Answers to the Queries published in the *London Chronicle* dated September 16–19, 1758." *Maryland Historical Magazine,* Vol. 33 (September, 1933).

Bemis, Samuel Flagg, "British Secret Service and the French-American Alliance." *American Historical Review,* Vol. 29 (October, 1923–July, 1924).

Bigelow, John, "Franklin's Home and Host in France." *Century Magazine,* Vol. 35 (serial, 1887–1888).

Calvert, Cecilius, Letter to Gov. Horatio Sharpe, December 5, 1758. *Maryland Archives,* Vol. 31, p. 507.

Crawford, Mary Caroline, "Franklin and the French Intriguers." *Appleton's Booklovers Magazine,* Vol. II, No. 2 (February, 1906).

Hill, David Jayne, "A Missing Chapter of Franco-American History." *American Historical Review*, Vol. 21 (October, 1915; July, 1916).

Miles, Richard Donald, "The American Image of Benjamin Franklin." *American Quarterly*, Vol. IX (Summer, 1957).

Quinlan, Maurice J., "Dr. Franklin Meets Dr. Johnson." *The Pennsylvania Magazine of History and Biography* (January, 1949), p. 34.

Read, Conyers, "The English Elements in Benjamin Franklin." *The Pennsylvania Magazine of History and Biography* (July, 1940).

Woodburn, James A., "Benjamin Franklin and the Peace Treaty of 1783." *Indiana Magazine of History* (September, 1934).

INDEX